MW00574165

Theodore Roosevelt and Six Friends
of the Indian

Theodore Roosevelt and Indian. Theodore Roosevelt Collection, Harvard College Library

Theodore Roosevelt and Six Friends of the Indian

By William T. Hagan

UNIVERSITY OF OKLAHOMA PRESS
NORMAN AND LONDON

Also by William T. Hagan

The Sac and Fox Indians (Norman, 1958; 1980; 1989; 1993)
American Indians (Chicago, 1961; 1979; 1993; Hokkaido, Japan, 1983)
Indian Police and Judges (New Haven, 1966; Lincoln, 1980)
United States–Comanche Relations (New Haven, 1976;
    Norman, 1990)
The Indian Rights Association (Tucson, 1985)
Quanah Parker, Comanche Chief (Norman, 1993)

Library of Congress Cataloging-in-Publication Data

Hagan, William Thomas.
    Theodore Roosevelt and six friends of the Indian / by William T.
Hagan.
        p.   cm.
    Includes bibliographical references and index.
    ISBN 0-8061-2954-9 (cloth : alk. paper)
    1. Indians of North America—Government relations—1869–1934.
2. Indians, Treatment of—North America—History—20th century.
3. Indians of North America—History—20th century—Sources.
4. Roosevelt, Theodore, 1859–1919.   5. Garland, Hamlin, 1860–1940.
6. Grinnell, George Bird, 1849–1938.   7. Leupp, Francis Ellington,
1849–1918.   8. Lummis, George Fletcher, 1859–1928.   9. Merriam,
C. Hart (Clinton Hart), 1855–1942.   10. Welsh, Herbert, 1851–1941.
11. Indian Rights Association—History.   12. Bureau of Catholic
Indian Missions (U.S.)—History.   I. Title.
E93.H227   1997   97-4517
973.0497—dc21   CIP

Text design by Debora Hackworth.

The paper in this book meets the guidelines for permanence and durability of the Committee on Production Guidelines for Book Longevity of the Council on Library Resources, Inc. ∞

To Robert M. Kvasnicka,
whose knowledge of the holdings
of the National Archives and dedication
to service made my task easier

Contents

 Illustrations

 Preface

      This is an account of the efforts of six individuals (Hamlin Garland, George Bird Grinnell, Francis E. Leupp, Charles F. Lummis, C. Hart Merriam, and Herbert Welsh) and two organizations (the Indian Rights Association and the Bureau of Catholic Indian Missions) to capitalize on their acquaintance with President Theodore Roosevelt to influence his administration's conduct of Indian affairs. To provide a proper background, I have traced relevant portions of his upbringing and his views on Indians as reflected in his writings. My objective has not been to write a history of the Indian policy of the Roosevelt administration, but rather to reveal the tenor of its approach to the complex problems of the Native Americans and the efforts of the six friends to educate Roosevelt on Indian issues.

      This study also depicts a different Roosevelt than the anti-Indian frequently encountered in print and based on his effusions in *The Winning of the West*. I do not maintain that Indians were ever a major Roosevelt interest; he did, however, respond frequently and readily to those for whom they were. Moreover, he demonstrated a willingness to try to include them in his Square Deal and to encourage the preservation of their arts and music.

Over the years many institutions and individuals have contributed to this project. The State University of New York College at Fredonia and the University of Oklahoma provided research funds, and their library staffs performed countless services. A Huntington Library fellowship enabled me to spend two rewarding months in that scholarly environment.

Other institutions whose staffs were most helpful include the National Archives, the Library of Congress, the Smithsonian Institution's Anthropological Archives, the Braun Research Library of the Southwest Museum, Marquette University's Memorial Library, Harvard University's Widener and Houghton libraries, Yale University's Sterling Memorial and Beinecke libraries, the University of Southern California Library, the State Historical Society of Wisconsin, the Massachusetts Historical Society, the State Historical Society of Pennsylvania, and the Sagamore Hill National Historic Site.

I am particularly indebted to Mark Thiel of Marquette University, Wallace Finley Dailey of Harvard University, and Patricia Bodark Stark of Yale University for guidance through collections under their supervision.

Martin Ridge made my fellowship at the Huntington Library more pleasant by his efforts to create, among the transients there, a sense that one is a member of a community of scholars. Francis Paul Prucha, S.J., was most hospitable during my research at Marquette University. Individuals who responded graciously to specific inquiries include Henry E. Fritz, Donald L. Parman, Laurence M. Hauptman, and Tsianina Lomawaima.

One of our children, Martha Ruffman, took time from

her busy schedule to track down elusive data in Los Angeles. As always, my wife, Charlotte N. Hagan, provided constant support, ranging from word processing to faultless navigation on research trips.

Finally, I am grateful to Lewis L. Gould and Donald J. Berthrong for their careful and most helpful readings of the entire manuscript.

WILLIAM T. HAGAN

Norman, Oklahoma

Theodore Roosevelt and Six Friends
of the Indian

1

An Education in Indian Advocacy

On the afternoon of September 13, 1901, Theodore Roosevelt descended gloomy Mount Marcy in the Adirondacks in response to alarming reports from the bedside of President William McKinley. The president's death dropped onto Roosevelt's sturdy shoulders the wide-ranging responsibilities of one of the most powerful offices in the world. Among his new roles was that of Great Father to the roughly 270,000 American Indians who were wards of the federal government.

As a boy Roosevelt had manifested no particular interest in Indians, despite his delight in the great outdoors. Throughout his life he loved horses, hiking, and hunting, and he developed into a naturalist of considerable competence. In time Roosevelt would correspond with some of the leaders in the field, including people of the caliber of John Muir of Yosemite fame and C. Hart Merriam of the Smithsonian Institution. Merriam, as an outgrowth of his own western travels, became an advocate for tribes that he had encountered; in contrast, Roosevelt's journals and letters dating from the time of his early ventures into Indian lands reveal little interest in the first Americans. Nevertheless, as a result of the passage of time, his immersion in the history of the American frontier, and the responsibilities associated with being a civil service commissioner, Roosevelt became well informed on the subject and even an advocate for some Indian causes. He would enter the White House better acquainted with Indians and the Indian Service than any chief executive since William Henry Harrison. In addition, he knew, like few other Americans, the history of Indian-white relations on the cis-Mississippi frontier through the research that went into his four-volume *Winning of the West.*

In eight volumes published before he entered the White House and in numerous letters and public addresses, Roosevelt documented his views on Indians and their resistance to white expansion. He frequently is dismissed as a racist on the basis of quotations such as the one drawn from a speech he made in New York in January 1886: "I don't go so far as to think that the only good Indians are the dead Indians, but I believe nine out of ten are, and I shouldn't like to inquire too closely into the case of the tenth. The most vicious cowboy has more moral principle than the average Indian."[1]

This was typical Roosevelt hyperbole; he seldom was accused of understatement. And he could issue diametrically opposed views on an issue, and with equal vigor. As political rival Robert M. La Follette observed, "This cannonading, first in one direction and then in another, filled the air with noise and smoke" but frequently left Roosevelt in the neutral zone.[2] It is not surprising then that abundant evidence also can be found that Roosevelt was not a racist in the sense in which the term is currently employed. For example, he detected wide variations among peoples then being lumped together as the

Yellow Peril. The Chinese he regarded as weak and incompetent, while he admired—and feared—the strength and efficiency of the Japanese.[3]

While Roosevelt believed that the Indians had lagged behind the whites, he was confident that any people had the capacity to improve, and among the tribes he perceived marked differences, something many Americans have yet to grasp. As he phrased it in 1888, "An upper-class Cherokee is nowadays as good as a white. The Nez Perces differ from the Apaches as much as a Scotch laird from a Calabrian bandit. A Cheyenne warrior is one of the most redoubtable foes in the whole world; a 'digger' Snake one of the most despicable. The Pueblo is as thrifty, industrious, and peaceful as any European peasant, and no Arab of the Soudan is a lazier, wilder robber than is the Arapahoe."[4]

Roosevelt, however, stressed even more the differences between individuals. Himself a man with a tremendous capacity for work and a driving need to be productive, he had nothing but scorn for the shiftless and inefficient of whatever color. He denounced the profligate life of his own beloved younger brother, Elliott, and deplored his daughter Alice's consorting with the hedonistic Four Hundred, whom he described as leading lives "which vary from rotten frivolity to rotten vice."[5] Nor did he permit group stereotypes to cloud his assessment of the worth of an individual member. Thus he could describe one of his cowboys, a Pueblo Indian whose people Roosevelt admired, as "an excellent rider and roper, but a drunken, worthless, lazy devil" and praise two other employees, "a Sioux half-breed, a quiet hard-working, faithful fellow, and a mulatto, who was one of the best cow-hands in the whole roundup."[6]

The Rough Riders whom Roosevelt led in battle in Cuba included Indians as well as cowboys and Ivy Leaguers, and he described a Pawnee trooper as "one of the gamest fighters and best soldiers in the regiment."[7] As a bespectacled "dude" who had had to prove himself in the strenuous life of the cow-men of Dakota Territory, Roosevelt respected anyone, re-gardless of color or class, who could produce under pressure.

Although he strove to be fair to individuals, even a casual reading of his works on frontier history reveals Roosevelt's chauvinism. He wrote of "The Winning of the West" by the white man, not "The Losing of the West" by the Native Amer-ican, and was unapologetic about justifying in florid prose how whites wrested the continent from America's original in-habitants. In a passage reminiscent of Andrew Jackson's ref-erence to the questionable claim of Indians to lands "on which they have never dwelt nor made improvements, merely because they have seen them from the mountain or passed them in the chase,"[8] Roosevelt ridiculed Indian land claims: "To consider the dozen squalid savages who hunted at long intervals over a territory of a thousand square miles as own-ing it outright—necessarily implies a similar recognition of the claims of every white hunter, squatter, horse-thief or wan-dering cattle-man."[9]

Roosevelt employed the land utilization argument com-mon to invaders since time immemorial: "Let sentimentalists say what they will, the man who puts the soil to use must of right dispossess the man who does not, or the world will come to a standstill."[10] But even here he made distinctions, ac-knowledging that the Cherokee claim was superior to that of some other Indians because Cherokees used the land more intensively.

Although he characterized the white man's conquest of the continent as both inevitable and desirable, the historian Roosevelt could describe Indians and frontiersmen in equally harsh terms. He spoke of the Indians' "silence, their cunning and stealth, their terrible prowess and merciless cruelty . . . the tigers of the human race."[11] But on occasion their white adversaries fared little better at Roosevelt's pen. "Their feats of terrible prowess," he wrote, "are interspersed with deeds of the foulest and most wanton aggression, the darkest treachery, the most revolting cruelty . . . We see but little of such qualities as mercy for the fallen, the weak, and the helpless, or pity for a gallant and vanquished foe."[12] Nor did Roosevelt portray the whites as generally superior to their Indian opponents. He maintained that Indians were never defeated by a white force of equal or lesser numbers.[13]

In his dealing with individuals Roosevelt did not restrict his depiction of heroism to the whites, nor his depiction of villainy to the Indians, although his is definitely a history written from white sources and focusing on white conquest of the continent. His description of the Mingo chief Logan is an oft-cited example of his effort at some balance: "A skilled marksman and mighty hunter, of commanding dignity, who treated all men with a grave courtesy that exacted the same treatment in return, he was greatly liked and respected by all the white hunters and frontiersmen whose friendship and respect were worth having."[14]

For a contrasting white villain, Roosevelt did not have to look far. The notorious Greathouse, a trader who sold rum to the Indians, is remembered in history only as the leader of the massacre of nine of Logan's family, including children. "It was an inhuman and revolting deed, which should consign the names of the perpetrators to eternal infamy," was Roosevelt's judgment.[15]

While prepared to recognize merit in individuals at any level of society, Roosevelt was not a true egalitarian, although he mellowed over time. Until his graduation from Harvard there was little that set him apart from the other young men of his social class. Like them he inherited wealth and social position and had had little contact with the masses. Roosevelt had been schooled by tutors before entering Harvard, and he had the smug assumption of superiority that went with his family's position. On one occasion he was happy to report to a sister that his Harvard academic ranking was nineteen in what had originally been a class of 230. Moreover, Roosevelt noted, of the eighteen ahead of him, only one was a "gentleman."[16] Given the virtual monopoly of higher education by the upper classes in the 1870s, one can only conclude that even in the rarified atmosphere of Harvard, Roosevelt considered himself among the elite. This comforting thought was validated by his selection for membership in Porcillian, the most exclusive of Harvard's clubs. Throughout his life he regarded those tapped for Porc as a special breed.

But the man grew. A quarter-century later he would confide to his son Ted that Seth Bulloch and Bill Sewall "represent the type of man with whom I really believe I have more in common . . . than almost any others."[17] Sewall was a rough-hewn Maine guide when the young Theodore first encountered him, and later he persuaded Sewall to join him in the cattle business in Dakota Territory. Seth Bulloch was the prototype western sheriff and had killed two men in the line of duty.

Not that this member of the eastern aristocracy ever forgot his class origins. The twenty-one-year-old Theodore could be amused that rough Illinois farmers acted as if they were the equals of him and his brother Elliott.[18] A more mature Roosevelt shared the campfire and drudgery of the roundup for weeks on end—remaining "Mr. Roosevelt" to his cowboys. First-name acquaintanceship was something members of his class reserved for only a very few intimate friends. Even Bill Sewell, of whom he remarked that "we have hunted together and lived on the roundup together and have always been good friends," came under this proscription, Roosevelt commenting, in wry amusement, on his "invariably writing me by my christian name!"[19]

None of the six men—George Bird Grinnell, C. Hart Merriam, Herbert Welsh, Hamlin Garland, Francis E. Leupp, and Charles F. Lummis—who knew President Roosevelt well and most often attempted to influence him on Indian affairs was on a first name acquaintance with the man. Each, however, had had some connection with Roosevelt before he entered the White House. Even Grinnell, probably the closest to him, addressed him as "My dear Roosevelt" when congratulating him on his appointment to the Civil Service Commission: "It is encouraging . . . to see an office held by a decent man who is also a gentleman."[20] And when Roosevelt was elevated to the presidency, Grinnell persisted in addressing him in the same way.

Although Grinnell had admiringly followed Roosevelt's tumultous career in the New York state legislature, their first real encounter resulted from an 1885 review by Grinnell of Roosevelt's *Hunting Trips of a Ranchman*. It was rather barbed and Roosevelt went to Grinnell's office to discuss it, but he was persuaded of the accuracy of the comments.[21]

The two men found that they had much in common. Both had inherited money and social position, and both had deep interests in nature and the West. Grinnell was the senior, both in age and western experience. After earning a Yale degree he had spent the summer of 1870 with a fossil-collecting expedition that ranged from Kansas to Utah. This brought him into contact with Pawnee scouts attached to the army and led by the North brothers, Frank and Luther. Grinnell developed a close relationship with both the Indians and their white commanders. Two years later Grinnell returned to hunt buffalo in company with Luther North, and for a time the white men joined with a Pawnee hunting party.

Twice that summer Grinnell encountered hostile Indians, probably Sioux or Cheyenne. The first time was an attempt to steal some Pawnee ponies, the second was potentially more serious. Grinnell, Luther North, and another white man were attacked on the open prairie, but under North's experienced leadership they were able to drive off the raiders. A dozen years later Roosevelt, riding alone, held off at rifle point several Sioux who may or may not have meant him harm.[22] Given Roosevelt's temperament, he must have envied the older man's actually having traded gunfire with Plains warriors.

After a brief exposure to the business world, Grinnell decided to return to Yale for graduate study that eventually resulted in a Ph.D. in paleontology. But he did not forget the West. In the summer of 1873 he engaged Luther North to guide him on another hunting trip, and the following year Grinnell accompanied Col. George A. Custer's Black Hills expedition as a naturalist, with North as his assistant. In 1875 he again interrupted his graduate training to join the expedition to Yellowstone Park led by Colonel William Ludlow, and he later published well-received accounts of the park's wildlife. Fortunately for Grinnell, the professor he was assisting at Harvard's Peabody Museum refused to grant him leave in 1876 when Custer telegraphed an invitation to accompany the 7th Cavalry on an expedition that climaxed on the Little Big Horn.[23]

In the summer of 1878 Grinnell again traveled west. This time his employment on a western Nebraska ranch owned by "Buffalo Bill" Cody and the North brothers helped set the stage for his own venture into ranching in Wyoming's Shirley Basin. Like Roosevelt, who entered the cattle business in Dakota Territory at about the same time, Grinnell found ranching a losing financial proposition, while at the same time becoming more enamoured with the region.

Meanwhile, Grinnell had begun contributing to *Forest and Stream,* and in time he and his father purchased a controlling interest in the magazine and he became its editor.

With this as a platform he became a leading spokesman for the embryonic conservation movement. The founder of the Audubon Society, Grinnell as a child had been a neighbor of the widow and children of the great naturalist and painter. Grinnell also was in at the birth in 1888 of the Boone & Crockett Club, which Roosevelt had taken the lead in organizing. Together with Roosevelt and another sportsman, Grinnell defined the goals of Boone & Crockett, which, according to John F. Regier, was "the first private organization to deal effectively with conservation issues of national scope."[24] Until Roosevelt became president, the two jointly edited the club's several publications. In Regier's judgment, when differences arose, Roosevelt tended to defer to the older and more experienced Grinnell.

The two men also shared an interest in politics, Grinnell largely from the sidelines, Roosevelt in the thick of it. How he had determined after graduating from Harvard to involve himself in practical politics, beginning with a Republican organization quartered in an unsavory district of New York City, is a familiar story. His reputation as an able young reformer was well established by 1886. In that year he, Carl Schurz, and George William Curtis represented the Civil Service Reform Association in discussions with the Indian Rights Association (IRA) about extending the merit system to the Indian Service.[25]

Roosevelt's real education in Indian affairs began when President Benjamin Harrison appointed him to the Civil Service Commission, a post he would hold until May 1895. Arriving in Washington in May 1889, he immediately galvanized an agency that had been virtually moribund. And while his principal battles would be with the Post Office Department, in his six years on the commission Roosevelt often would have problems in the Indian Service called to his attention. Occasionally it was George Bird Grinnell who approached him, but

Roosevelt's most frequent gadfly was Herbert Welsh, founder and principal force behind the IRA.

The IRA had become in its brief six years' existence the most influential organization of eastern friends of the Indian. Welsh ran the IRA through its Philadelphia office while it maintained an agent, old Washington hand Charles C. Painter, in the nation's capital. The IRA was alone among Indian reform groups in having either a Washington-based lobbyist or a permanent office. As a result, other groups such as the Boston Indian Citizenship Committee and Amelia Quinton's Women's National Indian Association usually followed the lead of the IRA on political issues.

Theodore Roosevelt could be comfortable in dealing with Welsh; they were both "men of good family," to use a Roosevelt term. The Philadelphian also had inherited social position and an independent income, his father being a merchant prince who had served as minister to England. A graduate of the University of Pennsylvania, he had studied painting in Paris before deciding to devote his life to good causes. A devout Christian, he had a strong belief in the brotherhood of man. Like Roosevelt, Welsh was prominent in the civil service movement; unlike Roosevelt, he chose to operate from outside the party system, being a classic Mugwump, a type that Roosevelt derided as impractical theorists, mere critics as opposed to doers like himself. Nevertheless, Roosevelt was willing to work with the Mugwumps to advance the goal of good government. He did not quarrel with Welsh's belief that "the solution of the whole Indian problem lies quite as much in the wise, unpartisan administration as in wise legislation."[26] And that meant recruiting and retaining personnel for the Indian Service on the basis of merit.

While still new to the Civil Service Commission, Roosevelt received the first of what would be hundreds of communications from Welsh. This one dealt with a campaign the

IRA had launched to persuade the new Harrison administration to retain Commissioner of Indian Affairs John H. Oberly, a Grover Cleveland appointee. George Bird Grinnell, however, had gotten to Roosevelt first with an account of how the commissioner had failed to get blankets to the Blackfeet Agency before winter set in. Grinnell castigated Oberly as "easy going, a shirker at his work," someone who had "the support of the cranks, the sentimentalists and the old women," and who had "long fed at the public crib."[27]

Welsh persisted for a time in seeking Roosevelt's assistance for Oberly, sending Charles Painter to make the case personally. Painter left a graphic description of his encounter with the new civil service commissioner, whom he disparaged as "immensely green" and unaware of the restrictions limiting the actions of subordinate officials like the Indian commissioner. Painter said Roosevelt gave the appearance of being "in great haste. Commenced to read me the letter [Grinnell's] upon which he planks his disbelief in Mr. Oberly before I could sit down; and finished it with the air of one who had effectively *crushed* an adversary, and there was nothing more to be said." Painter concluded his report to Welsh: "I must say that I was not favorably impressed either with the good sense or fairness of the Hon. Theo."[28]

Roosevelt would have ample opportunity to redeem himself in their eyes, because the IRA frequently importuned him to assist in its many crusades. Two months after the initial contact, he responded immediately to a request from Welsh for aid in the campaign to extend the civil service to the Indian Service. To emphasize the need, Welsh had cited examples of incompetent agency employees such as the physician who had prescribed carbolic acid for a cough, and another whose treatment for a sore throat was tincture of iodine taken internally. Roosevelt assured Welsh that he would take the matter up with his fellow commissioners: "The patronage system is degrading at the best; but when applied to the poor Indians it is simply infamous."[29] This inspired Welsh to brief Roosevelt on the evils of the Home Rule system by which the Republican Party reserved patronage on Indian reservations for local politicians.

The Civil Service Commission did not command all of Roosevelt's energies, and his life proceeded at an exhausting pace—or at what would have been an exhausting pace for an ordinary man. The first two volumes of his *Winning of the West* came out in 1889, one of his reviewers being an obscure professor of history at the University of Wisconsin, Frederick Jackson Turner. This scholar, who later would give legitimacy to the field of western history, concluded that Roosevelt had handled "impartially and sensibly the relations of the pioneers and Indians whom they dispossessed."[30] Turner did suggest that the research could have been more thorough. The author, however, was unrepentant, and while planning additional volumes in the series Roosevelt dashed off a history of New York City for a British publisher. Nor did his social life slacken. He was welcomed to the salons of the most interesting and discriminating hosts in Washington, including Henry Adams and John Hay, who viewed their young friend's exuberant energy with wry amusement. A wide range of people found Roosevelt's companionship delightfully stimulating. As one put it, "He was the prism through which the light of day took on more colors than could be seen in anybody else's company."[31]

Despite Roosevelt's many other interests and activities, his education in Indian affairs continued at the hands of friends of the Indian. In early 1890 Herbert Welsh was endeavoring to prevent Utes' being removed from Colorado to Utah, and he enlisted George Bird Grinnell in this fight; for Roosevelt he had a more appropriate assignment. Welsh asked him again for help in getting an extension of civil service to employees of the Indian Service. Roosevelt's task would be to brief Oberly's successor as commissioner of Indian affairs, Thomas J. Morgan. Roosevelt responded that it might be a fortnight before he could work it into his heavy schedule, although he would be happy to do so. He also invited Welsh to dine with him on his next visit to Washington, and took that occasion to introduce Welsh to one of his fellow commissioners.[32]

There was a lull of about six months in the contacts between Roosevelt and Welsh, but in December 1890 they were again corresponding relative to an unsavory situation at the Philadelphia post office. Nevertheless, it was Indian affairs that was the principal topic when they met later in the month at the Century Club in New York. Welsh followed that up by sharing with Roosevelt copies of two confidential letters relating to the increasing tension on the Sioux reservations as a result of the Ghost Dance movement.[33]

By this time time, blood had already been shed in Sioux country. Agency police had attempted to take Sitting Bull into custody. The chief, seven of his supporters, and six of the policemen died when Sitting Bull's followers resisted the arrest.

This was but a prelude to the Massacre of Wounded Knee in late December 1890, which resulted in the deaths of about 150 Indians, many of them women and children, as well as 25 cavalrymen. In a letter to Roosevelt, Welsh described it as "a horrible sequel to the whole wretched affair!"[34] He was convinced that the spoils system was largely responsible for the Sioux problems because it had installed inexperienced agents at Cheyenne River and Pine Ridge, two critical points. Roosevelt took up this refrain and was soon writing: "The Indian problem is difficult enough, heaven only knows, and it is cruel to complicate it by having the Indian service administered on patronage principles."[35]

Because of trouble he already was having with the heads

of the Census Bureau and the Post Office Department, Roosevelt declined to permit Welsh to circulate his letter concerning the impact of the patronage system on Indians. He sensed that President Harrison was nearing the limits of his tolerance for criticism of his administration by the brash young civil service commissioner. Roosevelt did, however, offer to write a letter endorsing "generous recognition" for the Indian police who had stood by the government in the crisis.[36]

Subsequently he wrote an article for *Century* in which he argued for government pensions for the survivors of the policemen killed arresting Sitting Bull. He had no sympathy for the Sioux chief, depicting him as "for many years the mainspring of hostility to the United States among the Dakota tribes being even a greater bane to his own people than to ours." Roosevelt saved all his compassion for the Indian police "killed while doing their duty (in the interest not only of their own people, but of all the white settlers)." He concluded, "No white veteran, of no matter what war, can have a better claim on the Government."[37]

Roosevelt earlier had expressed equal enthusiasm for punishing cowboys who had killed an Indian named Few Tails, whose party they attacked as the Sioux were returning from an authorized hunt. "Such scoundrels as those who murdered Few Tails party should be hunted down and dealt with summarily by any of the military who overtake them," he declared. "If the whites of the neighborhood won't punish their men who murder Indians then the National Government should."[38]

Writing three weeks later to Welsh, Roosevelt was even more emphatic in his reaction to the violence on the Sioux reservations:

> I am inclined to think that the killing of Sitting Bull and of the Indians in the Forsyth fight was all right; but if all accounts are true there were . . . peaceable men, or women and children,

killed under circumstances that ought to have called for the most rigid investigation. In particular as to the murder of Few Tails' people I would like to have it stated publicly . . . that as long as the civil authorities . . . fail to rigorously punish the white aggressors the Indians would be left in possession of their weapons to protect themselves. . . . I would put down an Indian outbreak as I would put down a mob uprising with the strongest possible hand . . . but I would also strain every nerve and stretch the federal power to the utmost to protect and avenge the Indians when molested by lawless whites. If it is impossible to procure the punishment of the whites by their local tribunals, then in some way they ought to be put under martial law. The hanging of a few white scoundrels implicated in such deeds as that of the murder of Few Tails' party would do incredible good.[39]

Nevertheless, Roosevelt did not speak out publicly in 1890. His excuse was that as a member of the administration he was prepared to fight on issues directly related to his responsibilities as civil service commissioner—and he certainly had—but that he could not involve himself in matters that did not.

Roosevelt was willing to speak up in behalf of bringing the Indian Service under civil service rules, and he advocated modifying the rules so as "to have most of the positions at the Indian agencies that are now filled by whites filled by civilized Indians." Such Indian preference would be instituted in time, but meanwhile whites were favored under Home Rule, which Roosevelt denounced as "all nonsense." After he became president, some would remember the stand he had taken as civil service commissioner: "No Indian agent should ever be removed on any pretense whatsoever save for charges directly affecting his capacity as an Indian agent."[40]

Roosevelt shared these views with Indian Commissioner Morgan in February 1891. Morgan then forwarded his own proposals to President Harrison, who in April issued an executive order placing nearly seven hundred positions in the Indian Service under civil service. Although the order did not go nearly so far as the reformers had wished, they were pleased. Perhaps the deaths of the innocents at Wounded Knee had been a factor in moving President Harrison to action and had not been entirely in vain.

Meanwhile Roosevelt was responding to other requests for assistance. One of them led him to propose an acquaintance as someone the IRA should back for membership on the House Indian Affairs Committee. When the congressman did get the seat, Roosevelt was then persuaded to ask him to help block the Ute removal from Colorado.

Despite Welsh's constant importunings, Roosevelt did not try to sever the relationship. Indeed, he congratulated the head of the IRA for a *Scribner's Magazine* piece entitled, "The Meaning of the Dakota Outbreak," which he declared to be "by *all* odds the best article of its length on the Indian question which I have ever seen."[41] Roosevelt always could be counted on to be lavish in his praise of the writings of those whom he favored. He also helped plan a trip for Welsh's son to his old stomping grounds near Medora, South Dakota. And Roosevelt proposed that he and Welsh inspect South Dakota reservations, something that he could work in with a check on his remaining cattle interests.

It would be eighteen months before the inspection of the reservations would take place, as the two men had difficulty coordinating their heavy schedules. When it did take place the experience provided Roosevelt the most concentrated education in Indians and the Indian Service he would have. He threw himself into it wholeheartedly, and Welsh described arriving at the Cheyenne River Agency to find him "engaged in a conference with the corps of Agency and camp school teachers . . . with that intense energy and sparkling enthusiasm so characteristic of him."[42]

Roosevelt sought information from every segment of the reservation population. His sources included Captain Hugh Leroy Brown, an army officer on detached service as the Pine Ridge agent, and William Hobart Hare, since 1873 bishop of the Episcopal Church's Dakota diocese with jurisdiction over the church's missionary work among the Sioux. But he also interviewed George Sword, a full-blood and a judge of Pine Ridge's Court of Indian Offenses, and Luther Standing Bear, another full-blood and a former student at Carlisle Institute. And by Roosevelt's side for several days was Herbert Welsh, thoroughly conversant with the Sioux reservations as a result of several visits and a network of both Indian and white contacts, and eager to indoctrinate the civil service commissioner.

In a little over two weeks Roosevelt visited four Sioux agencies, plus the Omaha and Winnebago reservations and the Haskell Indian school. His longest exposure to any one group was six days at Pine Ridge, home of seven thousand Oglala Sioux. There he was the guest of Captain Brown, and they covered 250 miles of the reservation on horseback and by wagon. Brown was captivated by the energetic and ebullient Roosevelt, the very antithesis of the image of a Washington bureaucrat, observing, "I *enjoyed* his visit more than I can tell."[43] A quick study with a phenomenal memory, Roosevelt closely observed conditions while inspecting schools, offices and shops, and the homes of a number of the Indians and intermarried whites.

Roosevelt's next stop was at Cheyenne River, where he was joined by Welsh, who also would accompany him to the Yankton and Santee agencies, with Roosevelt going on alone to the Omaha and Winnebago Reservation with a final stop at Haskell Institute at Lawrence, Kansas. At every point there were things that engaged Roosevelt's attention.

At Cheyenne River an Episcopal convocation had attracted nearly two thousand Indians. Roosevelt described it for his friend Endicott Peabody, founder of Groton School, which had ties to the Episcopal Church: "One of the most interesting sights I saw . . . many earnest and intelligent native preachers and catechists."[44] And he found time to drop a line about the Sioux to George Bird Grinnell, who responded, "I have no strong affection for the Sioux; they have killed too many of my old 'partners' [Pawnees]."[45]

On all the reservations he saw, Roosevelt visited schools and tried to get away from the agency headquarters, to get a feel for the life of the Indians. He was struck by the differences between the Sioux of Pine Ridge and Cheyenne River, real Plains Sioux, and the relatively more acculturated Yankton and Santee Sioux.

Roosevelt was sometimes shocked at what he learned. The Santee agent volunteered, with no suggestion of embarrassment, that he had mobilized his charges to support Republican candidates at a recent local election. Roosevelt was also disturbed at evidence of the spoils system and the contribution it made to the lack of continuity in agency staffs. At Cheyenne River there had been four agents in the previous twelve months, and the incumbent, only several weeks in the position, had yet to venture as far as two miles from his office.[46]

Roosevelt had ample opportunity to get his views on what he had learned before the public. He gave a statement to the press even before leaving the area, damning the "infamy of meanness" of local politicians who demanded campaign contributions from both whites and Indians on the government payroll.[47] In mid-October he and Mrs. Roosevelt joined a group sympathetic to the cause of the Indians at their tenth annual get-together of the Lake Mohonk Conference of Friends of the Indian near New Paltz, New York, to enjoy the hospitality of resort operator A. K. Smiley and to try to reach consensus on Indian issues. Roosevelt was unintimidated by the presence of veteran self-styled "friends" such as chairman of the Board of Indian Commissioners Merrill E. Gates, founder and president of the Women's National Indian Association Amelia E. Quinton, Henry L. Dawes, who frequently spoke for them in the Senate, and dozens of others who had devoted years to their vision of what was good for Native Americans.

Roosevelt's remarks were well received—as they did not deviate significantly from the conventional wisdom expounded at Lake Mohonk—and they were delivered with the usual Roosevelt verve.[48] Crusty old Charles Painter, the IRA lobbyist who had dubbed him "immensely green" on first meeting the freshman commissioner, reported that the debates at Mohonk were "spicy and of great interest" and that "Roosevelt contributed very greatly to this interest."[49] Senator Dawes's daughter Anna, active in Indian work herself, was even more enthusiastic: "You have no idea how much good Mr. Roosevelt did by his commendation of the school work and church work. It was so to speak outside testimony, and had a great effect."[50]

Roosevelt also was prevailed upon to share his thoughts with those attending a meeting sponsored by the Board of Indian Commissioners in Washington and to give a talk at the IRA's annual meeting. A reporter for a Philadelphia newspaper described Roosevelt's talk to the IRA as "bright, and witty, as well as full of practical information and suggestions." He opened with this observation: "I have seen both red men and white men pretty near to the bone, and where they are both unpromisingly raw, and I have found on occasion that the so-called civilized white man is only a little less savage than the

Indian." Later on he assured his pro-Indian audience that the Native American had one "immense advantage as compared with the majority of the non-white races—there is little or no race prejudice operating against him." To make his point abundantly clear, he continued, "In every Western community will be found men of Indian blood who enjoy, socially, politically and in every way, advantages which would be unattainable, notably, for instance, to the negro." He also addressed the problem of the educated Indian girl: "To return her to the degradation of her original surrounds is but to infinitely increase her capacity for suffering." But the best he could offer was to propose that at least some of these girls might be employed by the government in reservation schools and offices.[51]

Herbert Welsh found Roosevelt's presentation "original, wise, and highly amusing."[52] When newspaper editors ignored the commissioner's official report on his travels, the IRA printed and distributed three thousand copies.

Roosevelt had reached some general conclusions as a result of his tour of inspection. "It is on the one hand encouraging to see how much progress has been made in certain directions and at certain places," he maintained, "and on the other disheartening to see the harm wrought by greed of many white frontiersmen, the sentimentality of many sincere but impracticable philanthropists, and the culpable spoils-mongering of the politicians, acting upon the very defective character of the Indians themselves."[53]

Roosevelt believed that the Indians lagged far behind the whites in their cultural evolution. "It is three thousand years since our race produced the poems of Homer," he reminded the group at Mohonk, and warned against thinking the Indians could close the gap in one generation.[54] He believed, however, that it could be done in three or four, although not all would make it. Darwinian that he was, Roosevelt thought that, when all had been done for the Indians that could be done, "we must turn them loose, hardening our hearts to the fact that many will sink, exactly as many will swim."[55]

Roosevelt had no quarrel with the general thrust of Indian policy, finding it impossible to believe that the Indians should be permitted to remain at what contemporary social scientists referred to as the stage of barbarism. He believed that to accelerate their cultural evolution communal ownership of land should be ended, as provided for in the Dawes Severalty Act of 1887, but the timing was critical for the Indian: "It must not be done too quickly, for he will then be helpless and perish, nor must it be delayed too long, for he will then become accustomed to being petted and cared for and will be too weak to stand when finally left alone."[56]

Roosevelt was confident that schools could play a major role in preparing Indian boys for their new status. He favored placing them in reservation schools because there they were most likely to encounter the climatic and soil conditions they would face as neophyte farmers and stockmen. In his judgment, local boarding schools were more effective than day schools. And he counseled against permitting too many youths to waste time learning trades they would have no opportunity to practice on returning to their families.

Roosevelt admitted, after interviewing about two hundred of them, that he had been too critical of the performance of the so-called "returned students." He had dinner at the home of Carlisle graduate Luther Standing Bear, married to another Carlisle alumnus, and found "his spotless house a centre of civilizing influence to all the Indians round about."[57] Standing Bear seemed to Roosevelt to have derived an additional potential benefit from off-reservation school experience—the weakening of his tribal ties, which the Lake Mohonk attendees considered a major barrier to Indian advancement.

Disturbed by the paucity of opportunity for returned students to employ skills acquired in school, Roosevelt passed on the suggestion of agency employees that the former students themselves make the large quantities of wagons, harness, tin ware, and clothing that otherwise were purchased on the open market. The Indian Office, however, found this idea incompatible with the objective of dissolving the tribes. The employment situation for returned students would remain bleak.

Other groups reevaluated by Roosevelt as a result of his tour of the reservations were intermarried whites, referred to as "squaw men," and the mixed-bloods. He suggested that what teachers and missionaries really objected to in the mixed-blood was that he "was becoming more and more like the white man, and was therefore less docile."[58] Even if the intermarried white was rather shiftless, Roosevelt defended him for providing an educated Indian girl "a chance to keep the standard she has reached, and to have her children educated in white ways, whereas she has no chance at all if she goes back to the Indian tepee."[59] He saw the mixed-bloods as offering their wives more opportunity as well, judging their homes to be "more comfortable and cleaner . . . and their farms were likewise far superior."[60] He even managed to locate a white woman married to a mixed-blood and, ever ready to rate individuals on their merits, described her as "one of the most intelligent, capable, and genuinely philanthropic women I have ever met."[61] It was to be hoped that she and other whites among the Indians would provide them with models of the work ethic that Roosevelt and all friends of the Indian felt the Native Americans must develop to progress.

"The present system has a very evil tendency toward pauperizing the Indians," Roosevelt warned in his official report.[62] The annuities, which were installments on the purchase price the United States had agreed to pay tribes for land, together with gratuitous issues of supplies, enabled most

Indians to survive at a marginal level without working. He believed that as soon as possible they should be required to become self-supporting, and the first step would be to make the individual "understand that to live he must work."[63] By the same logic Roosevelt opposed an able-bodied tribesman's leasing his newly allotted farm, referring to it as a "great evil." Too frequently the Indian landlord "lives in idleness and drunkeness on his income and becomes absolutely unable to take care of himself."[64]

Landlord-tenant relationships inevitably gave rise to legal problems, and there were other difficulties resulting from Indian-white contacts that could be solved only in court. Unfortunately, the Indian-staffed Courts of Indian Offenses existing on most reservations had limited jurisdiction. If the case went off the reservation, Roosevelt had no confidence that the Indian would receive justice. When it was an Indian committing a crime against a fellow Indian, the white man's court was reluctant to assume jurisdiction because the financial burden fell on the white community, the Indians not paying taxes. Roosevelt suggested that the government pay their local taxes from proceeds of tribal land sales held in the U.S. Treasury. But even if the Indians appeared before off-reservation judges, there was one fundamental problem in Roosevelt's opinion: "The whites will not give them a fair show."[65] In another context he highlighted another reason for Indian vulnerability: "On the Indian agency you have a little group of beings cut off from the rest of the world, who don't know their rights and who are easily wronged; and you expose these helpless creatures, whom it is our business to protect, to all the evils of the spoils system."[66]

From time to time friends of the Indian continued to call upon Commissioner Roosevelt for assistance. He aided in a long but losing battle to save Captain Brown's job at Pine Ridge, a fight that revealed some serious splits among friends of the Indian. The situation had been complicated by a quarrel between Captain Brown and agency physician Charles Eastman, a Santee Sioux married to a white woman, Elaine Goodale. Eastman and Goodale had excellent connections among eastern friends, and he was frequently cited at gatherings like Mohonk as a role model for all Indians. His difference with the captain originated in a dispute over which Sioux should be eligible for government compensation for damages suffered during the Ghost Dance disturbances.

After having heard both sides of the Brown-Eastman dispute while at Pine Ridge, Roosevelt came down on the side of the captain. At the 1892 Mohonk Conference, he made a special effort to praise Brown to counteract glowing words about Dr. Eastman from one of the speakers. In December, Roosevelt and Charles Painter received an appointment to meet with Commissioner Morgan to press Brown's case, but Morgan persisted in his hostility to the agent. Roosevelt concluded that it would be useless to see the commissioner again, although he did speak to Interior Secretary John W. Noble.

While learning more about factionalism among friends of the Indian, Roosevelt continued to be helpful to them. He agreed with the IRA that it was "monumental pig-headed folly" not to provide carbines to the Indian police, criminals usually being better armed than the police.[67] Roosevelt promised Welsh to bring the subject up with Henry Cabot Lodge, then in the House of Representatives, and with his and Lodge's friend, Thomas B. Reed, a Republican power in the House. He also responded favorably to the suggestion that the IRA might support a Catholic, Agent James McLaughlin of Standing Rock, to be the commissioner of Indian affairs in the second Cleveland administration. "I think it would emphasize the liberality of the Association's record . . . and it would make it all the easier for us to oppose any improper encroachment by the Catholics," wrote Roosevelt, who as president would make a special effort to give Catholics a larger voice in Indian affairs.[68]

Roosevelt also was being educated about encroachments of a more serious kind, the schemes of land-hungry whites to acquire land of the Southern Utes in Colorado and of the Lower Brule Sioux in South Dakota. Early in 1892 Welsh approached him for support in the fight the IRA had been waging against Colorado's effort to move a thousand Southern Utes to Utah. At stake was access by Colorado settlers to the Ute reservation of over one million acres. Even though the overwhelming majority of Utes themselves wished to move to Utah in the hope that there they could continue a hunting and gathering existence, friends of the Indian insisted that they should be allotted Colorado land that could be irrigated. The IRA led the fight, supported by the Women's National Indian Association and the Lake Mohonk Conference. Even Indian Commissioner Morgan urged Secretary Noble to hold fast against the Coloradans' demands.

When Roosevelt was contacted, a bill to remove the Utes was in the House Indian Committee. Welsh wanted Roosevelt to try to influence a congressman whom the IRA, at the suggestion of Roosevelt, had successfully backed for membership on the committee. Roosevelt's response was prompt, and typical: "All right. Of course I am with you entirely in the fight."[69] He also later would help persuade Lodge of the correctness of the IRA's position on the Utes.

When Roosevelt's aid was sought to keep the Lower Brule Sioux on their own reservation, it again was an instance of the friends' willingness to do battle to keep Indians in place in order to facilitate their transformation into farmers and stockmen. Many of the Lower Brule, however, were prepared to accede to the wishes of whites desiring their reservation— if they were permitted to move to the nearby Rosebud Reservation of the Upper Brule. Herbert Welsh, ever the paternalist, described the Brule willing to move to Rosebud as "poor, ignorant people whose real welfare depends upon their being told firmly and positively by the Government that they must settle down on their own lands."[70] In his first appeal to Roosevelt, Welsh had blamed South Dakota's Senator Richard Pettigrew, "again at his evil work," and wanted Roosevelt to try to reach Senator Dawes and possibly others on the issue.[71] Roosevelt's immediate response was that he would try to see Dawes "about the new atrocity of Bro. Pettigrew."[72]

During this period Roosevelt received from Welsh a Navajo blanket "as a slight expression of my strong personal friendship," and the Philadelphian tried to further exploit that connection.[73] Welsh previously had attempted to get at Lodge through Roosevelt, and now he sought his help in influencing the editorial policy of *Good Government,* the journal of the National Civil Service Reform League.

The editor of that journal was Francis E. Leupp, also head of the Washington bureau of the *New York Evening Post.* Roosevelt had recommended him to Welsh in 1891 for the editorship when Welsh was on the League's publications committee. At that time Roosevelt referred to Leupp, whom in 1905 he would make commissioner of Indian affairs, as "a thorough gentleman, a radical believer in the civil service law and principles, and, on the whole, the best and most trustworthy correspondent I know in Washington."[74]

Roosevelt gave the same advice to Baltimore civil service reformer Charles J. Bonaparte, a grandson of Napoleon's brother Jerome. Charles Bonaparte also was on the publications committee of the Civil Service Reform League, and this time Roosevelt was a little more frank in his appraisal. He described Leupp as "a first rate fellow in spite of his association with that villainous paper the Evening Post." And then Roosevelt added: "He has some very cranky notions however, as I suppose is inevitable with a man of his associations."[75] Leupp could be difficult, although he appears to have been one of a host of ruggedly independent people who succumbed to Roosevelt's charisma.

Leupp consulted him about the IRA position that opened when Charles Painter died in January 1895. This led Roosevelt to suggest the journalist to Herbert Welsh: "He has courage, tact, clear-sightedness, a knowledge of men, and he is a devoted civil service reformer and a believer in decency and justice."[76] Welsh needed little persuasion, and Leupp became the IRA's Washington agent and served in that capacity until he resigned in early 1898.

Being employed by the IRA would be excellent training for the future commissioner of Indian affairs. In those three years Leupp visited a number of reservations and was introduced to a wide variety of their problems, becoming acquainted with many people in the Indian Service. And for those three years he was plugged into the network of reservation contacts that helped keep the IRA the best informed of the associations of eastern reformers. Meanwhile, his boss, Welsh, continued to turn to Leupp's friend Roosevelt for help, seeking his advice and assistance in dealing with members of Congress and the new Cleveland administration.

Roosevelt had expected the new president to request his resignation, but Grover Cleveland continued him in office. When Roosevelt did leave the post in May 1895, it was to take a position as a New York City police commissioner. In the two years that he remained on the Civil Service Commission he would continue to be bombarded by requests for help from friends of the Indian.

Roosevelt heard most frequently from Herbert Welsh, who sometimes used Leupp as a means of getting to the Indian commissioner about personnel problems in the Indian Service. The IRA was constantly importuned by government employees who felt they were being treated unfairly. Some of these complaints originated among the staff of the Carlisle Institute, where Captain Richard Henry Pratt, its founder, was vigorously opposing civil service regulations.

Captain Pratt, an army officer who had been on detached service working with Indians since 1875, was as articulate and forceful as Theodore Roosevelt, and neither was prepared to give ground under attack. Pratt's position was that he, rather than the Civil Service Commission, should determine who should teach at Carlisle. The Civil Service Commission, he charged, sent him "the scum, the refuse" that was left for the Indian Service after other schools had filled their staffs.[77] In an effort to get Carlisle exempted from civil service regulations, Pratt appealed directly to President Cleveland. Asked by the president to comment on the letter, Roosevelt and a colleague defended the system and attacked Pratt for his "strong aversion to co-operating with anybody, his resolute determination as far as possible to have his own way at all times, his strong prejudices, likes and dislikes."[78] When Welsh brought to his attention a complaint against Captain Pratt from one of Carlisle's staff, Roosevelt assured him that he would fight Pratt "tooth and nail to the last."[79]

In this battle the captain stood virtually alone, devotion to the principle of civil service being a vital part of the canon of the friends. When one of them counseled Pratt against resisting this "car of juggernaut," the defiant captain vowed to fight on.[80] His stand so antagonized Roosevelt that he concluded that Pratt had become "insupportable, and that he ought to be turned away."[81] Despite growing criticism of the captain, that would not take place until Roosevelt became president.

In his last two years on the Civil Service Commission, Roosevelt also helped develop a closer relationship between Grinnell and Welsh, two of the men who would seek to advise him on Indian affairs when he became president. As early as

1889 Grinnell had approached the IRA for aid for two tribes in which he was interested, the Blackfeet and the Pawnee. The Blackfeet had been suffering under an agent whom Grinnell declared "a thief, who is robbing both the Indians and the Government."[82] In the case of the Pawnees, he was concerned about their unreadiness for allotment in severalty, which the government was proposing. Subsequently he acknowledged Welsh's help in getting the agent removed. Several months later Welsh approached Grinnell for his support—which he promised—in opposing the removal of the Southern Utes from Colorado.[83] What Welsh did not know was that on occasion Grinnell, like Roosevelt, could be caustic in discussing the eastern reformers. Both men liked to think of themselves as practical people, not sentimentalists.

It is fortunate for Grinnell that Welsh was unaware of these sentiments when he was called upon to write a review in 1893 of the naturalist's collection of Blackfeet and Pawnee stories. Welsh's request to Roosevelt for information on Grinnell elicited this response: "Grinnell is the editor of the *Forest and Stream,* a member of the Boone and Crockett Club, a great lover of sport and natural history. He is an adopted member of the Pawnee tribe, and has always taken the greatest interest in every effort to improve the condition of the red man."[84] Welsh sent a copy of his review to Roosevelt, who responded that he was "really pleased with it" and "was heartily glad that [Grinnell] had as a reviewer a man who possesses your sympathy for the subject and your knowledge of Indian life."[85]

After it was published Grinnell thanked Welsh for "one of the pleasantest reviews" that he had received. He concluded by wishing that he "might feel free to bring to the notice of your association abuses that every now and then come to my knowledge."[86] Welsh promptly assured him that he would try to correct any problem that Grinnell called to his attention.

Within a few months Grinnell communicated to Welsh

his concern about alcoholism among the Blackfeet. He suggested that perhaps a statement he had drafted could be circulated among W.C.T.U. chapters and other temperance societies to generate pressure on the government to make a greater effort to stop the liquor traffic. Welsh found it an "admirable tract"; with the dispatch that made the IRA the most effective of the reform organizations, he within three weeks had three thousand copies of Grinnell's "The Enforcement of Liquor Laws a Necessary Protection to the Indians" ready for mailing.[87]

By the time of Roosevelt's departure from the Civil Service Commission in 1895, he had earned the admiration of many of the friends of the Indian. Some had worked closely with him; others had heard him speak at Lake Mohonk or the annual meetings of the IRA or the Board of Indian Commissioners. In these settings he had reiterated the conventional wisdom, but with the flair and dynamism that were uniquely Roosevelt. Nor did anyone ever point out that there might be some inconsistency between his warm advocacy of Indians at these meetings and the tone of his *Winning of the West,* three volumes of which had appeared by 1895. If the question had arisen, Roosevelt might have pointed out the difference between the Indians of the cis-Mississippi frontier, fighting desperately to defend their homeland and way of life, and the pathetic wards of the United States on remote reservations in the 1890s.

2

A Heartbeat from the Presidency

In just five years Theodore Roosevelt moved from a relatively obscure agency, to which only someone as articulate and magnetic as he could give visibility, to being a heartbeat from the presidency. In the same period he became more enmeshed in the network of friends of the Indian, as he developed relationships with Hamlin Garland and Charles F. Lummis to match those already established with Francis Leupp, George Bird Grinnell, Herbert Welsh, and C. Hart Merriam.

As early as August 1893 Roosevelt had concluded that the civil service post "leads 'no forrader [forwarder].'"[1] His friend and confidant Henry Cabot Lodge was now a U.S. senator, and comparing himself with Lodge he felt a failure. Older by several years, Lodge always seemed to be steps ahead of Roosevelt. In 1886 the younger man failed in a race for mayor of New York, but Lodge was elected to Congress. Now, a decade later, Roosevelt would turn to Senator Lodge to handle the final negotiations for the position on the New York City Police Board. The New York legislature had just authorized the board, and Roosevelt saw in it an opportunity to escape from the dead-end civil service post. Moreover, the post of police commissioner certainly was more attractive than another city job that he had declined earlier, street cleaning commissioner.

Taking office in May 1895, Roosevelt again demonstrated his ability to invest a relatively minor post with glamour and excitement. Aided by two newspapermen who would make names for themselves as reformers, Jacob Riis and Lincoln Steffens, Roosevelt was soon the talk of the town. Nothing gave him more publicity than his practice of touring the city at night to check on the activities of patrolmen. Jacob Riis accompanied him on his first outing, and later Roosevelt would invite others, including Hamlin Garland, the chronicler of the Middle Border, to join him on his midnight inspection tours.

At first glance Garland and Roosevelt would appear to have little in common other than their interest in literature. In contrast to Roosevelt's aristocratic background, Garland's was one of numbing drudgery on frontier farms. They both had been in the Dakota Territory in the early 1880s, but Roosevelt, as the owner of a ranch, consorted with glamorous figures such as fellow cattleman Marquis de Mores, while a hundred miles away Garland was failing as a homesteader. Given the facts of Garland's early life, it is little wonder that others were struck by his morbid outlook on life, his utter lack of a sense of humor.

By the time he became acquainted with Roosevelt, Garland had begun to enjoy success as a writer, and Roosevelt delighted in the company of those with ideas and an ability to express them. Indeed, he prided himself on being a "literary man."[2] And he cultivated friends like James Brander Matthews, a Columbia University literature professor who suggested in 1894 that Roosevelt read Garland's latest publication, *Crumbling Idols.* On the basis of a review he had seen, Roosevelt already had concluded that he would not like it and that Garland was a "hopeless crank."[3] At Matthews's urging, however, Roosevelt did read *Crumbling Idols* and accepted Garland's main thesis that authors should write about what they knew best. He did not agree, however, with Garland's view of the literary greats. "I think that his ignorance, crudity, and utter lack of cultivation make him entirely unfit to understand the effect of the great masters of thought," Roosevelt fulminated.[4]

Fortunately for their relationship, several months later Roosevelt read a Garland article on lumberjacks that he did like. Yet even then he faulted Garland's "jaundiced view of life," and referred to the midwesterner's earlier writing and "the utter crudity of his half-baked ideas."[5] Nevertheless, Roosevelt invited Garland to lunch and introduced him to another writer gaining distinction, Stephen Crane. As was so often the case, Roosevelt made Garland an instant admirer by expressing appreciation for his tales of the Middle Border and actually quoting from them. Later, at Roosevelt's instigation, they exchanged autographed copies of their books, and in September 1896 Roosevelt took Garland along on one of his midnight inspections and permitted him to sit by his side as he passed judgment on shirkers.

Although Garland had published a piece in 1890 about Indian-white relations, it was not until trips west in 1895 and 1896 that he became seriously interested in Native Americans. The first year he visited the Southern Ute and Navajo reservations and several pueblos. Everywhere he went Garland carefully observed the lives of the Indians, recording his impressions in notebooks he would mine for essays, short stories, and novels. "No other of my trips was ever so inspirational," he would remark later.[6]

It had been educational, bringing Garland into contact with a few of the many Indian cultures. While visiting the Utes he became interested in their naming practices, and later, when his friend Theodore Roosevelt was in the White House, Garland would embark upon an officially endorsed project to rename tribal members. He also was impressed by the richness of Indian spiritual life and was fortunate in having ethnologists Jesse W. Fewkes and Frederick W. Hodge help him to appreciate the nuances of the Hopi snake dance ceremony. The Pueblos gave the failed homesteader a new perspective on the virtues of cultivating the earth, and Garland concluded his first extensive trip among the Indians convinced that much of value would be lost if they were hurried down the white man's road to civilization.

The following year Garland was back in the Southwest for a quick visit to the Southern Ute reservation and then on to see the Jicarilla Apaches. Both the Utes and the Jicarillas were being exposed to the blessings of private property by having individual farms allotted them. Garland recognized that satisfaction of the white man's greed for land was a principal explanation for allotment's popularity in Congress. This he would begin pointing out in a series of publications that would soon make him one of the most widely read popular writers on Indians. Garland was not yet actively seeking to influence Indian policy in the same way as George Bird Grinnell and Herbert Welsh, but that would come.

In 1897 Grinnell was delighted to learn of Garland's intention to "serve the Indians." "I am sure that if you and I can form an alliance we can do very much to awaken public interest in these Indians," he responded. Grinnell explained that while acquainted with the Cheyennes, he did not claim to know them as he did the Blackfeet, as "I have not summered them and wintered them for many years as I have the [Blackfeet]."[7] It was the beginning of a relationship between the two writers based on their mutual interest in improving the lot of the Native Americans, a relationship that would flourish during Roosevelt's presidency.

During the two years that Roosevelt served on the New York police board, Herbert Welsh sought his assistance on IRA matters. When Francis Leupp indicated some ambivalence about remaining in the employment of the IRA, Welsh turned to Roosevelt for help, reminding him that he had first recommended Leupp for the position. The IRA's head also took the opportunity to ask the commissioner to write an occasional piece on police matters for *City and State*, a reform weekly that Welsh had launched. Less than six months after Roosevelt took office in New York, *City and State* was lauding him effusively: "Certainly to no one man should Americans, who see in their country something more than size and wealth, and who believe her institutions worthy of some sacrifice, look with stronger feelings and gratitude, or sustain with more united sentiment."[8]

Despite the ringing endorsement, Roosevelt declined to pressure Leupp to remain on the IRA staff, nor did he submit anything for publication in *City and State*. Roosevelt's failure to do so may simply have resulted from his intimidating burden of other commitments. The police commissionership demanded much time and energy. A midnight patrol, for example, meant that he might have to go as much as forty hours without sleep. And he was very active politically, speaking to Republican audiences in many states while engaged in intermittent warfare with his own state political machine. Meanwhile, Roosevelt continued to write, getting out the fourth volume of *Winning of the West* while coauthoring a book of essays with Lodge and publishing articles in *Scribners, North American Review, Century, Forum,* and other journals. He also somehow found time to dash off a note to a young boy who had read Roosevelt's description of frying-pan bread in his *Wilderness Hunter* and wanted the recipe.[9]

Journals like *Scribner's* paid standard rates, and the checks were always welcome to a man who had trouble keeping his expenditures in line with his income. Although Roosevelt depended on a brother-in-law to monitor his accounts and try to keep him solvent, he frequently was in distress. Yet it was to this financial incompetent that Herbert Welsh turned for advice when he was considering investing some of his own inheritance in a publishing company.

Roosevelt and Grinnell also maintained close contact in this period, usually in connection with Boone & Crockett Club business. Grinnell, however, also was actively engaged in the affairs of the Blackfeet and the Northern Cheyennes. In 1895 he was one of three U.S. commissioners appointed to bargain with the Blackfeet for the purchase of a portion of their reservation. The mountainous area was little utilized by the Indians; it was rumored to have gold and had begun to attract prospectors, who never were respectful of reservation boundaries. George Steel, the Blackfoot agent whom Grinnell admired, had concluded that it was in the Indians' interest to dispose of the potentially troublesome strip, getting as good a price for it as the United States could be brought to pay. Grinnell believed, however, that the asking price of $3 million for the 800,000 acres was too high. He capitalized on his contacts within the tribe to help persuade the Indians to accept half that sum while retaining hunting, fishing, and timber rights in the cession.[10] After the agreement had been negotiated, Grinnell wrote a mixed-blood Blackfoot friend, "I hope that you are well pleased with the bargain. . . . I myself think the treaty a liberal one on both sides."[11]

Although now given free rein on the cession, prospectors were unable to locate the gold that they had fantasized to be available in great quantity. In 1901 Grinnell launched a campaign to create what in 1910 would become Glacier National Park and would include the 800,000 acres formerly a part of the Blackfoot Reservation. The episode revealed both Grinnell's active role in the national park movement and the belief he shared with other friends that the tribes could not realistically hope to retain intact large reservations.

Nevertheless, when a plan was afoot in 1896 to move the Northern Cheyennes to the Crow Reservation, Grinnell enlisted the IRA's help to block the proposed transfer. He referred to it as "really an outrage" and approached both Herbert Welsh and Francis Leupp in behalf of the tribe.[12] On his own, Grinnell tried to arouse public indignation by writing for the *New York Post* on the proposed removal.

A year later he sought and received the cooperation of the IRA in saving Spotted Hawk, a Northern Cheyenne, from the gallows. Spotted Hawk and his brother Little Whirlwind had been convicted of murdering a sheepherder. Grinnell was convinced of their innocence and persuaded Welsh to commit his association to the fight for justice. One of the IRA's publications on the issue included a letter from Hamlin Garland testifying to the "malevolently eager" efforts of Montana officials to prosecute the Cheyennes.[13] The unified campaign of the friends of the Indian paid off. Although the campaign took four years, Spotted Hawk's life was saved and his brother was finally released from prison.

The cooperation Grinnell had received from the IRA encouraged him to enlist its help for four hundred Northern Cheyennes threatened with relocation. Their portion of the reservation was being eyed by cattlemen who lobbied to get the government to buy the land. Grinnell argued that because the area concerned was one of the few that was well watered, the Indians "would be made to suffer in order that half a dozen wealthy cattlemen might have a larger and better range for their cattle."[14]

Meanwhile, Grinnell was attracting attention by his books and articles on Indians, which he aimed at a popular audience although he was somewhat defensive about that approach. Indeed, he felt a need to justify his method to Smithsonian ethnographer James Mooney, who had reviewed one of his publications: "It has seemed to me that I could do better work for the Indian both from a scientific and humanitarian point of view, by making him interesting to the public," Grinnell wrote, "than I could any other way. Personally I should more enjoy studying Indians from a purely scientific standpoint," he went on, "but the number of people influenced by the scientific student is so limited that I believe more can be accomplished by general work like mine."[15]

Roosevelt would have agreed with him on that subject, as he himself was a caustic critic of the scholar who, by choice or inability to reach a broader audience, engaged in "intolerable antiquarian minuteness."[16] Indeed, when dashing off a hasty biography of Thomas Hart Benton while on his ranch in Dakota Territory and cut off from libraries, Roosevelt could describe his own approach as "evolving him from my inner consciousness," a technique not stressed in graduate schools.[17] But his preference was a middle ground, where the historian did basic research but not to the extent that he got bogged down in an effort to "again thrash out the straw."[18]

Despite Roosevelt's failure to show much personal interest in Indian affairs after his move to New York City, he was proposed by the IRA for the position of commissioner of Indian affairs after the Republicans regained the White House in 1896. Indeed, the election had hardly taken place when Leupp, still the IRA's Washington representative, was suggesting the possibility. Welsh did not need much persuasion to support Roosevelt for the post. In the three months that elapsed before the IRA made its formal recommendation to McKinley, Roosevelt's name usually headed the association's short list. The list also included Francis Leupp, whom Welsh described as possibly unqualified politically, as he was a

Democrat, but whose knowledge of the political system, "his absolute courage and general good sense, would make him, also, an ideal man." The Republican Roosevelt did not suffer the same political handicap, and Welsh discussed him in glowing terms: "He has every qualification for a first class commissioner . . . rigid integrity . . . fearlessness . . . sound judgement in all the details of administration . . . hold upon the public . . . knowledge of the subject."[19]

Late in the game, Leupp urged that Secretary of the Interior Cornelius N. Bliss be approached about making Roosevelt an assistant secretary and having him head the Indian Service. "He knows the subject so well and in so practical a way," urged Leupp, "and is so admirable a character, that the appointment would give an indelible stamp to the administration."[20]

What apparently neither Leupp nor Welsh knew was that Roosevelt had set his heart on becoming navy assistant secretary and was working through Lodge and others to obtain that position. Naval history had been a major Roosevelt interest since college days, when he began writing *The Naval War of 1812*. With no false modesty he could confide in a sister, "I am intensely interested in our navy, and know a great deal about it."[21] His fear was that McKinley regarded him as "hot-headed and harum-scarum,"[22] an attitude reinforced, he believed, by members of the New York Republican machine whom he suspected of painting him as "headstrong, impractical and insubordinate."[23] Roosevelt, in typical fashion, balanced his expressions of strong interest in the Navy Department with avowals of his willingness to continue as police commissioner. Nevertheless, his joy and relief were apparent when finally, in early April, he was offered the Washington post. Roosevelt took office ready and eager to assume his duties under Secretary J. D. Long, who had little knowledge of or interest in naval affairs and thus was not likely to resent an activist subordinate.

Roosevelt delighted in his new position, one daily growing in importance as war loomed. Three months before entering office he had been convinced that the United States should intervene in Cuba, confiding in a sister that he was a "quietly rampant 'Cuba Libre' man." Confident that if Spain resisted it could be defeated without "very serious fighting," he had wanted Cleveland to recognize Cuba's independence and send a fleet to Havana.[24] Now assistant secretary, Roosevelt would do what he could to prepare the navy for the war he regarded as inevitable.

Hamlin Garland, Herbert Welsh, and George Bird Grinnell followed Roosevelt's new career with interest. Garland himself was in and out of Washington in 1897 and 1898, doing research for a biography of Ulysses S. Grant. Within two weeks of his moving to the Navy Department, Roosevelt invited Garland to join him for lunch with Brooks Adams and for dinner with Cabot Lodge. Later, Roosevelt showed Garland around his office and the two saw each other occasionally at the Cosmos Club, which attracted Washington's intellectual elite. Years after the event Garland recalled an uncomfortable dinner in Senator Lodge's home at which he was vigorously interrogated by Roosevelt and Henry Adams about his populist leanings.[25] But he also remembered a pleasanter occasion when he and Senator Lodge's son were Roosevelt's guests and they discussed Garland's plans for a trip to Alaska. It involved packhorses, and Roosevelt had exclaimed at his pleasure at having at his table "a man [Garland] who knows the difference between an *apparejo* [a packsaddle] and *parfleche* [a container made of buffalo hide]."[26]

Before seeing Alaska, Garland broadened his knowledge of Indians by visiting eight reservations in the Northwest. At Standing Rock he was interested in learning more about Sitting Bull and interviewed a number of Indians, mixed-bloods, and white employees about the chief, who had been killed by

Indian police in 1890. The writer was attracted to Lame Deer by exaggerated reports of a Northern Cheyenne uprising after the murder of a white sheepherder. This led to his becoming acquainted with the local agent, George W. H. Stouch, who would serve as a model for the protagonist in *The Captain of the Gray-Horse Troop,* Garland's best-selling novel about an Indian agent.[27] The author returned from this trip even more sensitized to the plight of Indians pressured by missionaries and officials to change their way of life, while other whites conspired to get access to their land. He also carried messages to George Bird Grinnell from Blackfeet who had told Garland of their white friend.

Garland was in Alaska when Roosevelt abruptly resigned his navy post to join a volunteer cavalry regiment with the rank of lieutenant colonel and fight in the Spanish-American War. He had done this against the wishes of his family and closest friends, but military service was something Roosevelt had considered during previous national crises. In 1886, when Mexican-American relations had been tense, Roosevelt had written the secretary of war from Dakota Territory proposing that he recruit some "harum-scarum rough riders out here," should hostilities erupt.[28] Nearly ten years later, when the Venezuela/British Guiana boundary dispute brought the United States and Great Britain into angry confrontation, he declared his readiness to "try to have a hand in it myself! They'll have to employ a lot of men just as green as I am even for the conquest of Canada."[29] It was not a surprise then, that, in anticipation of a war with Spain and months before the sinking of the *Maine,* Roosevelt was considering raising a regiment of volunteers of which he would be deputy commander. When war came, he reminded those who argued that he could make a greater contribution in the Navy Department, or that he had obligations to his wife and six children to stay out of combat, of his being accused for two years of trying to get the

United States involved in a war with Spain. "One of the com-
monest taunts directed at men like myself," Roosevelt confided to one correspondent, "is that we are armchair and par-
lor jingoes who wish to see others do what we only advocate
doing." Nor could he ignore how his sitting out the war could
affect his political future: "I cannot afford to disregard the
fact that my power for good, whatever it may be, would be
gone."[30]

Eastern friends of the Indian were divided on the merits
of the war. Roosevelt could count on the warm support of
George Bird Grinnell, with whom he currently was coediting
a Boone & Crockett Club publication and for whom he had
obtained an audience with the secretary of the interior to discuss Blackfoot problems. And it was to Roosevelt that Grinnell turned when he sought a role for himself in the coming
war. The same day that Roosevelt accepted appointment as
lieutenant colonel in the 1st U.S. Volunteer Cavalry, Grinnell
wrote Roosevelt asking his reaction to Grinnell's proposal to
raise a regiment of Indians to fight in Cuba. Grinnell also
mentioned the possibility of recruiting a Cuban regiment instead, although, "I do not know how these dagoes fight, nor
how much dependence is to be placed on them, whereas I
know that Indians could be trusted."[31] There is no evidence
that Roosevelt encouraged Grinnell to pursue his ambition to
get in the war.

Through the columns of *City and State* and in private
correspondence, Herbert Welsh had been one of the most
vocal critics of the administration's drift toward war and of
Roosevelt's bellicose statements. When, however, President
McKinley had appointed Roosevelt assistant secretary of the
navy, *City and State* was positively effusive. He was described
as a "natural fighter" who "has shown rare judgment in the
thick of many fights," a man of "indefatigable energy," "sweet-
ness of temper" and "keen, practical good sense." Indeed, ac-

cording to *City and State,* he was "*sui generis.*" But Welsh could not refrain from adding: "Mr. Roosevelt is something of a jingo . . . and his utterances on questions of foreign policy are not always wise. . . . But this limitation is as fine dust in the balance, compared with his sterling qualities."[32]

A month after this appeared in print, Welsh was asking Roosevelt to intercede on behalf of Francis Leupp, whom Secretary of the Interior Bliss was about to oust from the Board of Indian Commissioners. Like that of Charles Painter, Leupp's service on the board had made him a more effective lobbyist for the IRA and had helped pay for some of his travel to reservations. Generally a strong supporter of Roosevelt, Welsh failed to recognize that his occasional harping on Roosevelt's jingoism, and his own antiimperialist stance, put their relationship in jeopardy. Welsh's longtime correspondent and ally in the fights for civil service reform and better treatment of the Indian tended to regard any criticism of himself as, at best, evidence of faulty mental processes or, at worst, rank disloyalty.

While Roosevelt and Welsh, unperceived by the latter, were drifting apart, Francis Leupp's relationship with Roosevelt remained solid. It was through its former Washington agent that in early 1898 the IRA sought Roosevelt's help in persuading President McKinley to retain Superintendent of Indian Schools William N. Hailmann. His response to "Brother Leupp" was to advise him to seek instead the cooperation of the secretary of the interior, because "I find it almost impossible to see the President. The last time I was there by appointment I waited nearly two hours, and then wasn't able to see him."[33] After the exploits of the Rough Riders in Cuba, however, Roosevelt would have no trouble getting McKinley's attention.

Despite his belief that the United States should have tried arbitration before resorting to force, Welsh also became a cheerleader for the troops, and particularly Roosevelt. On June 23, the day before the Rough Riders saw their first combat, *City and State* called for his appointment as secretary of war to replace an obvious incompetent. Referring to Roosevelt as a "genius for action" and attributing the navy's readiness for war to his "extraordinary energy and ability," *City and State* claimed that he could do for the army what he had done previously for the navy.[34]

Thanks to the vivid writing of correspondents like Richard Harding Davis who dogged his footsteps, Roosevelt's exploits were front-page news. In prose that equaled that of the Hearst press, Welsh's *City and State* lauded the colonel for having "exhibited to the full the dazzling quality of military heroism" by his "cool bravery and reckless dash . . . under a murderous fusillade from Spaniards in ambush." But Welsh could not refrain from concluding the nearly page-long paean with a qualifier: "We recognize the dangers of Mr. Roosevelt's temperament, not alone to himself but to the country . . . but, that being said, we would render to him the highest tribute."[35]

Even before the climactic assault on San Juan Hill overlooking Havana, a movement was underway among New York Republicans to draft Roosevelt as their gubernatorial candidate that autumn. And he was not yet back from Cuba when Welsh endorsed the draft. Among the throng who volunteered support were Leupp and Grinnell, both of whom offered Roosevelt advice should he become a candidate. Grinnell's was that he refuse the nomination of the Citizens Union, an independent group that he believed would support Roosevelt anyway. His advice was strengthened by his admission: "For some years I have been a goo goo and a cit."[36]

Roosevelt won in November, although by an uncomfortably narrow margin that he explained to James Bryce, an English friend and the author of the classic *The American Com-*

monwealth: "I was opposed by the professional independents . . . and the idiot variety of 'Goo-Goos,' partly because they objected to my being for the war with Spain, and partly because they feared lest somebody they did not like might vote for me." At this point in his political career Roosevelt prided himself on his party regularity: "One who while always acting ultimately on his own best judgment and according to his own beliefs in right and wrong, was yet always anxious to consult with and if possible come to an agreement with the party leaders."[37]

Roosevelt may have been reacting to a letter just received from William Dudley Foulke, an Indianian active in the civil service movement. Foulke had written of his disgust at the "so-called reformers" who opposed Roosevelt in the campaign, and he reported having chided Welsh for criticism of Roosevelt. "I would not mention this matter at all," Foulke wrote, "but for the fact that it comes from a man who is so honest and sincere in all that he does that I thought you ought to know about it." Roosevelt responded, "The attitude of the bulk of our associates [in the civil service movement] did not much surprise me, but it gave an illustration of why they so rarely accomplish good results and filled me with gratitude for having kept within party lines." He gave Foulke permission to show the letter to Welsh, whom Roosevelt described as one "whose honesty and sincerity I entirely appreciate, though what you tell me of his attitude . . . shows that he is suffering from prolonged and excessive indulgence in the [New York] Evening Post."[38]

City and State had not actually endorsed Roosevelt's opponent, but its constant carping about Roosevelt's bellicose pronouncements and his support of national expansion had possibly contributed to dilution of reformers' enthusiasm for his candidacy. Welsh's role would not be forgotten by Roosevelt, particularly after *City and State* began to boom the new

Anti-Imperialist League. Welsh would continue to solicit Roosevelt's support on Indian matters, but the warm relationship that had peaked during the 1892 tour of the Sioux reservations had cooled perceptibly—at least on Roosevelt's side. When Welsh wrote him defending an Independent who differed with the governor-elect, he gave Welsh a lecture on the difference between the undependability of the "champions of good government" and the loyalty of professional politicians who might oppose him on some issues but could be expected to close ranks behind him on "those contests which really determine the fate of good government."[39] Roosevelt was clearly fed up with the holier-than-thou reformers in general and with Welsh in particular.

If Welsh was aware of the Lowell Institute Lectures that Roosevelt delivered in Boston shortly after the election, they must have made him even unhappier with the governor-elect. Drawing on material accumulated for *The Winning of the West* and speaking on the theme "The Western Movement of the American People," the frontier historian's second presentation focused on Indians. According to a newspaper account, Roosevelt defended the treatment of the tribesmen by the United States with his usual chauvinism:

> Let us remember that it was absolutely impossible in the past to do such justice to the Indians as we expect to be done today. This continent had to be won. We need not waste our time in dealing with any sentimentalist who believes that, on account of any abstract principle, it would have been right to leave this continent to the domain, the hunting ground of squalid savages. It had to be taken by the white race. Our Government has tried to be just—it has been more than just—it has been generous. . . . No other nation—not the English in South Africa or Australia, not the French in Africa, not the Russian in Siberia—has ever purchased land with the attempt at entire fair play to the aboriginal owners that we have shown.[40]

It is unlikely that anyone in Roosevelt's audience was sufficiently acquainted with how Indians were bribed, deceived, and intimidated into selling land to have challenged this statement.

Although New York had a population of about five thousand reservation Indians, they were not a subject on which the governor-elect anticipated spending much time. Indeed, Roosevelt foresaw a rather quiet term with little innovation. "Just at present, all that seems to be necessary is honest administration" was his opinion before taking office.[41] But someone with his tremendous vitality could not be passive, and he proved one of the most exciting and newsworthy governors the Empire State ever had.

Within weeks of Roosevelt's taking office, Welsh wrote William Dudley Foulke about having had "some very pleasant correspondence" with the governor, exclaiming, "How finely he has done!" Unaware of how Foulke had shared with Roosevelt Welsh's criticism of him, he concluded: "I am also glad to say that even those who differed with him last fall among the independents give him now very high praise for his course."[42]

Meanwhile, Welsh continued to seek Roosevelt's help on Indian issues. Early in 1900 he turned to the governor for assistance in getting the agent at the Rosebud Sioux Reservation reappointed, only to be told, "You must remember that I have not got great influence with the administration at all."[43] This was an odd observation to come from one who already was being discussed as a possible vice-president for McKinley's second term.

Roosevelt would be more responsive when Welsh approached him a few weeks later about the possibility of New York's assuming the burden of educating the Indians of that state. Many of them were enrolled at the expense of the federal government in The Educational Home in Philadelphia.

This institution was about to lose its federal funding because of abuses uncovered by the IRA. By return mail the governor assured Welsh that, although the press of other affairs had prevented him from visiting the reservations, he was concerned about the welfare of New York's Indians. Nevertheless, "unless we have something strong to go on," he doubted that the legislature would assume the burden of Indian education. Roosevelt believed that a formal investigation might give him some leverage, and he asked Welsh for the names of "two or three thoroughly rational sensible people" who might conduct it and report on what was needed. "I have felt uneasy about the Indians here all through my administration," he concluded, "simply because it seemed to me that the State has absolutely neglected its duty to them for over a century."[44]

Roosevelt's proposal for a committee was not implemented until just shortly before he left Albany. He obviously was distracted by the issue of the vice presidency, something that he not only did not seek but hoped to avoid. His interest was in the 1904 presidential race, and if he did not run for a second term as governor his idea of a desirable position was to be the first civilian governor general of the Philippines. In April he confided in Lodge that the "machine men, and above all, the big corporation men . . . are especially anxious to have me gotten out of New York somehow. In default of any other way, they would like to kick me upstairs."[45] And kick him upstairs they did.

Roosevelt might have blocked his nomination for the vice presidency at the last moment, but he refused the advice of friends to write a statement irrevocably closing the door. The New York Republican machine then capitalized on his national popularity and forced him on President McKinley over the strenuous opposition of that presumed master of political tactics and Republican national chairman, Mark Hanna.

As McKinley again chose to wage a front-porch campaign that kept him off the campaign trail, the burden in the fall of taking the Republican message to the provinces fell upon Roosevelt. During the campaign he gave "a total of 673 speeches in 567 towns in 24 states; he had travelled 21,209 miles and spoken an average of 20,000 words a day to 3 million people."[46] Needless to say, this left him no time to reflect on the needs of New York's Indians.

Without Roosevelt to push it, the committee that was to investigate the Indians' status was not even organized and ready to function until early December.[47] Long before the committee actually came into being, its original concern for education had given way to broader objectives. Samuel M. Brosuis, Leupp's successor as the IRA's Washington agent, discussed the matter with Indian Commissioner William A. Jones, and his report was relayed to the governor: "The Commissioner is . . . clearly of the opinion that these wards would be in a position to care for themselves if their lands were allotted to them."[48] He also reported that Jones agreed with Welsh's earlier suggestion that Philip C. Garrett, the IRA's president and a member of the Board of Indian Commissioners who also was acquainted with the Iroquois, should be on the committee.

As finally constituted by Roosevelt the committee was chaired by Garrett, and serving with him were four New Yorkers including the chairman of the Board of Indian Commissioners; a member of the Smiley family, which hosted the annual Lake Mohonk Conference; and an Episcopal bishop also on the Board of Indian Commissioners. The fifth member was Oscar S. Straus, then serving as U.S. minister to Turkey, who was surprised at the appointment, given his ignorance of Indian affairs.

In a letter to Garrett, Governor Roosevelt had signaled that he wanted a report that would justify legislation to "do away with the antiquated reservation system and make the Indians United States citizens."[49] In a similar letter to Welsh he added, "I need not go over with you the undesirability of continuing the reservation system with its attendant and inevitable demoralization."[50] Those views, of course, were the conventional wisdom of the day. The Board of Indian Commissioners' annual report for 1900 referred to "the mass of tribal community in ignorance, which the old system of an isolated reservation perpetuated with sinister ingenuity."[51]

That annual report also carried the findings of the Garrett committee. It noted that conditions on some reservations were "repugnant to Christian civilization. Among some, barbarous feasts and ceremonies are still continued." And why were these so deplorable? "The effect of it all is deteriorating to commercial enterprise and to land values," stated the committee. Their answer to this threat to the state's economy was a familiar one: "All jurisdiction over the Indians in this State [should] be relegated to the National Government, and steps taken for the allotment of their lands in severalty under . . . the 'Dawes Act.'"[52]

Although only three members were acquainted with the reservations, the committee had made no effort to visit the tribes or seek the views of Indian leaders. Garrett believed that the prospect of shifting the burden to the federal government "is possible with Col. Roosevelt . . . in the influential position of Vice President."[53] There is no evidence, however, that Vice President Roosevelt made any effort to have the Garrett report implemented.

Roosevelt was not happy in his new office, and he made no secret of it in correspondence with old friends. To one, Roosevelt complained about the drawbacks of his new position: "The vice-president has no power and is really a fifth wheel. . . . It is not a stepping stone to anything except oblivion. I fear my bolt is shot."[54] That he indeed calculated that this might be the last stage of his political career is evidenced by his casting around for a possible new occupation. Becoming an attorney or a history professor were two options he considered.[55] He would have made a great trial lawyer, and certainly no one would have nodded off in his history classes.

Meanwhile, the vice president was badgered by people seeking his support for themselves or their friends. They ranged from former Rough Riders seeking places in the regular army or a federal appointment in one of the territories, to a friend who envisioned herself as the spouse of a U.S. minister to a leading European power. The former Rough Riders were particularly burdensome because there were so many of them. "They have driven me nearly wild. As Edith says at times, we feel as if we were the parents of a thousand very large and very bad children. Many of them have strong homicidal proclivities and are always shooting somebody or getting shot," was how Roosevelt described his predicament.[56]

Herbert Welsh applied to Roosevelt, even before he had been sworn into office, for help in keeping Indian Commissioner Jones in office. In support of this request, he invoked the name of "our mutual friend, Mr. Leupp."[57] In March 1901 it was Roosevelt's turn to pass on to Jones a request he had received on behalf of an Indian agent whose job was threatened. The vice president commented plaintively, "For some reason or other people interested in the Indians persist in thinking that I still have some concern with them. Of course, this is not true, and all I can do is to send letters like the inclosed to you."[58] The commissioner's response was tactful as always: "I regret very much the tone of your letter. . . . While the Insular possessions have largely absorbed the attention of the country, we still have an Indian question, and I sincerely hope that you may find some time occasionally to give it attention, as I understand that you have been accustomed to doing."[59]

Even as Jones wrote, the groundwork for a new organization of friends of the Indian was being laid and the driving force behind it was someone as energetic as Roosevelt and even more flamboyant, Charles F. Lummis. Although he and Roosevelt had shared three years at Harvard, they moved in different circles. Lummis did recall with pride his being congratulated as a freshman by the lordly sophomore for defying a hazing ban on long hair. Apparently, however, Roosevelt never really became aware of him until the 1890s, when Lummis became a prolific writer on the Southwest, a term he popularized.

Lummis first encountered western Indians during his epic thirty-five-hundred-mile walk from Chillicothe, Ohio, to Los Angeles in 1884. He embarked on this trek after being promised a job with the *Los Angeles Times*. En route he wrote travel letters that were published in the *Times* and also, in somewhat more realistic versions, in the Chillicothe paper that had employed him.[60] His career with the *Times* was interrupted when a stroke felled him in 1887. Retiring to the ranch of a Hispanic friend in New Mexico, Lummis forced himself, much as the young Roosevelt had done, to overcome physical weakness.

The ranch was near the pueblo of Isleta; Lummis, when partially recovered, moved there in late 1888. For the next four years his home would be Isleta while he supported himself by churning out numerous articles and books dealing with the region and its peoples. He also was able to photograph several pueblos, taking rare shots of ceremonies. In all of his work Lummis presented the Native Americans as nonmaterialistic, hospitable, dignified, wise, and moral.

The people of Isleta, although initially friendly, began to cool when Lummis showed no indication of leaving. Pueblo officials then suggested that he move on. Lummis ignored these admonitions. As he demonstrated his respect for their culture and labored to understand it, meanwhile displaying a generosity with his candy and tobacco that earned him the nickname Por Todos (for everyone), the people came to accept him. A few even came to love him when he joined their fight against the government's policy of coercing parents to send their children to a boarding school in Albuquerque. The family from whom he rented lodgings had three children enrolled, the youngest having been virtually kidnapped when only four. Lummis waged a white man's war to get the children back to their parents, arousing public opinion by writing newspaper articles and finally getting a lawyer to obtain a writ freeing the children. Out of gratitude his Isleta host family adopted this strange white man who had cast his lot with them.[61]

Lummis's charges that the Indian schools were brutally stripping the children of their culture and attempting to turn them against their parents brought him notoriety in the East. Indian Office officials and the class of people who attended Lake Mohonk conferences were incensed at these attacks on what they conceived to be the heart of the civilization program. Commissioner of Indian Affairs Thomas J. Morgan spoke for them when he charged Lummis with "a slandrous attack upon the entire government system of schools." He denied that Indian parents had "any right to forcibly keep their children out of school to grow up like themselves—a race of barbarians and semi-savages."[62]

The year following his triumph over the boarding school superintendent, Lummis returned to Los Angeles, where he became a local celebrity. Attired in his trademark corduroy suits set off by a red sash on ceremonial occasions, he lived at a frantic pace. Somehow he managed to continue his writing while launching a new journal and being a strong advocate of historic preservation and a patron of art and literature.

Lummis closely followed the rise of Theodore Roosevelt, or "Teddy" as he liked to refer to him—evidence of his unfamiliarity with the man. In the columns of his journal, *The Land of Sunshine* (later *Out West*), Lummis endorsed Roosevelt for the presidency while he was still governor. After he had accepted the nomination for the vice presidency, Lummis denounced Roosevelt for selling out: "The Lion [a Lummis term for himself] loved and mourns for the Real Teddy." He also criticized his foreign policy, which he described as "buncoing Cubans, suppressing Puerto Ricans, killing Filipinos and allowing Boers to be killed!"[63]

Through the columns of *The Land of Sunshine* its editor and publisher continued to attack government Indian policy, and Lummis also kept a close eye on new literary work. Hamlin Garland could not have enjoyed some of the notice he received. Lummis caustically dismissed a Garland piece about Mexico, "where he passed a few weeks as a peripatetic deaf-mute. He did not see very much, and understood less than he saw; and the result is naturally painful."[64] A few months later, however, Lummis was pleased with an article Garland had written on the Hopi snake dance ceremony. "It is encouraging and warming when a traveller can see the human and elemental in a primitive race," the editor wrote. But Garland must have flinched at what followed: "Perhaps all that Mr. Garland needs . . . is to get out West and stay long enough for it to soak in—but the real West, and not the Nebraska farm-hand area with its pig-pen horizon."[65]

Lummis also was coming to know C. Hart Merriam, another individual interested in California's Indian population. Merriam was one of those remarkably versatile people whose acquaintance Roosevelt enjoyed. Like Grinnell, who believed him "one of God's people, a strong man, an honest man and a good fighter," Merriam had first seen the West with a government exploring expedition.[66] Only seventeen, he served as an ornithologist. While birds remained an interest—he was founder of the American Ornithologists' Union—Merriam had wide-ranging scientific experience. He earned a Yale M.D. and practiced medicine for several years before becoming an ornithologist with the Department of Agriculture. By 1896 Merriam was heading the department's new division of biological survey, and he was on his way to becoming one of America's great naturalists.

One criticism of Merriam was that he was a "splitter," one inclined to discover new species when, in the opinion of others, he was only describing variations of known species. One of his severest critics was Assistant Secretary of the Navy Theodore Roosevelt, who engaged him in a scholarly debate before the Biological Society of Washington and in the pages of *Science.* In a lengthy letter to the president of the American Museum of Natural History, Roosevelt made clear why he disagreed with Merriam's propensity to identify new species: "I may as well confess that I have certain conservative instincts which are jarred when an old familiar friend is suddenly cut up into eleven brand new acquaintances."[67] But on this Merriam may have had the last word when two years later he identified and named a new type of elk—*Cervus Roosevelti.* "It is fitting that the noblest deer of America," he proclaimed, "should perpetuate the name of one who, in the midst of a busy public career, has found time to study our larger mammals in their native haunts and has written the best accounts we have ever had of their habits and chase."[68]

By the time President McKinley had that fatal rendezvous with Leon Czolgosz in Buffalo, his vice president's circle of admirers included Merriam as well as George Bird Grinnell, Francis Leupp, Herbert Welsh, Hamlin Garland, and Charles Lummis. With Garland and Lummis he shared literary interests, and Welsh and Leupp had collaborated with Roosevelt to advance the cause of civil service reform; in the process they had helped educate him about the Indian problem. Roosevelt and Grinnell had been drawn together by their mutual

interest in hunting and conservation, and Roosevelt had supplied Merriam with mammal specimens, although they might
debate the classification of species.

In the same period during which Roosevelt had come to
know these men, they met each other and began to share their
common interest in Native Americans. Grinnell and Garland
had cooperated with the IRA, which Welsh headed and of
which Leupp had been an employee, on a variety of Indian
causes. Grinnell, Garland, and Merriam had become sufficiently well acquainted to help Lummis organize, early in
Roosevelt's presidency, the Sequoya League to advance their
vision of Indian welfare.

Theodore Roosevelt would be the best informed individual on Indian affairs to enter the White House since the very
brief tenure of William Henry Harrison. Paradoxically, however, President Roosevelt never exhibited a deep and abiding
interest in the subject. But Grinnell, Welsh, Garland, Lummis, Merriam, and Leupp, in varying combinations and with
varying degrees of success, would seek to capitalize on their
connections with the new chief executive to influence his administration of Indian affairs. And to some of them Roosevelt would turn for help when confronted with problems relating to Native Americans.

3

The Wards and Their Guardians

The roughly 270,000 Indians, a small fraction of the 76 million people of the United States, would pose problems out of all proportion to their numbers for the new president. As wards of the government they required a sprawling bureaucracy of nearly 6,000 to administer their affairs. In 1901 forty-nine agency staffs, some of them with more than thirty members, administered one or more of the 160 reservations that were home to more than 300 tribes. A major component of the Indian Service was a system of 250 schools that accounted for over half of its total workforce and had an enrollment of nearly 20,000.

To monitor this large force, the secretary of the interior relied on seven inspectors, and the Indian commissioner had a corps of five special agents and six supervisors of Indian schools. These officials spent their time in the field moving from one agency to another investigating conditions, but a year or two might pass without an agency's seeing one of these long arms of Washington.

The Indian Service was a growing financial burden for the American taxpayer. In 1901 the total cost of administering Indian affairs was approximately $10 million—in those days a substantial sum. When William A. Jones became Indian commissioner in 1897 he was shocked to learn that the government would purchase for the Indian Service that year "nearly 600,000 pounds of bacon; over 26,000,000 pounds of beef cattle; between nine and ten million pounds of flour; one million pounds of sugar and half that quantity of coffee."[1]

There was no such thing as an average tribe, and reservations were as varied as their occupants. Although government policy for its wards was usually framed as though Indians were a homogenous entity, in actuality they still were a bewildering variety of peoples. Theodore Roosevelt knew this well. Addressing a missionary conference a year and a half before assuming the role of Great Father, Roosevelt reminded his audience of Indian diversity: "Out there you see every grade of the struggle of the last 2,000 years repeated, from the painted heathen savage . . . till you come to the Christian worker of a dusky skin, but as devoted to the work . . . as anyone here tonight."[2]

The Office of Indian Affairs, which supervised these wards of the nation, was a branch of the Department of the Interior. The commissioner of Indian affairs headed the office and reported to the secretary of the interior, and those who knew the administrative setup deplored the commissioner's lack of power. Agents might report to him, but in most situations he could only recommend action to the secretary. His proposals were received by the Indian Division of the secretary's office and its chief clerk screened all Indian-related matters before submitting them to the secretary. Thus the commissioner received credit or blame for many things that actually were determined by the clerk heading the Indian Division. Nevertheless, George Bird Grinnell overstated the case when he remarked to Hamlin Garland that the commissioner was "a mere head clerk without any power."[3]

Both the secretary and the Indian commissioner had lost some influence by 1901, as patronage at their disposal had diminished. In the aftermath of the 1890 Wounded Knee Massacre, Civil Service Commissioner Roosevelt had declared, "The Indian problem is difficult enough, heaven only knows, and it is cruel to complicate it by having the Indian Service administered on patronage principles."[4]

The friends used the massacre to help persuade President Harrison to extend the classified civil service to cover about one-third of the positions in the Indian Service. In 1896 President Cleveland added most of the remaining, with the exception of agents that required Senate confirmation. The Roosevelt-dominated Civil Service Commission also had ruled that Indians who had graduated from an off-reservation boarding school need not pass a civil service examination to be eligible for employment. Roosevelt thought it desirable to fill most of the agency positions with Indians.[5]

That did not occur. Indeed, before Roosevelt entered the White House a commissioner of Indian affairs had concluded that young Indians should be discouraged from thinking that "after their school career is closed the Government will continue to furnish support and maintenance as employees of schools or agencies. The general public is not thus called upon to support either Indians or whites under such circumstances."[6]

The author of those sentiments was William A. Jones, appointed commissioner by William McKinley in 1897 and in office until January 1, 1905, the second-longest tenure of any commissioner. Like that of almost all of his predecessors, Jones's principal qualification for the post was political. A native of Wales, he had grown up near Mineral Point, Wisconsin. After graduating from Platteville Normal School he taught several terms before being elected county superintendent of schools. Jones left education for banking and then, with his two brothers, took over what would become the largest zinc oxide works in the country. Jones also began to dabble in Republican politics and in 1894 was elected to the lower house of the Wisconsin legislature, where he became associated with the Republican faction headed by U.S. Senator John C. Spooner. The senator apparently was responsible for McKinley's appointing Jones to head the Indian Office, after Jones advanced his cause by campaigning for McKinley in 1896. It was not a position that he sought, but it must have provided him some satisfaction, as Jones remained in it for so long. Certainly it was not so burdensome that he had to give up his several business interests, which in time would make him a millionaire.[7]

As commissioner, Jones revealed real administrative talent. Politically astute and socially adept, he was able to survive for eight years although caught between members of Congress seeking favors for their constituents and friends of the Indian who regarded the spoils system as the root of all evil. That Jones somehow managed to remain on good terms with both groups over a long period also suggests a capacity for duplicity.

The extension of civil service to include most positions in the Indian Service had not quieted the demands of politicians for preferential treatment for constituents. Although he might voice momentary irritation with someone as persistent as Representative Charles Curtis of Kansas, himself a mixed-blood Kaw and later Herbert Hoover's vice-president, Jones always managed to let favor-seekers down easily when he could not help. And he could exercise the same grace in dealing with Indians. When communicating to Philip Deloria, a

Yankton Sioux, his inability to provide the house that Deloria sought for his allotment, Jones closed his letter in his usual consoling style: "I am sorry that I am unable to do more for you, as I believe that your case is a deserving one. If at any time in the future something develops to your interest and by which I am able to assist you, I will be very glad to take it up."[8]

The ranks of those who perceived the Indian Service as a potential employer for relatives and political supporters included Henry Cabot Lodge. He interceded for a Judge Ely of Dedham who was seeking a temporary job for a young man headed for Princeton. Jones promised to help find something for him in Indian Territory, expressing particular interest because he saw it as "an opportunity to gain a desirable student for that college, which, by the way, is our family college [his two brothers had gone to Princeton], and to deprive *your* 'Fair Harvard' of one." How Platteville State Normal, Jones's alma mater, fitted into this equation is not clear.[9]

Senator Mark Hanna and President Roosevelt also were among those who sought to procure positions in the Indian Service. Hanna's candidate was a clerk wishing to be promoted to agent. The commissioner must have enjoyed reminding the senator of the political realities: "You know that the positions of Indian Agents are considered the political perquisites of the Senators from the State in which the Agency is located, the home rule doctrine governing in such cases." Moreover, Hanna's protégé labored under a fatal disadvantage, as Jones reminded the senator in a "Confidential" postscript; being "tarred with the wrong political stick."[10] He was a Democrat and owed his original appointment to President Cleveland.

There was no talk of home rule, however, when Jones received word that President Roosevelt was seeking a place in Indian Territory paying $1,200 to $1,500 for a brother of Buckey O'Neill, who had died serving under Colonel Roosevelt in

Cuba. The commissioner promptly contacted the head of the Union Agency at Muskogee, urging him to find something for the president's candidate.[11] Nor would this be the only time Roosevelt intervened to find people jobs in the Indian Service.

Commissioner Jones not only took care of his own friends, but also his family. For a son he found temporary employment at a government warehouse in San Francisco and later with the Five Civilized Tribes (Dawes) Commission. Jobs in Indian Territory not associated with the Union Agency were particularly difficult for Jones to produce. Most patronage there had been, according to him, disposed of in "a great deal of trading and bartering done in Congress" to grease the way for the passage of the Curtis Act of 1898 that extinguished the Five Civilized Tribes' governments.[12]

Nor did Jones neglect the personnel interests of friends of the Indian like Grinnell, who usually were trying to save the jobs of deserving agents or superintendents. Grinnell sought on occasion to influence appointments at the Blackfoot and Northern Cheyenne agencies. He finally concluded, however, after seeing one of his own nominees proved a crook, that "there seems to be something about the business of Indian agent, which saps the morals of almost every man who takes the position."[13]

The influence of the reformers also could be seen in the refusal of the commissioner to move against Supervisor of Pueblo Schools Mary E. Dissette, an able but fractious employee, on the grounds that "she has powerful and influential friends in the east."[14] But Jones seemed to have real reluctance to discharge even incompetent employees, all of whom seemed to have supporters somewhere, preferring to transfer them to another agency to give them a second or even a third chance.

The commissioner charmed the eastern friends by egregious flattery. Invited to speak at the 1897 annual meeting of the IRA, he declined, explaining, "I am just learning, and I do not think there is a member of the Association but that knows a great deal more about Indian affairs than I do." He concluded by declaring that "any suggestions that you can make that you think will be helpful to me in the discharge of my duties will be thankfully received."[15] Later he apologized to Senator Henry L. Dawes for missing the Mohonk Conference. "I certainly should have been with them," he wrote, "more to learn from those who know more than I do of the Indian service than to take part in the discussions. I . . . had promised myself a rare treat in sitting at the feet of those Gamaliels."[16] The man was shameless.

By the time Roosevelt became president, Jones had attended two Mohonk conferences and the members had embraced him as one of their own. Flattered by his protestations of ignorance while acknowledging their superior grasp of Indian affairs, they found little to complain of in Commissioner Jones. Certainly their views on such issues as the desirability of gradually reducing distribution of rations to Indians, and expediting allotment of reservations while discouraging leasing of these allotments to non-Indians, were all echoed in Jones's annual reports. Little wonder that the platform of the 1899 Mohonk Conference called for "enlarging the power of the Commissioner of Indian affairs so that he may no longer be held responsible for that which he cannot control."[17] In January 1901 Herbert Welsh sought help from Vice-President Elect Roosevelt in keeping Jones in office: "an excellent man in every way; one of the best Commissioners I have known."[18]

Welsh had particular reason to feel grateful to Jones. Secretary of the Interior Ethan Allen Hitchcock, a curmudgeon suspicious of everyone and not receptive to suggestions on how he should run his department, denied Welsh a letter introducing him to agents of reservations he wished to visit in

1899. Disregarding his superior's action, Commissioner Jones supplied one. In it he stated that he knew of no one "who has done more toward purifying and elevating the Indian Service than Mr. Welsh."[19]

Welsh and the other reformers were unaware of a dark side of William Jones, one documented in papers he took with him when he left office in 1905 and which became available to researchers over half a century later. These reveal him to have been just as charming when soliciting favors from those doing business with the government or responding to the political needs of his fellow Republicans. For example, on one occasion at the request of a Republican senator he ordered an Indian Service special agent to the senator's state, supposedly to inspect an Indian agency but actually to campaign for the senator. Similarly, Jones connived with Senator Spooner's brother, who ran the Indian Service warehouse in Chicago, to send a government clerk to Wisconsin to help defeat Robert M. La Follette's bid in 1904 to take control of the state Republican Party. Jones himself was pressured by his patron Senator Spooner into campaigning in his home county, which Spooner thought to be pivotal in quelling the La Follette threat. Later that same year Commissioner Jones sought a pass from the Chicago & Northwestern Railroad so that the private secretary of a congressman might return to his district, free of charge, to campaign for the reelection of his boss.[20]

Jones was not only a partisan politician, but he also was a businessman with wide-ranging mining interests. He needed to travel to inspect his properties and scout out others worth acquiring. And what cheaper way to do it than by a railroad pass? The Indian Service shipped millions of pounds of supplies by railroad, and officials of competing lines were more than happy to accommodate a commissioner of Indian affairs capable of throwing some business their way. In all these dealings Jones was his usual tactful and ingratiating self. To a

Santa Fe freight traffic manager he expressed his appreciation for passes issued him and his brother, and then requested one for a friend of his wife's, adding that he did not want to impose and that he hoped the man would "not hesitate to refuse . . . whenever I am 'riding a willing horse to death.'" In the same letter he assured the Santa Fe official that favors done him and his family "will not be forgotten."[21] Other obliging railroad people, for example, a traffic manager for the Great Northern, received more specific assurances. After providing Jones an annual pass he was told, "In relation to the routing of freight to Devil's Lake [Agency] . . . I have issued instructions that hereafter the stuff will go via the Great Northern."[22]

During his long tenure Jones routinely accepted, and sometimes sought, gifts from those doing business with the Indian Service. Some of them were of slight value, but the cumulative effect is to raise questions about the commissioner's ethics. He did seem to have a well-developed streak of acquisitiveness, accepting boxes of canned goods from a wholesaler, free use of a postal telegraph system, and sets of books (including Roosevelt's *Winning of the West*) from a book dealer. Acknowledging one gift from the dealer, Jones disingenuously remarked, "I do not know what I have done that deserves such consideration on your part," adding almost in the same breath, "I will send you in a day or so a complete list of the estimates sent out to the various agencies and schools."[23] This advance information, of course, would give the businessman an edge over his competitors. Jones also intervened to include books handled by the dealer on the list of acceptable texts for agency schools.

The commissioner and his wife collected Indian arts and crafts, and several individuals holding licenses to trade— including the well-known Navajo trader J. L. Hubbell— presented him with blankets, baskets, and beadwork. Agency personnel were equally interested in courting the commissioner, and from them he received a variety of gifts including a saddle of venison, a canoe paddle for his son, and rubies for his wife.

Accepting gifts from people doing business with his office raised questions of conflict of interest, and in fact Jones was engaged in other even more serious activities. He kept one hometown acquaintance (and possible business associate), who manufactured pipe coverings, apprised of government school-construction plans and worked to make him the exclusive supplier of the coverings for the Indian Service.[24]

Jones trod on still more dangerous ground in his mining business, in which another Platteville man seems to have been involved. At least one of their areas of activity was the Uncompahgre Ute Reservation. And Jones also took an unhealthy interest in the Raven Mining Company's operations on the Uintah Ute Reservation. In the mining game he played his cards very close to his vest; not even his brothers, with whom he was in business, always were kept informed of his ventures. In using a former agent to scout properties for him on a Ute reservation, and a current government employee to prospect for zinc deposits in Indian Territory, Jones was flirting with malfeasance in office.[25]

Jones, however, was sufficiently discreet that his use of his office to advance his financial interests did not become public knowledge. And so long as he was able to delude the reformers and his superiors, his job was safe and he could choose when to leave it. Certainly Jones received little supervision from President Roosevelt, who preferred not to be bothered by Indian Service problems and was happy to have an Indian commissioner with whom friends of the Indian generally were happy.

This was not the case with Secretary of the Interior Hitchcock. He rejected their friendly overtures inspired by their belief that, as a brother of a well-known civil service reformer, Hitchcock would be a great improvement over his predecessor. By the time Roosevelt entered the presidency, however, people like Herbert Welsh had been thoroughly disillusioned. Secretary Hitchcock had been in what Welsh dubbed "a state of bubbling irritation" when he finally got an audience with him.[26]

It is little wonder that the friends of the Indian responded with enthusiasm to Roosevelt's assumption of the mantle of the presidency. He was an old ally in the fight to extend the merit system to the Indian Service, and they were confident that things could only improve.

4

The Honeymoon Period for the Roosevelt Administration

Roosevelt's first acts as president were designed to reassure McKinley Republicans like Mark Hanna that the "damned cowboy"—in Hanna's phrase—would not launch the nation on a new and radical course. Roosevelt was well aware that others who had succeeded to the presidency through the death of incumbents had alienated party leaders who then denied them nomination for a full term, and he was intent on being elected in 1904. Although a much more dynamic leader than McKinley, he at least initially would attempt to avoid controversial initiatives or personnel changes. One area was particularly volatile, however. He inherited a war in the Philippines that would drive a wedge between him and friends of the Indian who saw a parallel between the country's treatment of Native Americans and of occupants of territories the United States had recently acquired. In 1900 the Lake Mohonk Conference had its first sessions on these colonials, and by 1904 it had become "The Lake Mohonk

Conference of Friends of the Indians and Other Dependent Peoples."

In the fall of 1901, however, the friends seemed united in applauding Roosevelt's accession. At Lake Mohonk the presiding officer alluded to Roosevelt's attendance in 1892 and expressed confidence that the new chief executive, "knowing the actual condition of affairs upon our Western Indian reservations by personal observation as no other President has ever known them," would cooperate fully in improving the quality of Indian agents.[1]

Those at Mohonk also heard Roosevelt praised by William Dudley Foulke, who delivered an address entitled, "Indian Agents and the Spoils System." He and others had launched a campaign to try to reinvigorate the Civil Service Commission, which had lapsed into the doldrums from which Roosevelt had rescued it in 1886. There was a vacancy on the commission that the reformers hoped President McKinley would fill with their kind of candidate. One thing Foulke had done was to persuade Vice President Roosevelt to advise McKinley on the subject. Roosevelt approached the president with caution: "If you do not care to hear from me, just tear this letter up, and I shall understand perfectly." Although this suggests something less than an intimate working relationship between the two top officers in the executive branch, Roosevelt went on to suggest a few names. Heading the list was Foulke's: "a practical fellow, a straight-out republican who was on the stump day in and day out throughout the campaigns of '96 and 1900 on your behalf."[2]

McKinley ignored the advice—he seldom sought the counsel of his young vice president—but by October 1901 the authority was Roosevelt's and he acted. He requested the resignation of an incumbent and appointed Foulke to the Civil Service Commission. Having visited with the president a few days before reaching Mohonk, Foulke knew of his pending appointment and it helped fuel his enthusiasm for Roosevelt, to whom he referred in his talk: "There is at the head of our government . . . a man who has . . . shown his interest in the Indians; a man whose name stands as the synonym for civic righteousness."[3]

George Bird Grinnell, Hamlin Garland, Charles Lummis, Herbert Welsh, and Francis Leupp were among those who wrote congratulatory notes or otherwise expressed their pleasure with the new occupant of the White House. Garland, who had seen Roosevelt that summer in Colorado, wrote him of his happiness at having a president "who has written books and whose vocabulary is not made up from the briefs of country lawyers and stump orations."[4] Roosevelt replied as he did often in these circumstances: "Come and see me when you are in Washington."[5]

Garland made a point to stop by Washington and call on Roosevelt, who welcomed him warmly. The president did twit him about a novel he was writing featuring an Indian agent who struggled to protect the reservation and its inhabitants from white intruders: "You have discovered the fact that the borderer is often the aggressor and sometimes the thief." Roosevelt went on to say that he would use Garland as a source for information on the reservations: "You and George Bird Grinnell know what is going on out there and I intend to use you both—unofficially."[6]

The next day the president permitted Garland to observe him at work in the executive chamber. That night the Garlands were invited to the William Dudley Foulkes', and after dining the party attended a White House musicale. The failed homesteader, who had become a successful author and a confidant of the man he considered "the most powerful and the most popular man in all America," felt on top of the world.[7]

Grinnell's first approach to the new president did not indicate a comparable euphoric state. Addressing him on September 25, as usual as "Dear Roosevelt," he asked to see him the next week. Roosevelt promptly responded with an invitation to lunch that Grinnell accepted, expressing pleasure at the prospect of seeing the entire first family.

What Grinnell and the president discussed is unknown, but it probably included matters relating to the Tongue River Reservation of the Northern Cheyennes. That week Grinnell did confer with personnel in the offices of the Indian commissioner and the secretary of the interior about getting cattle issued those Indians as herd foundation stock, and also about the necessity of restoring a cut that had been made in their beef ration. Early in December Grinnell would ask Roosevelt to reappoint the incumbent agent at Tongue River.[8] While in the city Grinnell also met with Samuel Brosius, who had been Francis Leupp's replacement as Washington agent for the IRA. Having a man in the White House whom they regarded as an old ally was leading to a strengthening of ties among the six friends of the Indian as they looked forward to a new day.

Although increasingly aware of how his criticism of Roosevelt as a jingo had eroded his standing with the president, Herbert Welsh professed delight at the change in leadership. An anticipated increase in influence by the IRA was alluded to in fund-raising letters, and the report of the organization's annual meeting in December 1901 lauded the new chief executive:

> We think that the present outlook for Indian affairs is . . . particularly bright. No man in the country has a fuller or more practical sympathy with the Indians than President Roosevelt, nor a better understanding of their conditions and needs. . . . Mr. Roosevelt first knew the Indians on the rougher, harder side, which he saw in his earlier experiences of frontier and cowboy life. Later he visited a number of Indian reservations and saw the governmental and philanthropic side of the question.[9]

Welsh's *City and State* also reflected his confidence. It declared in an article headed "Bad Agents Unnecessary" that "a better day has dawned for the Indian" with Roosevelt in the presidency and William Dudley Foulke on the Civil Service Commission.[10]

As an organization that took the lead in monitoring the Indian Service, the IRA already had alienated Secretary Hitchcock by bringing charges against his subordinates. Welsh did not intend to back off the tactic; the only question was how to bypass Hitchcock and go directly to the president. Brosius was on the scene but was not particularly adept politically, so Welsh concluded that the best approach was through "a close friend of the President," Washington-based Francis Leupp.[11]

Responding to a letter from Welsh, Leupp had agreed that it indeed was "a wonderful thing, seeing our old friend in the chief seat."[12] And Leupp would see Roosevelt often as the Washington correspondent of the *New York Evening Post,* and as a personal friend entrusted with sensitive assignments. After the outburst in the South over Roosevelt's having Booker T. Washington to dinner at the White House, the president was more circumspect. Leupp became one of the less visible channels by which Washington and other African Americans got their views before Roosevelt.[13]

Leupp urged Welsh and Brosuis not to push the president too hard. The journalist believed that Roosevelt would do the right thing where it was politically possible. The president's policy, as he himself confided to Henry Cabot Lodge, was to continue to accept nominations from members of Congress, "but I shall name the standard, and the men have got to come up to it."[14] Roosevelt would infrequently make the selection, but even then he would adhere to the Home Rule practice and seek the concurrence of any Republican senators from the nominee's home state.

Early on, Leupp was able to get before the president a plan for bypassing the politically charged method of appointing agents. This was to have those duties assumed by agency school superintendents who also were bonded and now under civil service, a tactic already employed on occasion by Commissioner Jones. Roosevelt responded favorably, and his administration would increasingly use this procedure to fill the chief administrative post at Indian agencies—without having to seek Senate approval.[15]

Leupp was the prototypical Washington insider; Charles F. Lummis was at home twenty-five hundred miles away but aspired to influence Roosevelt's administration of Indian affairs. Three weeks after McKinley's death, Lummis, in his own eccentric way, managed to convey his confidence in the new president while denouncing the policies the United States was pursuing in the Philippines. Salting his letter with Spanish and western expressions, Lummis closed with, "Away off here we are with you."[16] Roosevelt replied with a terse three sentences: "I thank you very much for your letter. Can't you get on to Washington? I should so like to see you."[17] Although the invitation to visit him was one Roosevelt was dispensing rather casually, Loomis took it as a presidential mandate. He asked, however, to postpone his trip to Washington for a month or two and cited two topics he would like to discuss with the president, irrigation and "our Indians who have been most ignorantly and infamously . . . treated." Lummis enclosed a clipping from his magazine, *The Land of Sunshine,* in which he stated: "It is in Theodore Roosevelt to be one of the greatest of our Presidents."[18] Roosevelt quickly agreed to a postponement of the visit of an editor so favorably disposed.

Before departing for Washington, Lummis launched a new association, "to make better Indians and better-treated ones." Its original focus was the Mission Indians of Southern California, and Lummis charged that there were "few darker and meaner chapters" in the "Century of Dishonor" than our treatment of these Indians.[19] The fifty-odd people who attended the organization meeting included Episcopal and Catholic bishops from the area. Once in Washington, Lummis discussed his plans with, among others, Garland, C. Hart Merriam, and ethnologists Frederick W. Hodge and W. J. McGhee of the Smithsonian. Merriam suggested that Grinnell be included, and Lummis wrote him.

Lummis hoped that the new organization would be able to work with the government rather than adopting an adversarial role. "Instead of fighting the Bureau and getting in such bad odor that it hates to see us coming—as the Indian Rights Association has done," he wrote Grinnell, "we must make ourselves so useful that the Bureau will find our way the line of least resistance." The Californian vowed that the new group "shall never fall into the hands of the impossible people. It is born of sentiment, but it must never admit sentimentality."[20] "Sentimental" was the disparaging adjective with which their critics damned eastern reformers.

Although it had begun as a West Coast operation, some of those with whom Lummis discussed it in the East, particularly Hamlin Garland, envisioned its operating nationwide. Grinnell unsuccessfully tried to dampen the enthusiasm of Garland, who dispatched Lummis unsolicited suggestions for a name, objectives, and organization for the infant association. Taken aback, founder Lummis responded, "I am glad to have your vigorous manhood harnessed to our car, but please don't run away with the hearse."[21] Later, when the eager Garland proposed keeping Indians in buckskins as a worthy objective of the league, Lummis replied tersely, "We must save our Indians first; afterwards we can decide about their tailoring."[22]

But Garland would have a free hand in the East and he began pushing for the formation of a New York City chapter of the Sequoya League, as it would be named after much discussion. A series of meetings at the home of Mrs. F. M. Doubleday, wife of the publisher, culminated in one that attracted at least eighty people who organized the chapter. Few, however, seem to have had Garland's zeal for the cause, and the League would remain focused on and run from the Southwest.

Lummis placed himself, Grinnell, and Merriam on the seven-member executive committee, and Mrs. Doubleday and Garland on the much larger advisory board. Garland's assignment was explained to Grinnell as a move, "since [Garland's] impetuous letter" with its flood of unsolicited ideas, "to get him where he will feel in honor bound not to spill the milk."[23] Despite the presence on the executive committee and the advisory board of people of the caliber of President David Starr Jordan of Stanford University and A. K. Smiley, who had founded the Lake Mohonk Conference, Lummis would make the Sequoya League essentially a one-man operation, with his magazine, which he would rename *Out West,* as its official voice.

While in Washington, Lummis had discussed his hopes for the League with President Roosevelt, Secretary Hitchcock, Commissioner of Indian Affairs Jones, and a few members of Congress. He claimed that "all found 'horse sense' in its plans . . . and all promised cooperation."[24] He already had given effusive endorsement to Jones's policy for the Indians as spelled out in the commissioner's 1901 annual report, proclaiming: "For the first time in the history of the United states, a policy of real mercy, justice and common sense . . . is at last officially announced."[25] As the basic objectives of Indian policy had not changed, and procedures to achieve them remained much the same, Lummis seems to have indulged in his customary hyperbole.

Commissioner Jones's tenure, from 1897 to 1905, encompassed the period during which the Plains tribes, which received national attention out of all proportion to their numbers, were scheduled to complete the assimilation process begun by the peace commission's treaties of 1867 and 1868. The assumption had been that within thirty years, through the agency of Christianity, education, private property, and the reservation's isolation from the dregs of white society, these Indians would have become self-sufficient farmers and stockmen. This had not occurred, and both government officials and friends were being forced to rethink not the objective of assimilation, but rather how to expedite the process. A return to the life of buffalo hunters was impossible, and the prospect of Indians' becoming permanent wards of the government was as unthinkable as was their retention of hundreds of millions of acres of underutilized land.

In his annual reports in 1900 and 1901, and in "A New Indian Policy" in the March 1902 issue of *World's Work,* Commissioner Jones inveighed against "Obstacles to Self-Support,"—the ration system, annuity payments, and the leasing of allotments. He got no criticism from friends of the Indian for the positions taken. The 1901 annual report of the Board of Indian Commissioners had stated, "With the . . . official utterances and actions of the present Commissioner for the most part we heartily concur."[26] And the IRA's chief, Herbert Welsh, assured Jones of his support for a cut in rations: "I could not do otherwise, for this is the very policy which . . . I myself strongly urged."[27]

Given the lack of serious disagreement between officials and the friends about broad objectives and means, it is not strange that there were no surprises in the brief section devoted to Native Americans in Roosevelt's first State of the Union message. He had sought ideas from the Board of Indian Commissioners and then asked Commissioner Jones to look over the board's contributions and submit his own suggestions. The result was that the Indian portion of the message struck only familiar notes. Roosevelt endorsed banning liquor from reservations, abolishing the ration system, individualizing tribal funds, and strictly limiting allotment leasing, all causes championed at Lake Mohonk. The phrase in his State of the Union message that most often has been highlighted by historians is this: "The General Allotment Act is a mighty pulverizing engine to break up the tribal mass."[28] Even that was not original with Roosevelt, Merrill Gates having used the metaphor in his keynote address at Mohonk in 1900.[29] Possibly Gates suggested the phrase when, in his capacity as secretary of the Board of Indian Commissioners, he advised the president on the message.

But the devil is in the details, as Commissioner Jones discovered when he attempted to reduce Indian rations, although such a move seemed to enjoy support everywhere that the friends gathered. In 1898, his first full year in office, Jones began to reduce rations, "this curse of the Indian service."[30] The Sioux were particular targets, although all of their agents opposed the action. Fear of an armed uprising, coupled with the feeling that it was unfair to deny rations to the diligent while continuing to issue them to those Jones referred to as "indolent and inefficient," were arguments advanced by one agent.[31] The commissioner held to his course, convinced that there were able-bodied Indians who would never take up the hoe and plow "until they are compelled by the withdrawal of Government aid."[32] In language similar to that of more recent fables of "welfare queens" arriving in their Cadillacs to pick up their government checks, Jones declaimed against "Indians driving into the agency regularly in buggies and carriages to receive a gratuitous distribution of supplies from an indulgent Government 'to keep them from starving.'"[33]

Grinnell was one of those who endorsed ration reduction. He reported to Hart Merriam that Cheyennes and Arapahoes were "clamoring for work" after their rations were curtailed.[34] He also heard from his friend James Willard Schultz, a white man intermarried with the Blackfoot who, incidentally, named his son Hart Merriam Schultz. A well-known author of stories about Indians, Schultz warned that the tribe was suffering. Grinnell was unmoved: "I am sorry to hear your gloomy forebodings with regard to shutting off the rations, but I do not think things will be as bad as you foretell, and I do not see how the Indians are ever to learn to do any work if they are supported by the government."[35]

Commissioner Jones's ration reductions stirred up more opposition when applied to children at nongovernment schools. An order issued August 27, 1901, specified that they would no longer receive aid. Jones maintained that this was a logical extension of the policy initiated in the 1890s to reduce support gradually for the contract school system, culminating in the failure to appropriate any funds for them for the fiscal year 1901. Coming just before the schools would reopen in September, the withdrawal of rations was a devastating blow to church administrators who had assumed that they would have food and other supplies allotted them for the 1901–1902 academic year.[36] At the Kiowa Agency, for example, four mission schools with a total of about 210 students would be losing rations worth almost $5,800 a year. Their agent protested that in event of closure of the mission schools the government facilites could not accommodate the pupils.[37]

An alarmed observer on the northern plains was Bishop William Hobart Hare. He was responsible for the operation of the Protestant Episcopal Church's four large boarding schools, attended by Sioux students for a quarter-century. The loss of $9,000 a year in rations, at very short notice, created a desperate situation for the bishop. While scrambling to collect sufficient funds to keep the schools open, he tried to bring pressure to bear on Commissioner Jones to alter his policy. Hare dispatched a long and well-reasoned protest to Secretary Hitchcock, and he called upon Herbert Welsh and the IRA for support.[38] Welsh was happy to cooperate, as he was an active Episcopal layman and it was his visit in 1882 to his church's schools among the Sioux that had been the beginning of his consuming interest in Indian affairs.

Welsh's first reaction was to consider writing President Roosevelt. In part this was because he had responded appreciatively to an article in Welsh's *City and State* defending his having Booker T. Washington to dine at the White House.[39] The IRA's executive committee, however, directed him first to approach Commissioner Jones on this issue and Welsh did so, incorporating many of the arguments the bishop had employed in his letter to Secretary Hitchcock, a copy of which he had sent Welsh. Weeks later Welsh was still waiting to hear from the commissioner, and within a year Hare was forced to close two of his church's boarding schools.

The Catholics had a much larger mission school operation than the Episcopalians and responded accordingly to the ration cutoff. Representing their interests was the Bureau of Catholic Indian Missions (BCIM), conveniently located in Washington. Founded in 1874, the BCIM had grown in influence and in 1901 was under the leadership of the Reverend William H. Ketcham, a convert to Catholicism who had studied at seminaries in Ohio and Indian Territory and then served in the territory for eight years as a missionary.[40]

Ketcham took over the BCIM at a time when the tide seemed to be running against church-sponsored education. Congress had ended the contract school arrangement, and the Browning Ruling specifying that agents must first fill government schools to capacity before permitting Indians to attend church schools had become policy in 1896. Now even ration and clothing issues were to be denied Indians enrolled in mission schools. Ketcham was determined, however, not to submit peacefully to policies that tried to confine Indians to government schools that were, in his judgment, "often bitterly anti-Catholic, and at the best totally indifferent in religious matters."[41]

Ketcham had not been one of those overjoyed at the succession of Theodore Roosevelt, commenting, "I am downcast at the death of President McKinley and our doubtful chances (I suppose) under the new President."[42] He was unduly pessimistic. Roosevelt would attempt to allay the pattern of government discrimination from which the Catholics had been suffering since the Grant administration. Catholics also had been conspicuous by their absence from Lake Mohonk. This was not strange, as the organizations that supplied most of the attendees at Mohonk—the Women's National Indian Association, the Boston Indian Citizenship Committee, and the IRA—were all Protestant dominated. Finally, the Board of Indian Commissioners had never had a Catholic member, despite that church's very active role among the Indians.

That the Catholics could expect more even-handed treatment from the new president quickly became apparent. In response to a congratulatory note from Archbishop John Ireland of St. Paul, an outspoken Republican, Roosevelt wrote: "I did not need to receive it, for you and I have been together in the past, and I have ever found that our loyalty was the same to the great ideals of our great nation." He closed with one of his casual invitations: "When you come to Washington I look forward to seeing you."[43]

By the end of October the archbishop had called on the president and shared with him some of the problems the BCIM faced. One related to the Browning Ruling and its denial to Indian parents of the option of sending their children to Catholic schools—if there were vacancies in the government schools on their reservation. Presumably the policy already had been revoked by Secretary Hitchcock on orders from Roosevelt, although Ketcham had told Ireland that the revocation was a "miserable subterfuge."[44] He communicated this to the president and was able to get Secretary Hitchcock to issue a new and unambiguous cancellation of the Browning Ruling.

Ketcham passed on the good news to Archbishop Patrick J. Ryan of Philadelphia, adding that Archbishop Ireland "promised to help me with the Department whenever it is necessary and he can accomplish anything." But the head of the BCIM could not take much comfort in this, because the archbishop "is bitterly opposed to our Society." What Ketcham had reference to was the Society for the Preservation of the Faith among Indian Children. He had established it to raise funds for Catholic schools that were in a perilous financial situation following the end of the contract system and the termination of rations. Ireland, however, objected strenuously to one fund-raising technique the society was employing. This was its offer to have masses read in exchange for donations. Ketcham described the archbishop as scandalized by the promise of "masses and other Spiritual benefits, and that it is all the worse because we have the Masses said in Rome, where the stipend is small." But to Ketcham there was "nothing either scandalous or shocking in offering the Spiritual benefits—indeed, it would be much more shocking and scandalous to suspend the schools and send the children to the Devil."[45]

Meanwhile President Roosevelt was moving to get Catholic representation on the Board of Indian Commissioners, and Archbishop Ireland would not be Ketcham's preference. When he and other local priests met with the president in mid-November, they suggested Archbishop John J. Keane of Dubuque, Iowa, whom Ketcham portrayed as "interested in Indian schools, knows how to get along with non-Catholics, and is a close personal friend of the President."[46] Roosevelt then sought Secretary Hitchcock's view, indicating his own preference for Keane. Nevertheless, it would be five months before the president would act, and, when he did, he appointed Archbishop Ryan of Philadelphia. At the same time Roosevelt filled another opening on the board with a second Catholic, Charles J. Bonaparte, the civil service reformer. Not Ketcham, but Herbert Welsh and Father Henry George Ganss had taken the lead in pushing Ryan and Bonaparte.

Welsh originally recommended Archbishop Keane and Bonaparte to the president, but switched from Keane to Ryan after meeting Father Ganss, with whom he was greatly impressed. The priest had become interested in Indians while serving a parish near Carlisle and had made arrangements with Captain Pratt for Catholic services and instruction for Carlisle's Catholic students. Indeed, Catholic equal access to Carlisle was offered by Commissioner Jones as a model that other schools might follow.[47] Father Ganss had proved his diplomatic skills in winning over Pratt, a notoriously prickly individual, and would do as well with Herbert Welsh, who in the past had manifested some anti-Catholic bias.

After an audience with President Roosevelt, in which he had plugged Archbishop Ryan, Ganss, now employed by the BCIM's Preservation Society as a fund-raiser, returned to Philadelphia, where he conferred with Welsh. The priest had no difficulty persuading him of Ryan's worth, as the IRA leader professed "a sincere regard for [the] Archbishop and a very high opinion of his abilities, good sense, and real desire for what is right, based on a good many years' acquaintance-ship."[48] Welsh also liked the idea of having a member of the Board of Indian Commissioners conveniently located in Philadelphia.

Welsh believed that he was observing the opening of a new era in relations between the Catholics and the Protestant friends of the Indian: "I am deeply impressed with the belief that there is a broad common ground on which our Catholic friends and ourselves can meet and work without compromise which would invade the essential principles of either party." And he gave due credit to Father Ganss, who "has shown so broad and humane a sympathy, so just an appreciation of what was good . . . that I feel quite sure this is not too bright a view to take of the situation."[49] Any remaining doubts Welsh might have had were quieted when Father Ganss subscribed to *City and State* and enthusiastically endorsed Welsh's attacks on American policy in the Philippines, promising to send copies of one letter by Welsh to editors of Catholic journals.

The man clearly responsible for setting the stage for this rapprochement of Catholics and Protestants active in the Indian field was Theodore Roosevelt, who enjoyed strong support from both groups. Aside from his personal commitment to tolerance and equity, the president had good political reasons for trying to right the wrongs done the Catholics by previous administrations. One of the most delicate problems he faced early in his administration was that of the friar lands in the Philippines. Catholic orders owned estates worked by thousands of tenants, and charges that these Filipinos were being exploited had been a factor in producing the Aguinaldo-led rebellion. The United States inherited the problem when it took over the Philippines, and its solution was to try to persuade the friars to sell the land and be replaced by American priests. This required negotiations with the Vatican, and that in turn meant navigating the shoals of prejudice in American public opinion.[50]

As a practical politician who had found it profitable to work with Catholic leaders in New York, and one who was mending his political fences in anticipation of a run for the presidency in 1904, Roosevelt had an additional reason to court the Catholic bishops. They had demonstrated an ability to deliver the vote that Protestant leaders could only envy. For his part, Father Ketcham recognized the need to lobby for the BCIM and realized that a president and members of Congress with significant numbers of Catholic constituents were worth cultivating and supporting.

To try to get legislation restoring rations to mission schools, Ketcham resorted to tried-and-true lobbying tactics. Identifying Senator William Ernest Mason of Illinois as someone who could help, Ketcham approached church leaders in Illinois in late 1901 to do what they could to ensure Mason's reelection. In a letter to Bishop James Ryan of Alton, Illinois, Ketcham opened with this observation: "It is not the wish of this Bureau to mix in politics, yet it is to our interest and to the interest of the Church to help our friends whenever we can." He then went on to say that Senator Mason was just such a friend and that the bishop could help the senator "in his canvass among Catholic and even non-Catholic Republicans, and possibly among Catholic Democratic voters." Clinching the argument for supporting Mason, Ketcham stated: "The Senator's attitude towards the A.P.A. [American Protective Association, a rabidly anti-Catholic group] and on the Philippine question ought to recommend him . . . to Catholics. Moreover, he is friendly to our Catholic Indian Schools."[51]

The BCIM had an ally in its lobbying, the Catholic Order of Foresters headquartered in Chicago. Theodore B. Thiele, an officer in this organization, had also taken up the ration matter with Illinois's other senator, Shelby M. Cullom. Thiele was confident of Catholic political clout in the state: "We defeated thirteen undesirable bills in the Illinois Legislature . . . secured the governor's veto on one that passed over our opposition. . . . I think we . . . have shown our strength sufficiently to impress the senators, and I think they will feel obliged to do the best they can for our cause."[52] Ketcham met with Senator Mason, and that led to Mason's getting an audience with Roosevelt to discuss the ration question. Ketcham's assistant, Charles Lusk, reported this to Thiele and asked him to keep up the pressure: "We want you to pull every string possible, with the view of inducing the President to take favorable action."[53] It would take, however, another two years of lobbying by both Catholics and Protestants to get rations restored to mission schools.

Commissioner of Indian Affairs Jones looked upon ration reduction for able-bodied Indians as a way of coercing them into greater efforts at self-support. Nor did he want them to believe that the government would always serve as an employer of last resort, so he encouraged the replacement of agency Indian employees by whites.[54] Jones was particularly concerned that students returning from four or five years at one of the off-reservation boarding schools like Carlisle would expect the government to continue to support them by providing jobs on the reservation. Moreover, he ordered an end to the practice of paying students for work performed at government boarding schools. A business man at heart, Jones referred to it as "paying the pupils for the privilege of allowing the government to expend $167 per capita for their benefit," that being the cost to the government of maintaining a student in a boarding school.[55] When the head of one school called it unfair not to pay students during their summer vacation for helping put up hay, he was told that 50 cents a day would be ample pay, as care should be taken not to "unfit them for . . . moderate wages after they leave school."[56]

That Indians should become self-sufficient was a goal that few could fault; the issue was how it should be accomplished. In a letter to agents in January 1902, Commissioner Jones proposed a 25 percent cut in rations and clothing issued Indians. Money saved in this fashion, however, could be used to hire Indians at $1.25 per day on reservation construction projects such as roads, fences, and irrigation ditches. Jones insisted that, if at all possible, the Indians should find employment in the private sector with railroads, local stockmen, and farmers. "Instead of an Indian agency being a center for the gratuitous distribution of supplies," Jones declared, "it should be an 'employment bureau.'" To further this objective he suggested that agents send circulars to potential employers informing them of their reservation's labor pool. And Jones reminded the agents that among their charges were girls recently returned from Carlisle and other off-reservation boarding schools who might find employment in "good respectable white families" in the area.[57]

The friends endorsed the commissioner's views, at least in theory. In an article in the *North American Review* in April 1902, Hamlin Garland commented on the problem of making Indians self-sufficient on land that could not support an experienced white farmer. He proposed an alternative form of employment—native crafts—citing the success of Reverend W. C. Roe, a missionary to the Southern Cheyennes, who had seventy Indians producing moccasins, bead work, and other items for which there was a growing market.[58] George Bird Grinnell was sufficiently impressed by Roe's operation to persuade Commissioner Jones to assign a government employee to assist the missionary, and to try himself to launch a comparable workshop among the Northern Cheyennes.[59] Grinnell and Garland must have led in persuading the New York chapter of the Sequoya League to make its first major project the financing of workshops on both reservations.

Commissioner Jones had the backing of President Roosevelt and the friends in what he chose to call "A New Indian Policy." But the controversy over rations for mission schools was only a portent of the opposition the commissioner would encounter in the remainder of his tenure as he strove to convert theory into practice. The friends had warmly welcomed the new president to power, but they would soon lapse into their more familiar roles as nagging critics of his subordinates.

5

Land Problems

Burdened by major problems in the Philippines, deteriorating relations with Colombia as the United States sought a canal route across the Isthmus of Panama, and domestic emergencies like a major coal strike, President Roosevelt had little time for Indian affairs. Nevertheless, he had that active corps of friends of the Indian who were not reluctant to seek his intervention. And Roosevelt was a hands-on president who would intercede personally in matters of no weightier national concern than the religious makeup of the board for a government school for the deaf, or locating a statue of Pulaski so as not to lose a "beautiful old elm."[1] If approached by one of the friends about a particular problem, the least he would do would be to direct the Interior Department to look into the matter and report to him.

Of critical importance to the Native Americans were issues relating to their land. Many of these concerns grew out of the effort of Indian Commissioner Jones to stimulate use by white ranchers of unallotted reservation land. The rationale for this was obvious, according to Jones: "Where the Indians . . . are receiving gratuitous rations they have no right to object to the Government developing the resources of the reservation for grazing purposes, because the grass goes to waste annually unless it is used as it grows."[2] Thus at two large Sioux reservations he approved rancher access even though the tribal councils refused to authorize leasing. A common argument for ignoring tribal views on the matter was that neighboring ranchers routinely ran their cattle on unfenced reservations, and usually only a few Indians profited.

What happened at a Sioux reservation, Standing Rock, is illustrative of how leasing was implemented and the furor it created among the friends. Standing Rock was a large reservation of about 2,700,000 acres with a population of thirty-six hundred Indians. The Sioux held some thirteen thousand head of cattle, but the unfenced range could support many more. In 1901 the Indian Office cut the first deals permitting ranchers access to the reservation. That October at Mohonk, Commissioner Jones defended the action: "There are millions of acres on the Sioux reservation unoccupied, except by squawmen [intermarried whites] and white cattlemen." Furthermore, he insisted, "These people have for years been using the grazing lands . . . without paying either to the Indians or to the government, one cent for the privilege." He pointed out too, that most of the Sioux had no cattle and that those who had one hundred head or fewer could graze them free. For any in excess of one hundred, however, the fee was $1.00 per head. Jones stressed that "it is eminently unfair to permit a few favored individuals to reap the benefit of the grazing lands without any recompense to those less fortunate or less energetic full-bloods."[3]

What Jones did not tell his audience at Mohonk was that the Chicago, Milwaukee & St. Paul Railroad was behind his efforts to open Standing Rock to non-Indian cattle. The C. M. & S. P. expected to profit by shipping ranchers' cattle to the reservation and from there to market. Jones also neglected to tell his audience that the Indians in two councils in May 1901 had refused to admit non-Indian cattle. Nevertheless he persisted, and in the fall of 1901 three-fourths of the adult males were persuaded to accept the leasing of about a million acres. The Sioux secured promises of safeguards for any families living in leased areas and reserved the right to stake out the land to be leased. The instrument drafted in the Indian Office, however, covered an area twice the size that the Indians had approved and ignored the promise to permit them to determine its location.

In December 1901 the Indian Rights Association learned of the situation from a Sioux delegation to Washington, shortly before bids were to be accepted for the grazing leases. Herbert Welsh was then devoting much of his time to investigating reports of atrocities being committed by American forces in the Philippines, and he drove himself so hard that he became ill and had to take an extended rest. Increasingly, Samuel Brosius was taking the initiative in determining the IRA's agenda. Brosius was aggressive in pursuing complaints coming from the reservations and filed many charges against personnel in the Indian Service. Often he lacked solid evidence to support the charges, but he operated on the principle that investigation could do no harm. The commissioner of Indian affairs and the secretary of the interior understandably resented the frequent and sometimes poorly documented accusations, as well as the expenditure of limited resources needed in dispatching inspectors to remote agencies to check on the charges.

Brosius's concern about the Standing Rock leases led him to recommend that the IRA investigate the situation. At its January 8, 1902, meeting its executive committee did authorize sending someone to Standing Rock. In addition it directed a letter be written asking the Interior Department to hold off further action on the leases until the rights of Sioux families in the leased area were ensured and the Indians had indeed given their consent. As Brosius phrased it, "There is a principle involved in this struggle that we should not lose sight of: the *right of the Indians to control their reservation.*"[4]

Brosius also contacted Bishop Hare and missionaries Mary C. Collins and Thomas L. Riggs, seeking information and help in blocking the leases. In Washington he turned to Arkansas senator James L. Jones to stall the leasing by calling on the Indian Office for relevant data for the consideration of the Senate Indian Committee. Senator Jones also arranged to have the Sioux delegation testify before the committee.

Meanwhile others, sometimes after being prompted by Brosius, were beginning to weigh in against the leases. Merrill E. Gates of the Board of Indian Commissioners wrote Jones and spoke to him personally. A representative of the American Missionary Association visited Washington to convey to Secretary Hitchcock the objections of some of its missionaries at Standing Rock, and Francis Leupp wrote an account for his paper that the commissioner thought serious enough to answer.

By late January, President Roosevelt was being contacted on the issue. Hamlin Garland, who said that he saw "grave danger in certain of the provisions of the lease," asked the president to receive the Sioux delegation, including mixed-blood interpreter Louis Primeau and John Carignan, a French Canadian.[5] Garland highly recommended Primeau and Carignan, based on his acquaintance with them while researching Sitting Bull. Roosevelt also granted an audience to Merrill Gates and other members of the Board of Indian Commissioners and asked Secretary Hitchcock to be present. A few days later Roosevelt sent Hitchcock a letter he had received from Garland and observed that the letter and what he had heard from Primeau had rendered him "not altogether easy about the leases." He could understand the advantage of the income for the Indians, but like others feared that leasing might delay the Indians' development as "productive occupiers of their own lands."[6]

By February other friends of the Indian were protesting the leases. The Women's National Indian Association and the Boston Indian Citizenship Committee joined the fight, and *City and State* was informing its subscribers of the problem. Welsh's journal deplored the role of Commissioner Jones, who "has always been regarded as a stanch friend of the red man." It was eloquent about what happened when Indians with cattle found themselves surrounded by ranchers: "The Indians' cows never have calves, whereas the white men's always have twins."[7]

From his post in Washington, C. Hart Merriam alerted George Bird Grinnell to the crisis at Standing Rock. Grinnell had never been there, and he had heard that Garland's confidence in Primeau might be misplaced. Grinnell, who tended to be caustic on occasion, remarked that Garland "claims to know a great deal about the Standing Rock reservation. . . . He is a good talker."[8] Grinnell was sufficiently concerned, nevertheless, that he wrote Brosius asking for additional information and apprised Lummis on the West Coast that "what appears to be a great swindle to me, has just been attempted, and perhaps perpetrated, on the Standing Rock Sioux."[9] News from Merriam that he had seen Roosevelt about the leases heartened Grinnell: "We all know that if Roosevelt can be made to see that a thing is wrong, he will put his foot on it hard."[10]

All the attention that the leases were getting, and particularly a suit Brosius had persuaded the Sioux delegation to file in federal court, had placed Commissioner Jones on the defensive. The Indian Office had divided the reservation area to be leased into two tracts of relatively equal size. The westernmost, the so-called Lemmon Lease, was formalized, but the Walker Lease, which contained most of the affected Indian families, was put on hold and later canceled. Jones tried to put the best possible face on the leases by insisting that the Indian rights in the pastures would be protected and only they would be permitted to sell fenceposts. Moreover, Jones proposed that the income from the leases be invested in cattle to serve as foundation herds for Sioux families. As he saw it, "Squaw-men and mixed-bloods, who are now occupying the reservation without paying anything for the privilege," were behind the opposition.[11] To undercut the credibility of the interpreter, Primeau, Jones sought confirmation of a report that the C. M. & S. P. had put the mixed-blood on its payroll the previous year to help sell leasing to the Sioux.[12]

The commissioner's damage control might have worked, as even his critics did not oppose leasing unused reservation land. But then the attacks on the leases revived with the publication in *Outlook* of George Kennan's "Have Reservation Indians Any Vested Rights?" Brosius had provided Kennan, a highly respected journalist, "some of his ammunition," and it was effort well spent.[13] The author sent President Roosevelt a copy of his article with a covering letter to which Roosevelt asked Jones to respond. The commissioner prepared a lengthy rebuttal for *Outlook* that the journal published, together with Kennan's rejoinder. Kennan added little in the way of new information to the debate, although he did publicize a charge by one William V. Wade, a North Dakota rancher, that Jones had some pecuniary interest in the leases. That led Jones to persuade the Senate Indian Committee to hold hearings, and in that forum Wade admitted having no tangible evidence to support the charge.[14] The vindicated Jones insisted that *City and State*, which had carried the charge, publish a retraction, and Herbert Welsh did. But Jones could hardly enjoy that triumph, because Roosevelt finally had decided that the mess at Standing Rock required an outside investigator and prevailed upon Grinnell to undertake the mission.

Hart Merriam, Hamlin Garland, and Samuel Brosius contributed to the selection. Brosius earlier had convinced the IRA executive committee that it would be worthwhile to finance a trip to Standing Rock by Grinnell, but the publisher of *Forest and Stream* was very reluctant to take on the assignment. Meanwhile, Merriam and Garland were urging the president to pick Grinnell to do the job for the government. Roosevelt first indicated him as a possibility in a letter to Secretary Hitchcock, and after George Kennan joined Merriam and Garland in support of Grinnell, the president wrote his old friend asking him to take on the task.[15] At that point Roosevelt was going along with the idea that the IRA would pay Grinnell's expenses; however, that would change after the New Yorker accepted the assignment. Grinnell would go to Standing Rock as "a special confidential Indian agent" of the Department of the Interior.

Grinnell's lack of enthusiasm for the assignment was apparent. On the one hand he had made a small contribution to the chorus of criticism of the leases, yet he also could refer to it as an excitement among "the Indian cranks." And he was going "at the cost of a good deal of time and money," as the government would cover only his expenses.[16] As he saw it, the Indians "need the money and the other people need the land," and Grinnell went intent on achieving a compromise.[17]

Aided by Inspector James McLaughlin, a former agent at Standing Rock, Grinnell spent over a week on the reservation and secured Sioux consent to a slightly revised Lemmon Lease. In a twenty-five-page report, Grinnell strayed from his assignment to attack general policies of the Indian Office and to blame many of the Indian Office's problems on "the extremely radical—not to say eccentric—moves of the Honorable Commissioner of Indian Affairs." According to Grinnell, Commissioner Jones "appears to believe that the savage can be turned into a civilized man by an act of Congress or by a Departmental order, and that the inheritance of 10,000 years can be swept away by the word of the chief of a bureau."[18] Garland and others began to circulate the rumor that Jones would soon be leaving his post. To an acquaintance Jones confided that "it is a matter of supreme indifference to me whether my official head goes off or not," but he refused "to run under fire" and remained in office another eighteen months.[19]

Roosevelt informed Grinnell that he was "uncomfortably surprised" at the report's depiction of Commissioner Jones. Grinnell, however, also had been very critical of Standing Rock agent George H. Bingenheimer, whom the president said would be discharged. He then delivered Grinnell a lecture on the appointment process and its stress on the role of local senators. Roosevelt did not take the easy way out, blaming politicians: "In the long run politicians exactly represent the people, their good qualities, their bad qualities, and their indifference." Nor could he pass up the opportunity to denigrate the efforts of the reformers, some of whom disagreed violently with him on the army's operations in the Philippines. "Wise eastern philanthropists can do a good deal," Roosevelt observed, "but many of the eastern philanthropists are anything but wise, and these are in the aggregate very harmful."[20] Certainly their attacks on U.S. policy in the Philippines were getting on his nerves.

Although they had not significantly changed conditions at Standing Rock, except to get the Walker Lease canceled, the reformers had demonstrated their potential. To at least some degree they had coordinated their campaign, attracted national press coverage, and persuaded President Roosevelt to intervene personally. Nevertheless, a year later Commissioner Jones was scheming with E. S. Keeley, the general freight agent for the C. M. & S. P., to try to coax the Indians into leasing more of Standing Rock. Jones told Keeley that "in view of the contentions we had last winter I hesitate somewhat to take the initiative myself."[21] Jones probably was reluctant to flatly refuse a railroad official from whom he had received favors, including an annual railroad pass for 1903.

The coalition of the six friends of the Indian was never tightly knit, in part because of the strong and disparate personalities involved. Within months of Grinnell's mission to Standing Rock the fragile connections would be further weakened as conflict broke out over a successor to Agent Bingenheimer. In February 1902, President Roosevelt himself had raised the question of the advisability of reappointing Bingenheimer, citing his conduct regarding the leases. And in June, as previously noted, Roosevelt had told Grinnell that Bingenheimer was on his way out. The president had set a high standard for himself: "When it comes to Indian agents I want the very minimum attention paid to politics. There have been great scandals in connection with these agencies, and I do not favor putting men into them as rewards for political service. The register of a land office has to deal with white men who can protect themselves, but the Indian agent is in a place where the chance of wrongdoing is great, where the temptation is great, and where the chances of detection are comparatively small."[22]

But Roosevelt was a political realist. He confided to Grinnell that if he ignored Home Rule, which placed agent patronage in the hands of senators, he "should probably bring the entire system of Indian appropriations and management to an abrupt halt."[23] And there always were other issues on which the president would need a senator's vote, so some flexibility was a necessity. Only those "eastern philanthropists," with whom he did not lump Grinnell, had no responsibility and could afford to ignore political reality. Grinnell, who advised the president and Secretary Hitchcock to remove Bingenheimer, had seen some of his own favorite agents turn sour and had become disillusioned in the process: "I sometimes think I would hesitate to recommend the angel Gabriel for the position of Indian agent, a place where temptation, opportunity, worriment and insufficient pay combine to break a man down."[24]

Bingenheimer had another detractor in Herbert Welsh, who listed him in *City and State* among several "undesirable" agents.[25] Welsh, however, had become an irritant to the administration and his influence with Roosevelt was declining proportionally. Together with Charles Francis Adams and Carl Schurz, Welsh had written the president to protest government actions in the Philippines and had published their letter for all to see. Roosevelt contented himself with dismissing it as "foolish," but when the antiimperialists began holding public meetings at which individuals testified as to atrocities they had witnessed in the Philippines, his patience was quickly exhausted.[26] From being a "foolish irreconcilable," the IRA's head had become "that swine Herbert Welsh."[27] With obvious pleasure he relayed to Secretary of War Elihu Root, William Howard Taft's denunciation of the "rhetorical mouthings of Moorfield Story and Herbert Welsh."[28] Despite this, Welsh continued to suffer from the delusion that he could attack the president viciously in that area yet have enough influence to rid the Indian Service of agents like Bingenheimer.

Bingenheimer had a friend in Commissioner Jones, who asked a North Dakota congressman to intercede on his behalf and blamed missionary Mary Collins for stirring up the IRA against him. Jones was well aware of Bingenheimer's main problem, and in early 1903 Jones informed the agent that his case was hopeless: "The President seems to be wedded to the suggestions and recommendations of Dr. Grinnell."[29] Indeed, Jones said that Roosevelt had even suggested to a North Dakota senator that he seek advice from Grinnell in selecting a new agent for Standing Rock, a suggestion the legislator indignantly rejected.

The problem for the six friends of the Indian was that they could not agree on who should replace Bingenheimer. Grinnell had sought the advice of James McLaughlin, who had had an uncommonly long tenure as agent at Standing Rock, and he recommended John Carignan, a fellow Catholic. A leader of North Dakota's Republican Party added his endorsement, and Father Ketcham of the BCIM and Catholic Bishop John Shanley of Jamestown, North Dakota, provided additional support.

Grinnell quickly became aware that his candidate would not have united support. As soon as he had learned of Carignan's candidacy, Samuel Brosius launched an attack against him, citing his fourteen-year employment by a Standing Rock trader and arousing fears that Carignan's former employer would be the one really running the reservation. In private correspondence Brosius made clear that he also strongly objected to a Catholic's taking over the agency. He complained that the church already controlled the two government schools at Standing Rock and ran them as if they were private religious institutions. "I have never thought that I was prejudiced against any particular religious denomination," confided Brosius to a fellow IRA employee, "but my experience is that it does not do to give the Catholics any leeway or they will run things to suit themselves." He closed with this admonition: "Perhaps better burn this letter."[30]

Brosius also enlisted Civil Service Commissioner William Dudley Foulke in the fight, and Foulke conferred with Roosevelt. His interview coincided with a visit of William Jones to the White House, and Roosevelt, in Foulke's presence, sought Jones's opinion. The Indian commissioner was happy to support the view that Carignan would not be an improvement on Bingenheimer. The president was not swayed, and several days later he dropped a brief note to Bishop Shanley telling him of his pleasure in being able to appoint Carignan. At the same time he informed Archbishop Ryan that he had made the appointment despite the fact that some of Ryan's colleagues on the Board of Indian Commissioners opposed Carignan.[31] Roosevelt clearly was courting the Catholic vote as the upcoming 1904 campaign loomed ever larger.

The struggle over the Standing Rock Agency had revealed the fragility of the alliances of Catholics and Protestants, and of the IRA and the Sequoya League. Brosius had concluded, given Grinnell's leadership in the Sequoya League, that "all this shows what we have to contend with in the Sequoya League and the Catholic organization. The Sequoya League is not practical at all, but I did have more faith in the practical work of Geo. Bird Grinnell. I cannot trust his work hereafter."[32]

Leasing communally held tribal land had been the principal issue at Standing Rock, but allotment in severalty also was accompanied by a host of problems. One was that allottees were dying and their heirs were usually without the inclination or capital to put their new property into production. For example, ten years after the Cheyennes and Arapahos had received allotments, a local editor estimated that a large percentage of them had died and their land lay idle.[33] Pressure from settlers seeking homesteads and local businessmen hoping for more customers led Congress to enact in 1902 what came to be known as the Dead Indian Act. A clause in the Indian appropriation bill, it provided that adults could sell their inherited land if the secretary of the interior approved, and he routinely did so on the recommendation of local agents.

The law originally had been drafted by the Indian Office to permit only heirs no longer resident in Indian country to sell their inheritance.[34] In Congress, however, it was broadened to apply to all adult heirs. The IRA's Brosius initially endorsed the legislation, citing the situation among the Pawnees, half of whose allottees had died leaving a very "unsettled" title situation.[35] The Board of Indian Commissioners also favored the legislation, seeing it as "putting . . . responsibility for the management of their land, upon Indians as fast as the Indians are capable of taking care of it."[36] They all soon realized their mistake.

Within three months Brosius was denouncing the legislation as "a great error" because of the way it was being administered.[37] Commissioner Jones also had "no doubt that a great deal of rascality will be attempted . . . and . . . it will take a great deal of hard persistent work to counteract the efforts of designing white people to get possession of Indian lands at less than their worth."[38] At least that was Jones's official response to a missionary's complaint about the Dead Indian Act. Privately, he already had advised an acquaintance that when the act went into effect, "anyone having the ready means to purchase will be able to pick up some good bargains."[39] A study published by the National Resources Board in 1935 described the 1902 act as "opening the sluiceway for a wholesale dissipation of the Indian landed estate."[40] The procedures established to implement it were badly flawed. There was no provision for competitive bidding, and agents were known to direct Indians wishing to sell inherited allotments to the offices of attorneys who then would arrange for the sale of the acreage to another client for a fraction of its value. *City and State* declared, "Attorneys . . . immediately discovered an avenue by which to enrich themselves, and dishonest officials . . . had only to connive with designing purchasers to greatly increase their salaries."[41] Brosius was able to get the procedure changed to include appraisals and sealed bids that would not be accepted unless they equaled the appraised value. Nevertheless, if it did not actually open the sluice gates, the Dead Indian Act did accelerate the sale of Indian land, frequently under suspicious circumstances. Within two years, the monthly rate of sales averaged 8,000 acres.[42]

Having urged the passage of the legislation, the Indian Office now deplored the heirs' access to the money and limited the government's wards to no more than $10 a month, and then only with the consent of the agent. For more than $10, approval had to come from Washington—an ironic result of legislation justified as helping Indians become more independent.

Of greater significance than the Dead Indian Act was the 1903 *Lone Wolf v. Hitchcock* decision for which the IRA inadvertently helped set the stage. *Lone Wolf* grew out of a situation on the Kiowa, Comanche, and Kiowa Apache Reservation. William M. Springer, an attorney who had served in Congress and on the Federal bench, had persuaded the Indians to employ him to try to block the opening to white settlement of the surplus land after allotment. Springer sought help from the IRA and it became involved, despite a warning from Francis Leupp that the attorney was principally interested in the possibility of a $5,000 fee. The IRA contributed $400 to help Springer appeal a lower court decision against the Indians. Moreover, it assumed additional costs in recruiting Hampton L. Carson, a prominent Philadelphia lawyer, to assist Springer in the presentation of the appeal.[43]

When the court handed down its decision in 1903, it was a catastrophic defeat for the Indians. Not only did the justices refuse to stay the opening of the reservation, but they also promulgated the principle that Congress had "plenary authority over the tribal relations of the Indians" and could intervene at will. As the IRA admitted, "It is now distinctly understood that Congress has a right to do as it pleases; that it is under no obligation to respect any treaty, for the Indians have no rights which command respect."[44] The practical impact of this on the tribes became apparent a year later in the purchase by the United States of 416,000 acres from the Rosebud Sioux.

Three years elapsed between the initial negotiation and the enaction by Congress of an amended Rosebud Agreement into law. At the insistence of South Dakota politicians acting on behalf of Gregory County, over half of which was part of Rosebud Reservation and generating no taxes and little business activity for local citizens, Congress had authorized negotiations with the Sioux in March 1901. Secretary Hitchcock delegated the duty to Inspector James McLaughlin, celebrated for his ability to deal with the Indians. The inspector encountered considerable resistance, the Sioux demanding $7 to $15 an acre while McLaughlin offered only $2.50, despite an estimate by local whites that the land was worth at least $5. Demonstrating the tactics that made him so successful in persuading Indians to sell, McLaughlin gave them to understand that they could either accept his figure or run the risk of the government's mandating that they sell at even less, only $1.25 per acre.[45]

The following spring, Congress, after a revealing debate in the Senate, declined to ratify the agreement, primarily because of opposition to paying over $1 million for land that it would then permit South Dakotans to occupy virtually free of charge. Senator Orville H. Platt of Connecticut pushed that argument and had the effrontery to criticize the "philanthropists and humanitarians" who insisted "that we ought to pay the Indians what their land is worth at the present time, upon the idea that it belongs to them." Platt also argued disingenuously that paying the Indians adequately for their land really was not good for them: "I think that when we make an

Indian tribe rich we delay its civilization."[46] The plight of the Native Americans became even more obvious when the chairman of the Senate Indian Committee, William M. Stewart of Nevada, insisted that Indians had no legal title to the land, only a "sentimental right."[47] Faced with such obstruction, the bill to ratify the agreement died in that session of Congress. The Indians had been spared that time, although for the wrong reasons.

The IRA, which was attacked by name by senators during the debate, struck back. In June 1902, Samuel Brosius wrote a pamphlet entitled, "A New Indian Policy—The Red Man's Rights in Jeopardy," three thousand copies of which were circulated. In it Brosius quoted Senator Stewart and cited the Rosebud negotiation as an example of the Indians' plight. Brosius concluded: "We are not ready to believe that the American people will sanction a policy of confiscation and injustice toward the Indian race."[48]

Commissioner Jones, as usual, talked out of both sides of his mouth. In late 1901 he had recommended passage of the original bill, maintaining that the $2.50 an acre being offered the Indians was "fair and reasonable."[49] In succeeding months, however, he agreed with a South Dakotan that the land actually was worth about $10 an acre.[50] Jones blamed the state's congressional delegation for opposing any renegotiation of the agreement, because that would delay making the land available to settlers—and cost them more. Nevertheless, the attempt would be made.

In August 1903 Secretary Hitchcock ordered Inspector McLaughlin to return to Rosebud to get Indian acceptance of a new agreement. He failed, and Congress determined to dispense with bargaining. The House Indian Committee had concluded that *Lone Wolf* eliminated the requirement for Indian consent, and Commissioner Jones agreed. Testifying before the committee, Jones said that the Supreme Court had given Congress authority to "do as it sees fit . . . without the consent of the Indians."[51] Speaking specifically to the case of the Rosebud Sioux, he justified ignoring their wishes, despite treaty commitments requiring the consent of the tribe: "Supposing you were the guardian or ward of a child 8 or 10 years of age, would you ask the consent of the child as to the investment of its funds?"[52]

Thus encouraged, Congress turned to consideration of a bill introduced by Representative Charles H. Burke of South Dakota. It employed a new procedure. Instead of the United States purchasing the cession, it would act as a broker between the tribe and the individual purchasers. But this broker arbitrarily set the price at which the Indians would sell the land. For the first six months of the sale the settler would pay $3 an acre, with the payments stretched over a five-year period. After the initial first six months of the sale, the price dropped to $2.50. Even if purchased at the higher figure, the land was sold for substantially less than the $5 the Rosebud Sioux now were asking, and they sought help from the friends of the Indian. Reuben Quick Bear, a Carlisle alumnus and president of the Rosebud Council, appealed to the IRA to try to block the Burke Bill.

Quick Bear's request set off a flurry of activity. Brosius contacted Commissioner Jones, Merrill Gates of the Board of Indian Commissioners, and Francis Leupp. All agreed that the $3 price was too low, and Brosius began providing Leupp with material from which he fashioned an article for the *New York Evening Post* that was headed, "Taking Indians' Lands."[53] *City and State* entitled its story, "Lo, the Fleeced Indian!" and, while admitting the force of the *Lone Wolf* decision, argued, "If the United States is to impress the stranger peoples who have been lately coming under our dominion or influence, it will have to set a better example in . . . its treatment of our wards at home."[54]

Brosius also provided George Kennan with information on the issue, and the journalist would play a key role in the fight. He was the first to try to involve President Roosevelt, writing him on February 12 that he already had conferred with Secretary Hitchcock and Commissioner Jones. The secretary, Kennan reported, had denounced the Burke Bill as "robbery and an outrage," and Jones agreed, while admitting that, "against his own judgment and . . . sense of right," he had "'yielded' to Congressional presssure." Kennan requested an audience with the president to discuss this "latest scheme of the land-grabbers" to plunder those made by *Lone Wolf* into "absolutely helpless and dependent wards of the nation."[55]

A few days later Roosevelt did inform South Dakota's Senator Robert J. Gamble that Kennan had brought the Burke Bill to his attention. He suggested that the price per acre was inadequate and the procedure by which settlers would purchase the land did not protect the Sioux against fraud. Ever the practical politician, Roosevelt concluded: "I know that in a way it is none of my business how you frame the law in Congress; that my duty comes when I have either to sign or refuse to sign the bill. But I am so anxious that the settlers shall have the right to obtain these lands on terms just, not only to them but also to the Indians, that I do not want to take the chance of the bill coming to me in such shape that I could not give my assent to it."[56] Roosevelt then assured Kennan that he had warned the bill's backers that he would not sign it into law in its present form. Commissioner Jones, of all people, had the gall to comment to Kennan that he was confident that the president would back him in trying to get $5 per acre for the Indians, "although he is but human and with all his aggressive honesty has not always been able to resist political pressure."[57]

For the next two months the friends of the Indian kept up their campaign to alert the public and bring pressure to bear upon Congress. The IRA distributed three thousand copies of "Another 'Century of Dishonor'?" which stressed the impact of *Lone Wolf:* "Since the court has clothed Congress with the authority of an absolute guardian, it is incumbent upon the law-making power to see that the interests of its wards are protected."[58] It was Roosevelt's warning to Senator Gamble, however, that proved most productive. Gamble got the bill amended to make $4 per acre the price during the first three months that the land was on sale, and Roosevelt accepted the compromise and signed the bill. "I think it is enough," he said, citing supporting opinion from the head of the General Land Office.[59]

The Indians' supporters also were willing to declare victory. The fact that fewer than half of the 160–acre tracts sold at the $4 figure indicates that talk of $10 an acre for the entire tract was unrealistic. Left to their own devices, however, the Rosebud Sioux would not have sold. And as if any final evidence of the vulnerability of the Indians' wardship status were needed, Congress authorized the federal government, their guardian, to buy for only $2.50 per acre two sections in each township for support of schools. This was half the price the president had originally insisted that private citizens pay.

By coincidence, the same day that the Rosebud land bill became law, April 23, 1904, another piece of legislation was enacted also bearing the friends' imprint. For over two years the IRA had been fretting about the lack of security for Indian allotments. Presumably the Dawes Severalty Act of 1887 had guaranteed that the Indians would receive patents to their allotments, free and unencumbered, after the expiration of the twenty-five-year trust period. Nevertheless, in 1900 the secretary of the interior had determined that he could issue patents anytime during the trust period, thus opening the door to Indians' selling their allotments prior to the expiration of the twenty-five years. Brosius, the IRA staff member most concerned, charged that the ruling "cannot be other than disastrous to the allottee, whose chief anchor has been felt to be an absolute and indefeasible title in an allotment of land upon which he might become a self-supporting citizen."[60]

To correct the situation, Brosius drafted a bill and persuaded Senator Matthew S. Quay of Pennsylvania to introduce it, and then sought allies to push it through. Merrill Gates of the Board of Indian Commissioners and Commissioner Jones agreed to cooperate, which in Jones's case was surprising inasmuch as his superior, Secretary Hitchcock, opposed it. Hitchcock's argument was that he needed the discretion to cancel allotments where fraud was a possibility.[61]

To get the issue before the public the IRA published a pamphlet, and it got results. One woman became so alarmed that she contributed $500, a laborer's wages for about a year, to the IRA to help protect allotments. The campaign also generated some letters to the president, one of them from Senator Quay. Brosius and Commissioner Jones testified briefly before the Senate Indian Committee, which reported the bill favorably. The House was slower to act, but by mid-April Roosevelt was trying to decide whether to ignore the recommendation of his secretary of the interior and sign the bill into law. To help him make up his mind he summoned Secretary Hitchcock and two others from his department to represent the opposition to the bill. They met in his presence with Brosius, Merrill Gates, and Commissioner Jones. As Brosius reported it, the president, after hearing them out, "was inclined to think that if the bill would prevent injustice to the Indian, he would overlook the opportunity it might give some persons to practice fraud temporarily against the Government."[62] Roosevelt signed the bill and again the allies of the Indians had succeeded because of his willingness to respond to their arguments, even if doing so pitted him against a member of his cabinet.

At the request of friends of the Indian, the president also interceded in cases involving the Navajos and the Delawares. The Navajo situation had been building since the 1860s. Nearly a hundred families had been living off the reservation on federal land in what became Coconino County, Arizona. There they competed with white stockmen for the scarce grass, and they had been driven from the area on more than one occasion. But the Navajos had a white friend in W. R. Johnson, a missionary. Less than two months after Roosevelt took office, Reverend Johnson appeared in Washington with two of the Indians and called at the office of the IRA seeking help. Brosius promptly arranged audiences with Commissioner Jones and the president. On hearing the Navajo story, Roosevelt moved quickly to implement a suggestion Brosius had made a year earlier and by executive order withdrew the area from the public domain and made it available to the Navajos. In 1908 the 452,171 acres became a permanent addition to the Navajo Reservation.[63]

The Delaware case was brought to Roosevelt's attention by Senator Quay, the Pennsylvania Republican Party boss and an unlikely ally of the eastern reformers. A Senate loner who survived by his complete grasp of the chamber's procedures, Quay was a cynic who saw only hypocritical posturing in the self-styled humanitarians. Nevertheless, perhaps because of his knowledge that a little Indian blood flowed in his veins, he was surprisingly receptive to tribal delegations seeking redress of grievances. In his autobiography Roosevelt recalled Quay's bringing one group to meet with him in what was obviously a lost cause. When they had left, the senator lingered to remark to Roosevelt that they reminded him of Thomas De Quincey's "The Flight of a Tartar Tribe."[64] Roosevelt enjoyed a good literary allusion, and it gave him a bond with a politician with whom he had little in common except dislike of sentimental reformers.

In January 1904 Senator Quay asked for the president's help on behalf of Delawares who in 1867 had purchased from the Cherokees 15,600 acres of land and had accepted incorporation into the Cherokee Nation. In the maneuvering to break up tribal holdings in Indian Territory after the passage of the 1898 Curtis Act, the Dawes Commission had set aside land for the Delawares, but not where they had been improving homesteads. The area where the Delawares originally located had been the site of a major oil strike, and it was rumored that Dawes Commission members were trying to shunt the Delawares aside to promote lucrative deals with the Cherokees.[65]

Roosevelt was sufficiently alarmed by what he had heard from Senator Quay to order Secretary Hitchcock and representatives of the Dawes Commission to meet with him, Quay, and the Cherokees at the White House. He then quickly decided to cancel the Dawes Commission's relocation of the Delawares. When Quay introduced legislation to protect the Indians, Roosevelt made it clear to Secretary Hitchcock that he did not want the Interior Department opposing it.[66] Weeks later the president would call on Quay, who lay on his deathbed. The senator's last request of Roosevelt was that he look after the Delawares.[67]

That Roosevelt could be moved by less laudatory forces is illustrated by a cession extorted from the Shoshones and Arapahoes in 1904. Roosevelt ordered Secretary Hitchcock to dispatch Inspector McLaughlin to accomplish the mission, adding: "The Wyoming people feel deeply about this, and I am very desirous that it should be done at the earliest moment."[68] And it was. McLaughlin brushed aside Indian objections by referring to *Lone Wolf,* which he said dispensed with the need for Indian consent.[69] The agreement the Indians felt forced to sign provided that they would surrender over half of their reservation, but as had been the case with the Rosebud Sioux, they would receive nothing for it until purchasers for individual tracts appeared. And when Congress ratified the agreement, it unilaterally amended it at the expense of the Indians. Had this happened to the Blackfeet, George Bird Grinnell would have rallied to their defense; other tribes might have appealed for help to the IRA or similar friends of the Indian. The Shoshones and Arapahoes had no influential white people to remind the president of his responsibilities as guardian, and they suffered accordingly.

What the various land transactions had demonstrated was that Roosevelt would respond to pressure and appeals to his good nature. Unfortunately for the Indians, there were more congressmen with constituents seeking Indian land than there were friends of the Indian.

In correspondence with a New York editor about the Rosebud Sioux Agreement, Roosevelt tried to justify his actions. He rejected a critic's charge that the Indians had been defrauded. He also ridiculed the proposal that the United States stop acquiring Indian land: "If we had made any substantial alterations in our present system, both the Dakotas would now be a huge Indian reservation." Moreover, Roosevelt argued, had the critic's views prevailed earlier, "there would not now be a white man in America."[70] In an earlier communication on the same subject, he had declared, "Every rational friend of the Indian wishes at the earliest possible date all the surplus land in all the Indian reservations sold, and the Indians to retain only the lands which they actually use."[71] He did believe that the Indians were entitled to a "fair price," but this was about as far as any chief executive attempting to serve two constituencies—Indians and citizens— and eager for another term, could go.

Theodore Roosevelt. Library of Congress, LC-USZ62-826

Above, George Bird Grinnell. Library of Congress, LC-USZ62-12109
Below, Herbert Welsh. Historical Society of Pennsylvania

Above, Charles F. Lummis. Library of Congress
Below, Hamlin Garland. Library of Congress

Above, C. Hart Merriam. Smithsonian Institution, 88-17,222
Below, Francis E. Leupp. From *The Red Man,* April 1909. Western
History Collections, University of Oklahoma

Above, Ethan Allen Hitchcock. Library of Congress, LC-USZ62-23508
Below, William H. Ketcham. Marquette University Library

Above, Matthew K. Sniffen. Historical Society of Pennsylvania
Below, Charles J. Bonaparte. Library of Congress, LC-USZ62-23275

Above, James R. Garfield. Library of Congress, LC-USZ62-74382
Below, Front row: Theodore Roosevelt and Frank Frantz (two men at back unidentified). DeGolyer Library, Southern Methodist University, Dallas, Texas, Ag86.590.10772 Box 2 Fd6

6

A Friend Self-Destructs

In the February 1902 issue of *Out West*, Charles Lummis launched the Sequoya League on its first campaign. It was to assist more than two hundred Cupeño Indians about to be evicted from Warner's Ranch in Southern California. In the same issue he denounced an Indian Office directive specifying the proper length of an adult male Indian's hair. This would lead to the League's second campaign, one on behalf of Hopis pressed by their agent to conform to the new edict. For its first two years the League's resources would be dedicated primarily to these campaigns. Unfortunately, each would terminate on a sour note and at significant cost to the League's standing with the Interior Department and President Roosevelt. Lummis's relations with other friends of the Indian also would suffer as some of them began to question his tactics and his unorthodox personal life.

The Warner's Ranch problem had come to the attention of eastern reformers four years earlier. The attorney for the small group of Cupeños had requested assistance in appealing to the California Supreme Court a lower court's eviction notice. The Indian Rights Association supplied the bond required for the appeal, but California's high court also decided against the Indians. The IRA had then been able to persuade the Interior Department to seek help from the attorney general in getting the case reviewed by the U.S. Supreme Court. That had resulted only in another adverse decision, and after four years of litigation the Warner's Ranch Indians seemed to be doomed to eviction.

Lummis had been following their ordeal and at one point had testified on behalf of the IRA when the estate of the deceased owner of Warner's Ranch, a former governor of California, sued the association for damages. When in Washington in December 1901, Lummis recommended the establishment of a commission to consist of himself, Grinnell, and Hart Merriam to relocate the Indians.[1] Meanwhile, the ubiquitous Inspector James McLaughlin had been ordered to California to search out a new home for them. After considering eleven other properties, the inspector recommended the purchase of the Monserrate Ranch in San Diego County.[2] Before that deal could be consummated, however, Congress would have to appropriate $100,000 to cover both the purchase of the property and the removal of the Indians from Warner's Ranch.

Meanwhile, Lummis achieved a minor victory when Commissioner Jones withdrew a recommendation he had made to Congress to abolish the Indian agency for Southern California. Lummis had protested the closure to the president, who asked Jones for an explanation, and that forced the commissioner to reverse himself.[3] The Californian was well on his way to alienating Jones, although he was too clever to reveal his ire to Lummis.

And Lummis had backing in Congress, also. California's Senator Thomas R. Bard was a member of the Sequoya

League's advisory board, and he obtained an audience with Roosevelt to discuss the need for a commission to find a solution to the predicament of the Warner's Ranch Indians. The senator then informed Jones that the president wanted some action on the matter.[4] With Indian Office backing, an item promptly appeared in the Indian appropriation bill providing for a commission and specifying that the members must be Californians. Jones informed Herbert Welsh of this development and asked the IRA's help in getting proper people on the commission. Jones's disenchantment with Lummis was apparent: "While the President means well and will do what he thinks proper, I am afraid he is entirely under the influence of a man in that country by the name of Lummis."[5] He went on to denigrate the Sequoya League in a way designed to humor Welsh as the head of a rival organization.

Unknown to Jones, a few weeks later Lummis would suggest to Roosevelt that Jones be ousted. He added that Grinnell was the League's first choice for a new commissioner, although it would also be happy with Hart Merriam or a named Californian.[6] Lummis might have been less enthusiastic about Grinnell had he known that the publisher of *Forest and Stream* had referred to him as "that picturesque person . . . possessed of great activity and energy, but, [who,] like the rest of us, has his peculiarities."[7]

While insisting to Roosevelt that he was not urging that Jones be fired, Lummis made clear his opinion that a more knowledgeable commissioner would be desirable. Jones had tried on Lummis the ploy that he had found so winning in dealings with eastern reformers: "I realize my handicap. Ever since I was a child I have seen Indians—but I never knew any."[8] This was a fatal admission to a man like the Californian, who prided himself on having lived intimately with a pueblo's inhabitants—some would say too intimately.

Roosevelt's response to Lummis's letter was noncommittal; "If I make any change I shall carefully consider what you have said." He did close, however, reassuringly: "Meanwhile, if there is any evidence of any kind or sort that you have that I ought to have, please give it to me."[9] Lummis needed no encouragement, and there were others also happy to advise the chief executive. One of them, a Californian, warned Roosevelt: "Lummis is awful sharp, but a consummate crank of the first water and will get you or any body else in trouble."[10] The president passed this tidbit on to Secretary Hitchcock.

Blithefully unaware of the questions being raised about him in Washington, Lummis applied his abundant energies to the work of the Warner's Ranch Commission, a task he shared with two fellow Californians. But it was Lummis, as chairman, who set the pace, and it was a grueling one. Four days after official notification of their appointments, the commission took to the field. A month and more than five hundred miles later, most of those miles by wagon or horseback, the commission had looked at a hundred properties. It rejected Inspector McLaughlin's choice of Monserrate Ranch in favor of the Pala tract, which, according to Lummis, contained a thousand more acres and five hundred times the water of Monserrate yet could be had for $23,770 less.[11]

It took Secretary Hitchcock as long to approve the Warner's Ranch Commission's report as it had to conduct the investigation. Hitchcock was on vacation in New Hampshire, and Commissioner Jones had to arrange to meet him in Boston to get his approval of the report. Jones himself had just returned from a month in California, where he attended the opening of bids at the San Francisco warehouse of the Indian Service. He also had found time to visit Los Angeles, and he and Lummis had socialized like old friends. The Californian not only entertained Jones in his home, but he also gave Mrs. Jones an Indian rug. The commissioner thanked him profusely for his "disinterested kindness shown both myself and Mrs. Jones while sojourning in California. You made it so very pleasant . . . that we were very loath to leave."[12]

It turned out that the Indians were very loath to leave Warner's Ranch. It would be a long and painful year before they were relocated to Pala. In *Out West* Lummis might crow "that the Sequoya League . . . Means Business and Knows How to Do It."[13] But like so many other white men who, sometimes with the best of intentions, had laid plans to shift Native Americans from their ancestral homelands, Lummis was to discover the depth of their attachment. He explained Indian intransigence as had others—they were being advised by irresponsible whites.

In Lummis's eyes the principal villain was an attorney whom he described as "this chivalric gentleman who seduces people poor enough and ignorant enough to pay him $25 to set aside the Supreme Court of the United States."[14] But Lummis also vented his wrath on "discharged reporters who take [Indians'] money . . . and just common muddle-headed visitors who 'feel sorry for the Indians' and show it by adding to their troubles."[15]

The "muddle-headed visitors" may have included a woman whose letter to Samuel Brosius the IRA agent forwarded to President Roosevelt. She was protesting the removal of the Warner's Ranch Indians, and Roosevelt passed the letter on to Jones. He felt it necessary to reassure the president of the validity of the policy by responding with a seven-page summary of the legal history of Warner's Ranch.[16]

Usually an elusive target, Jones now was getting it from all sides. Grinnell had assailed him in the report on the Standing Rock leases, and the rumor continued to circulate that Jones would resign. Lummis reported to Grinnell that he and Merriam had discussed the matter but he was reluctant "to worry our Man [Roosevelt]" unless "I could *kill* [Jones] *dead*." Lummis's problem was that his knowledge of "Jones' incompetency is . . . almost all hearsay." In all of the commissioner's dealings with Lummis, "he has been very docile and zealous and sensible . . . very glad to take our advice."[17] Jones had indeed worked hard to be accommodating in the same fashion that he tried to oblige members of Congress seeking favors for their constituents. As Grinnell observed, he "is a particularly nice fellow, and is equally nice to all who have dealings with him."[18]

In May 1903 Lummis had an excellent opportunity to get his views on Jones and other issues before Roosevelt. The president had planned a visit to California, and Lummis arranged to meet his train at the Grand Canyon and accompany it for the two and a half days on to Los Angeles. Arriving there with Roosevelt, the enterprising Lummis got himself included in the official party for some of the events in the Los Angeles area. As he confided to Hart Merriam before joining Roosevelt's special train, he intended "to rub in on Roosevelt" the Sequoya League's view of Indian affairs and Commissioner Jones. "So far as Indians go," he wrote Merriam, "Jones is more kinds of a damned fool than almost anyone within three doors of his official inner office, but I myself still believe that he is in business honest."[19] Like the other friends, Lummis was completely unaware of Jones's business activities and relations with government contractors.

The Californian needed all the influence he could muster in Washington because he had gone beyond the mandate of the Warner's Ranch Indian Commission, and he suggested a forced removal of the Cupeños to the Pala tract. For months after the acceptance of the Warner's Ranch report, the government did nothing. Lummis fretted about the effect of the delay on the Indians and on the over a dozen white farmers who had agreed to sell the land that in the aggregate was the Pala tract. Several letters to Washington went unanswered, and not until March 1903 did Commissioner Jones at last accept Lummis's offer to supervise the removal of the Cupeños to Pala.

Lummis must have regretted that offer many times, as it would link him with threats to use force to wrench the Indians from their homes. He concluded that it might be necessary as soon as he approached them about removing. Nor, in his judgment, could the job be done by the local sheriff without the danger of precipitating bloodshed. As Lummis explained it to Jones: "So many fool Americans have (in natural enough sympathy) told the Indians all sorts of things that the Indians do not know what nor whom to believe." Lummis's solution was to call in troops: "But they all know Uncle Sam's soldiers . . . and these Indians would obey them in a minute."[20]

Lummis had not counted upon Secretary Hitchcock's taking an active role in the Warner's Ranch problem. The secretary was chronically suspicious of outsiders meddling in Indian affairs, and in dealing with friends of the Indian he unconsciously played the "bad cop" to Commissioner Jones's "good cop." Jones may have accepted Lummis's proposal to supervise the removal to Pala, but his boss insisted on keeping the responsibility within the Interior Department. Hitchcock selected Inspector James E. Jenkins to supervise the move from Warner's Ranch and in his orders specified that "it is not presumed necessary for you to confer with Mr. Lummis."[21] When the secretary received a letter from him, relative to the removal, signed "Chairman of the Advisory Commission," he erupted. Hitchcock peremptorily ordered Lummis to cease using the title because the commission created by Congress had ceased to exist.[22] To Lummis's lengthy telegram (sent collect) to Hitchcock, urging that troops be employed, the secretary responded brusquely: "I will exhaust every resource in my power before resorting to the use of the Army."[23]

Secretary Hitchcock moved promptly to block Lummis from circumventing him to influence the president. Before

Roosevelt left for California, Hitchcock reminded him, "The authority of the [Warner's Ranch] Commission ceased to exist some time ago, and further action on the part of the Commission, or any of its members is entirely unnecessary, and is leading to much trouble." And he observed, "Mr. Lummis will doubtless appeal to you, and I respectfully request that this matter be left entirely in the hands of the Department." Hitchcock concluded by assuring Roosevelt that a first-class official would be in charge and could get the job done without the use of troops as suggested by Lummis.[24]

Roosevelt got the message. While Lummis had access to him during the train ride from the Grand Canyon to Los Angeles, the president did not undercut his secretary of the interior. When Captain Moat, a Cupeño leader of the opposition to removal, approached him with a memorial praying for presidential support, Roosevelt declined to intervene. Lummis likewise had gotten the word. A *Times* correspondent reported, "Mr. Lummis stated yesterday that he will not be present at the removal, and said that he had resigned the entire matter to the officials of the Interior Department."[25] The *Times* lead read, "Lummis Was Superseded," a characterization that must have nettled someone as hubristic as the founder of the Sequoya League.

The *Times* story on the actual removal was entitled, "Indians Bundled Away Like Cattle To Pala."[26] Inspector Jenkins attempted to satisfy Indian objections as to how the move would be accomplished; nevertheless he insisted that in one fashion or another it must take place: "My sympathies are all with you but it is a case of have to go." The *Times* reporter favorably compared the inspector's tactics with those of Lummis and the local Indian agent: "Lummis and Wright tried the bluff game, which did not work. . . . At one time, if they had appeared in camp it might have gone hard with them."[27] That judgment must have been hard for Lummis to take, as he prided himself on knowing Indians and being accepted by them as a friend and advisor.

Samuel Brosius was among those enjoying Lummis's discomfiture. He and other IRA officials had been annoyed by what Roosevelt had said in a speech at the Grand Canyon en route to California. He had addressed a few remarks to Indians in his audience and had alluded to Native Americans who had served with him in Cuba: "They were good enough to fight and to die, and they are good enough to have me treat them exactly as square as any white men." But then Roosevelt went on: "You have got to save them from corruption, save them from brutality, and I regret to say that at times we have to save them from the unregulated eastern philanthropist," and he coupled that with an allusion to "softness of head."[28]

The excerpt from Roosevelt's speech was read at an IRA executive committee meeting, and there were some present who saw it as evidence of Lummis's prejudicing the president against eastern reformers. Commissioner Jones, not reluctant to create dissension among the friends of the Indian, also put this interpretation on it in a letter to Amelia Quinton, head of the Women's National Indian Association.[29] For his part, Brosius was happy to pass on the latest Lummis gossip to Matthew Sniffen, who was running the IRA's Philadelphia headquarters while Herbert Welsh was on medical leave. He alluded to the Californian's "unenviable record" while living with the Pueblos—a veiled allusion to charges of sexual escapades—and cited Lummis's remarriage in the home of his first wife as, "a sort of free-love affair."[30] Brosius was particularly censorious of sexual indiscretions of Indian Service personnel, and he would have been morally outraged had he known that Lummis kept a log of his sexual conquests.

Brosius had other complaints against Lummis, claiming that he was "working with the Ethnological people to keep Indians what they are, so as to be a study for future generations."

He concluded by charging that while Lummis attacked un-named individuals for advocating force to remove the Cupeños, it was the founder of the Sequoya League himself who had urged employing the army. Brosius clearly had learned this from Commissioner Jones and was happy to observe, "This will come out against him, and show that he is a fake and his paper not to be relied upon."[31]

Under attack from eastern reformers for his role in the Warner's Ranch affair, Lummis was creating more problems for himself by his criticism of a "haircut order," which led the League to bring charges against Superintendent Charles E. Burton of the Hopi (Moqui) training school at Keams Canyon, Arizona. Burton also was responsible for three Hopi day schools, Polacca, Second Mesa, and Oraibi, and also for the Navajo school at Blue Canyon. Indeed, about half of the Indians in Burton's agency were Navajos.

In January 1902 Commissioner Jones began the controversy over hair by a letter to selected agents. In it he identified "a few customs among the Indians which . . . should be modified or discontinued." These included long hair, body paint, native dress, dances, and feasts. Jones rationalized that the action was necessary to accelerate the "civilization" of the Indians and also to reduce the incidence of blindness among them, which he attributed, in part, to face paint seeping into their eyes. Jones singled out the returned students from off-reservation boarding schools as in particular need of guidance, because of their lapsing into old ways. He was confident that most Indians would accept direction in these matters, and that for the rest, "considerable tact and perseverance on the part of yourself and your employees" would get the job done. If returned students did not fall into line, however, Jones authorized withholding jobs and rations, and "if they become obstreperous . . . a short confinement in the guard-house at hard labor, with shorn locks, should furnish a cure."[32]

Jones usually demonstrated consummate skill in dealing with people, but this time he had blundered badly. Within weeks he received protests from every section of the country. Charles Lummis's reaction was to assume that it was a "newspaper fake," as he had talked to both Jones and Hitchcock when in Washington several weeks earlier and had been impressed by "their general horse-sense."[33] Meanwhile, agents who had received the directive complained to Jones, as did private citizens like Ernest Thompson Seton, the well-known naturalist and author. A Sioux delegation to Washington also raised the issue with the commissioner.

Jones was not overburdened with principle and beat a hasty retreat. Responding to Seton, he blamed the uproar on "yellow journalism of the worst sort" and maintained that he had only "urged" agents "to *induce* the Indians by moral suasion."[34] The commissioner assured the Sioux delegation that it was not his intention "to use arbitrary means," and that he recognized that elderly Sioux were "so wedded to old customs that it would be very ill-advised to insist upon compliance with this request."[35] In a letter to Secretary Hitchcock, Jones represented the furor as principally an effort by newspaper editors "to get out of it all the fun they could." He maintained, however, that the policy behind the directive was sound: "It was not that long hair, paint, blankets, etc. are objectionable in themselves . . . but that they are a badge of servitude to savage ways and traditions which are effectual barriers to the uplifting of the race."[36] Nevertheless, Jones issued a circular clarifying his edict by stressing the need for agents to be tactful and avoid precipitating revolts.

The damage already had been done, as Jones had set a deadline of June 30 for reports on progress in curbing the practices proscribed. Within weeks, zealous agents had their reservations in turmoil. President Roosevelt received complaints on the subject, and in a letter to Secretary Hitchcock he lumped the haircut order with the effort to reduce rations as policies whose objective was "excellent" but were "certain to be misconstrued, and a misconstruction might for a time cause serious trouble."[37] A year later, Roosevelt recalled the haircutting order when communicating with Hitchcock and termed the action a "misfortune . . . even with [Indian] assent, much less against their will." He also struck a blow for "a number of Indian dances [that] are perfectly proper to keep up and encourage."[38]

One individual who implemented the order too enthusiastically was Charles Burton at the Hopi Agency. Burton normally was a joy to his supervisors, an agent who was honest, handled his paperwork efficiently, and promptly carried out directives from Washington. Well within the deadline he reported that the Hopi males had been persuaded to cut their hair and that many of the Navajos under his charge had cooperated. Burton heartily approved of the order and, even after the uproar over it, endorsed it in his annual report: "Their long hair is the last tie that binds them to their old customs of savagery, and the sooner it is cut, Gordian like, the better it will be for them." Indeed, this zealot expressed his unhappiness with Commissioner Jones's watered down version of the original directive, characterizing it as a "backward step."[39]

Months after Commissioner Jones modified his haircut order, Lummis opened his campaign against Superintendent Burton. His first step was to attempt to get evidence against the superintendent, and that task he delegated to Gertrude L. Gates, who with her husband had become acquainted with the Hopis. At first Mrs. Gates posed as an invalid seeking a drier climate. When she finally admitted her real mission, Burton ordered her from the reservation and reported his action to Commissioner Jones.

Jones was very supportive of Burton: "I will protect you to

the full extent of my ability. I do not have much fear that the league or any one else will succeed in doing you any harm." The commissioner confided that he had arranged a transfer for Herman Kampmeier, who headed the Oraibi Day School and was accused of brutality in dealing with students and their parents. Jones judged Kampmeier to be "a very good man," although "inclined to be a little hasty occasionally," and promised Burton that he would not "permit this Sequoia League, or any one else, to persecute him."[40] Thus, months before the League had finished its investigation of conditions at the Hopi Agency or had begun to frame charges against Burton, the head of the Indian Office had committed himself to defend the agent and his subordinate Kampmeier.

Lummis would get support from an unexpected source, Belle Axtell Kolp. A teacher at the Oraibi school for only seven weeks, she resigned her post to protest the harsh discipline imposed by Kampmeier's successor, John L. Ballinger, with the knowledge and consent of Superintendent Burton. In the July 1903 issue of *Out West,* Lummis published Kolp's testimony, including a vivid account of two raids on Oraibi by armed Navajos and agency personnel to seize students for the local school.

By coincidence, the same day that Jones was pledging his support to Burton, Lummis was writing George A. Dorsey, an ethnologist at Chicago's Field Museum, seeking his support in the campaign Lummis was planning against Burton. The *Out West* editor indicated that he intended to seek the removal of Burton and, hoping to "coordinate" his operation with "scholars of standing," would like a supporting statement from Dorsey.[41] Lummis would have been shocked had he known that Dorsey promptly reported this to Jones. The commissioner made his case for Burton and then, with his usual tact, stated that he was reluctant to counsel Dorsey on the matter and would continue to respect the scholar, "whatever course you may take."[42] Dorsey promptly wrote Lummis, declining to get involved and adopting essentially Jones's views on the issue.

Lummis was not discouraged by this rebuff and forged ahead, delivering in *Out West* a scathing attack on "Mr. Pinhead Burton." He announced that the League had completed an eight-month-long investigation, "with its special agent (of the highest character and common sense) [Gertrude Gates] directly on the ground for nearly six months." Lummis admitted that Burton was a "respectable citizen," but insisted that he "was not fitted by God or Nature to be Czar over the lives of the 1,800 Hopi." In his usual flamboyant style Lummis denounced "Suasion by Six-shooter, Civilizing by Scissors, and Education with a Club."[43] In more prosaic language, but equally damning, he filed with the Interior Department lengthy charges against Burton and suggested specific witnesses to be subpoenaed.

To make certain that the charges were not lost in the bureaucratic maze, Lummis sent a copy of them to President Roosevelt, who promptly dropped a curt note to Secretary Hitchcock: "Please take this up at once and go over it with me Wednesday or Thursday. I think Burton should be removed immediately."[44]

Commissioner Jones could not have been surprised at this development. Back in May, after learning that Lummis would be on the presidential train from Grand Canyon to Los Angeles, Jones had confided in Amelia Quinton: "I look with some anxiety for the return of the President to Washington as I feel sure that he will call upon me in relation to Mr. Burton's administration at Moqui."[45] The same day, Jones expressed his concern to Burton and promised to try to find him a new place in the Indian Service if Roosevelt insisted on his removal from Keams Canyon. Burton, a man of principle, was confident that the president would give him a "fair show" and refused to consider a transfer as a way out, preferring an investigation that would clear his name.[46]

In anticipation of the attack on Burton, Jones had sought from a school superintendent in Albuquerque documentation of Lummis's own conduct among the Indians, trying to verify rumors of sexual misconduct.[47] But at the same time he sought to avoid an open rupture with the editor. Jones did chide him, as one might an erring friend, for exaggerating the nature of the haircut order. In the next breath, however, he offered to go directly to the president to try to expedite the government's reimbursement of Lummis for expenses he had incurred with the Warner's Ranch Commission. To someone wishing to visit the Hopis, Jones affected bemusement at the antics of Lummis: "I sincerely hope that you do not take seriously all the effusion that Mr. Lummis prints in the "Out West" in regard to that reservation. While Lummis and I personally are good friends, I cannot agree with him in many of his ideas concerning Indian matters, but as he is somewhat of an ethnologist, like yourself, some of his ideas are cranky, and I am free to forgive him as I believe he is honest."[48]

Lummis truly must have been getting on Jones's nerves, particularly when the Hopi problem developed concurrently with trouble on several other Indian Service fronts. The commissioner revealed his growing irritation in a letter to a Wisconsin politician in which he admitted, "Just now I am sick and tired of Indians." He closed with a criticism of Robert La Follette's political style that revealed something of his own predilections: "I am very sorry that Bob seems to lack diplomacy and tact in the management of affairs, as otherwise he would be a very capable man."[49] Jones would prove a master of political infighting as he maneuvered to counter charges prejudged by President Roosevelt.

The commissioner quickly spotted a flaw in Lummis's tactics. Not content with bringing charges and proposing witnesses, the Californian had suggested the names of three possible investigators, among them Inspector Jenkins. After reading an earlier Jenkins report on the Hopi Agency, Jones concluded that he could be trusted to come up with the right verdict and recommended him to Secretary Hitchcock. The commissioner then reassured Burton: "Mr. Jenkins is fair-minded and I think appreciates the situation at Moqui thoroughly."[50]

In an article in "Out West" entitled, "Bullying the 'Quaker Indians,'" Lummis printed the charges filed against Burton, "the narrow-between-the-eyes agent." He predicted that "the reign of the Pinhead Tyrant will soon be at an end," and announced with obvious pleasure Jenkins's appointment: "an alert and competent man . . . named for this task by the League in recognition of his honorable record."[51] By taking credit for the selection of Jenkins to conduct the investigation, Lummis had played into the hands of the wily Jones. And he compounded his problem by arranging for a special representative of the Sequoya League, Charles A. Moody, to monitor the investigation of Inspector Jenkins.

The inspector and Moody arrived at Keams Canyon on July 27 and departed August 7. They visited seven of the eight Hopi villages, took testimony from white agency employees and Indians; among the latter were some that Lummis had suggested as witnesses. On August 15, Inspector Jenkins submitted his report to Secretary Hitchcock, who then shared it with Commissioner Jones and President Roosevelt.

Roosevelt's reaction was to agree with Hitchcock that the investigation had failed to sustain the charges and that the League and Lummis personally "should make full retraction." Indeed, the president declared with finality, "If they are willing in advance to make reckless charges and are determined upon insisting . . . as to their truthfulness, then their usefulness in co-operating with the Department is at an end."[52] He was particularly scornful of Moody, who had said publicly at the end of the investigation that the charges had not been proved, but then, once back in Los Angeles and under the influence of Lummis, had recanted. To one correspondent, the president described the League's charges as having fallen "absolutely flat—in fact, comically so."[53]

Unaware that the tide was turning against him in Washington, Lummis informed Roosevelt that he knew that Hart Merriam had discussed the issue with him, and said, "He was right in his assertion that Burton was unfit for the place. I hope this eye-sore can be cured."[54] The president's response would have chastened a normal person: "Why, my dear fellow, we would not hang a dog on such evidence!" He also dismissed Mrs. Gates's testimony as revealing "her utter unfitness to go into such work at all." Nor did he spare Charles Moody, whose erratic course he held up to scorn. Roosevelt concluded with his own judgment on Burton: "He should have removed, instead of reprimanding, the teacher who misbehaved, and for this he should himself be reprimanded; but no heavier punishment would be advisable if any regard for decency and justice is to obtain in the Interior Department."[55]

The same day that Roosevelt prepared this stinging rebuke of Lummis, Secretary Hitchcock wrote the editor proposing that he publish in *Out West* Jenkins's report and a retraction of the League's charges against Burton. Lummis's response was a lengthy defense of his actions and an attack on the accuracy of the report. He particularly objected to Jenkins's statement that Lummis had failed to persuade the Indians to leave Warner's Ranch and then had been reduced to threats to call out troops. Lummis hinted strongly that rather than comply with Hitchcock's wishes he would continue the battle in the pages of *Out West*.[56]

Secretary Hitchcock wired a concession; he would not include in the printed version of Jenkins's report the paragraph personally offensive to Lummis. In turn the editor, after a long recitation of the case from his perspective, enclosed a draft of a statement to appear in *Out West* that was as close as he could bring himself to an apology to Burton. Lummis forwarded a copy of it to Roosevelt in a long letter that defended the actions of Moody, Gates, and himself. He denied having asked for Burton's "removal," and claimed credit for the League in getting needed changes at the Hopi agency. Even with the president he found it impossible to avoid an implied threat: "The enclosed proof from the Oct. No. is my notion of Live and Let Live as between two dissimilar parties aiming to do the Indian Service good. But if the Department," he continued, "still Eastern (and I beg to say to you that I try to forgive Easterners as hard as I can) insists on Friction, I am ready for the Show-down."[57]

Roosevelt saw no advantage in continuing a long-range debate with a cantankerous editor with a talent for colorful invective. "I want to congratulate you and myself on your straightforward and manly letter," the president graciously said, concluding, "The investigation has been productive of real and great good, and of course you and the Sequoya League are responsible."[58]

A number of people must have enjoyed Lummis's discomfiture. George Bird Grinnell could not refrain from coolly analyzing the situation for Lummis: "It is of course an unfortunate thing that the Burton investigation fell to the ground, as practically it did fall, and, of course, it gives the League a blow in the Department it may take long to recover from."[59] Commissioner Jones happily arranged to have Inspector Jenkins's report printed and distributed to the press. He asssured Jenkins that Lummis "feels so chagrined with the outcome of the investigation that he is like a drowning man clutching at straws and trying to raise a great hullabaloo as to the great things the Sequoya League has done." Jones observed that he and Secretary Hitchcock "understand [Lummis] thoroughly and take him at his true value" and that "the President is gradually finding out what he is."[60] Samuel Brosius reported jubilantly to IRA headquarters that "the investigation of charges filed by Lummis was a dismal failure. . . . They had no case at all."[61]

Lummis could take some comfort that Burton had been reprimanded, Kampmeier discharged from the service, and John Ballenger reassigned. What he did not know was that Jones would arrange the transfer of Burton, in whom he retained "absolute confidence," to Grand Junction, Colorado, which would provide his children "contact with civilization."[62]

The failure to sustain the most serious charges against "Pin-head" Burton had been a body blow to Lummis and the Sequoya League. For several years the League continued to function, but even Lummis could not sustain the vision of it as the vehicle for reshaping Indian policy for the Southwest.

Not that Lummis entirely ceased to advise the president. Within a few months he was writing him regarding U.S. policy on Colombia, telling Roosevelt that "[if you] were as familiar with it as I am, [you]" would handle it differently.[63] Nettled, Roosevelt replied that "if anything, I did not go far enough. No more cruel despotism outside of Turkey exists than that of the so-called Colombia Republic."[64] The irrepressible Californian replied that he felt "in honor bound to fight what seems to me is a great and uncharacteristic mistake of the man I most believe in among public men."[65] To Lummis's six-page dissertation, Roosevelt responded with a single line: "I guess I shall have to wait until I see you and then tell you at length my point of view."[66] Jones was right; Lummis had outworn his welcome at the White House. The president had had enough lecturing from the eccentric head of the Sequoya League. Like Herbert Welsh's, Lummis's wound was self-inflicted.

7

More Trouble for the Friends

By the end of 1904 Charles Lummis had lost influence with President Roosevelt, and changes in the status of the other friends of the Indian would become apparent. There would be a winner, Francis Leupp, and another loser, Herbert Welsh, with George Bird Grinnell, Hamlin Garland, and Hart Merriam retaining some influence.

In an entry in his journal in early 1903, Garland penned a description of his friend Grinnell: "He seemed a singular mixture of the old Manhattan and the old borderman. No one would suspect . . . but he is honorary chief of several tribes of red people, that he was on the war path with the Pawnee in the Sixties, and that he is one of the best informed writers on these subjects in America."[1]

This was somewhat of an exaggeration, although Grinnell was acknowledged to be senior among the six friends of the Indian in terms of personal experience. His most extensive contacts had been with the Pawnees, Cheyennes, and

Blackfeet. With the latter Grinnell could claim twenty years of contact, and he had been adopted by a Northern Cheyenne family with whom he maintained a special relationship. He was careful not to profit by his tribal connections, at one time declining an invitation to join a friend in leasing Indian land on which to graze cattle: "I have always kept myself free from any financial connection with things on the Blackfoot Reservation."[2]

Grinnell opposed both permitting white men to lease reservation pasture for their cattle and the allotment in severalty policy championed by other friends of the Indian. A comment to an army officer revealed his jaundiced view of reformers: "The good people . . . interested in Indians have been looking for 25 or 30 years, for some panacea which should transform the primitive man into civilized man, but they have not found it in allotments any more than in any of the other schemes . . . that they have devised."[3] Grinnell believed that leasing interfered with the development of Indian herds, as the cattlemen usually occupied more land than they paid for, and their stock sometimes introduced diseases that devastated Indian stock. Allotment he found particularly impractical for the Blackfeet because their land was too high, cold, and wet for farming, and the 160-acre allotments that were the norm simply were not large enough to support a family trying to live by raising cattle.

Grinnell, of course, believed that ultimately the Indians must become self-sufficient. When in 1902 a contact on the reservation reported to him that the discontinuance of rations for most Indians, which Commissioner Jones was pushing, would be disastrous for the Blackfeet, Grinnell disagreed. "I do not think things will be as bad as you foretell," he wrote, "and I do not see how the Indians are ever to learn to do any work if they are supported by the government." And he added, "I feel sure that if I were guaranteed clothes and grub I should never do a lick of work."[4]

On the other hand, Grinnell recognized the peculiar circumstances found on some reservations. In November 1904 he assured Jones that he concurred in the Indian Bureau's work policy, although he would make an exception during winter when work was scarce and the Blackfeet might be forced to slaughter their own stock to survive.

Grinnell not only had long acquaintance with the Indians' problems, but also continued to enjoy, through the Boone & Crockett Club and their mutual interest in wildlife, a special relationship with President Roosevelt. They had been with the club since its inception and continued to play major roles, particularly regarding Boone & Crockett publications. They also disagreed occasionally, as when Roosevelt belabored him at length over an attack on the president's friend John Burroughs that appeared over the pseudonym "Hermit" in Grinnell's *Forest and Stream.* The publisher's unabashed response was, "You take the view that Mr. Burroughs should not be criticized at all, because of your affection for him; while I feel that it is more important to get at the facts than to spare his feelings."[5] Two months later Roosevelt told Burroughs that "I have not looked at the *Forest and Stream* since Hermit's article appeared because I was so thoroughly disgusted with the attitude of the paper."[6] But he got over it and had Grinnell to lunch at the summer White House at Oyster Bay, "to talk Indian reservations, and incidentally some points on big-game zoology."[7] A few days later he wrote Grinnell to warn him about confusing mountain sheep with the plains variety and enclosed photos for a piece on bears. Their friendship had survived the brouhaha over Burroughs.

Roosevelt also sought the advice of Grinnell on the Indian passages in his State of the Union messages. In 1902 he made the conventional call for the "ultimate absorption" of the Indians "into the body of our people."[8] But he also stressed the fact that the tribes lived under widely different circumstances, and that the Indians could not be expected to all advance at the same rate. For Plains tribes, he noted, stock-raising rather than agriculture was the best bet.

The 1903 annual message virtually ignored Indians; in 1904, however, Roosevelt again addressed the issue. This time the emphasis was on Indians working, and he again referred to the great disparity in conditions on reservations. While endorsing the elimination of rations to stimulate enterprise, he cautioned that it was "to be exercised only with judgment and with the full understanding of the conditions which exist in each community."[9] To a friend Grinnell wrote of his excitement and pleasure at anticipating and then seeing his views reflected in the message.

Before he was tapped in early 1902 by the president to investigate the leasing situation at Standing Rock, Grinnell had been at work trying to get an additional issue of cattle for the Northern Cheyennes at the Tongue River, Montana, agency. He believed them to be "a fine, energetic people, perfectly willing to do the hardest kind of work," and took credit for an Interior Department proposal to Congress for an appropriation to fence a Tongue River pasture and stock it with one thousand head of heifers.[10] To generate support for the bill, Grinnell approached the IRA and Hart Merriam, who might be able to help from his office in Washington. The lobbying was successful, and in June 1903 the thousand head were distributed among the Cheyenne families.

The previous year these Indians had been forced to eat colts when their government rations were reduced; one band headed by American Horse had slaughtered sixty. Alarmed, Grinnell used his influence at the Indian Office to secure an additional 150,000 pounds of beef for Northern Cheyenne

Reservation residents. This project required six months of pressuring Secretary Hitchcock and Commissioner Jones because, as Grinnell saw it, "they are so densely ignorant of conditions in the west."[11]

Not content just to get the thousand heifers delivered to Tongue River, Grinnell advised on their care. Writing Spotted Hawk, he cautioned the Cheyenne to take good care of the cattle he would be issued, "and after a while these cows will have calves" and he would be able to sell beef, and "then you would be earning your living like the white men." Grinnell concluded with messages to "White Bull, whom I often think of, White Shield, Little Whirlwind, and your mother."[12] A year later, Grinnell was again advising Spotted Hawk on the virtues of being employed and having a garden. He also cautioned the Cheyenne against expecting to share in any settlement of the title to the Black Hills: "You and I know that the Cheyennes used to own the Blackhills, but they let the Sioux sell it and get the pay."[13]

When Grinnell concluded that Tongue River Agent James C. Clifford might be discharged, he rallied to his defense. He described him to Merriam as "the best Indian agent I have ever known," and hastened to Washington to speak to Commissioner Jones on his behalf.[14] Jones reassured Grinnell about the agent's tenure. Not only had he been retained, but Jones had also had Clifford designated a bonded superintendent, which placed him under civil service. He practically oozed concern and cooperation in communicating this to Grinnell, also promising him that his suggestion about an irrigation ditch on the Tongue River Reservation would be attended to promptly.[15]

This was vintage Jones. The commissioner actually had conceived a considerable dislike for this private citizen who used his influence at the White House to meddle in Indian affairs. In an unusually frank letter to Francis Leupp several months earlier, Jones had declared, "I have never been impressed with anything [Grinnell] has either written or done," dismissing his publications on Indians as "simply a re-hash of something that others had written." Obviously irked by Grinnell's evaluation of him in his Standing Rock report, Jones denounced Roosevelt's Boone & Crockett colleague's handling of that investigation as "prejudiced, unfair, and to put it harshly, untruthful."[16]

At about the same time, Grinnell was working to get cattle and a fenced pasture for the Blackfeet as well. He had first become involved with that tribe as a result of their starving time in the winter of 1883–1884. James Willard Schultz, married to a Blackfoot woman and the author of articles on Indians in *Forest and Stream*, appealed to Grinnell to intercede for the tribe. He did, and some supplies reached the desperate people.

In September 1885 Grinnell met the Blackfeet for the first time. As Schultz remembered it, "He arrived on the mail stage—a slender, quiet, fine-appearing man of medium height; in outing clothes that showed much use, his baggage a canvas-covered bedroll, a war sack, a Sharp's .45 caliber rifle, and a fly rod. No tenderfoot he, we thought."[17] When the Blackfeet learned from Schultz that Grinnell had been responsible for their receiving supplies, they adopted him with the name "Fisher Hat," a name borne previously by a courageous, wise, and benevolent leader of the Blackfeet.

In the summer of 1903, Grinnell took his concern for the Blackfeet to Oyster Bay. Roosevelt responded with a terse directive to Commissioner Jones: "Please take up the enclosed [Grinnell's proposal] at once. Wire me what you have done and wire Grinnell immediately to meet you. He knows these Indians right down to the ground, far better than any inspector can know them. Unless there is grave reason to the contrary I wish his suggestions carried out."[18] Jones assured the president that he would implement Grinnell's suggestions at once; he demurred, however, at inviting him to Washington to confer. "I most earnestly ask you not to insist that I do this," he pleaded, indicating that he had "personal reasons."[19] The president did not insist. The whole episode demonstrated how an individual personally distasteful to a commissioner of Indian affairs could still affect policy if he had the ear of the chief executive.

Grinnell's campaign against Agent James H. Monteath of the Blackfeet revealed, however, that even someone with his access sometimes experienced setbacks. Grinnell regarded Monteath as a poor agent but had difficulty developing specific charges that would stand up under investigation. As he remarked to Lummis after the Californian's efforts to get Agent Burton removed had backfired, "I know some men who I think ought to be chucked out of the service, but I will never attack them until I have material that absolutely assures me a victory."[20] Or as he put it to another correspondent: "I have got through making fights where I am sure to be beaten."[21]

In early 1904 Monteath was coming up for reappointment, and Grinnell set out to deny him another four years. Apparently he persuaded the president that the agent was suspect, because, in Grinnell's presence, he drafted a brief note to Secretary Hitchcock: "When time comes to appoint agent for Blackfeet Indians make no appointment until George Bird Grinnell has been consulted."[22]

Grinnell could be forgiven for feeling that he had some voice in affairs at the Blackfoot Agency. The secretary had been ordered to seek his counsel and Commissioner Jones was receptive to his suggestion that the Indian Service distribute some Hereford bulls, "the best rustlers," to the Blackfeet that summer. As Grinnell gloated to J. B. Monroe, an intermarried white man who guided him on some of his hunting expeditions on the Blackfoot Reservation, "I am on good terms with the commissioner at present, thanks to the action of our Ruler, and [Jones] seems disposed to do just what I ask him."[23]

Two months later Grinnell's euphoria evaporated when he read in the morning paper that the president had nominated James H. Monteath for reappointment. He dashed off a letter to Roosevelt declaring the news a "shock" and expressing the hope that he could see him shortly to discuss the matter.[24] At the same time Grinnell wired Senator Quay requesting his help in delaying ratification of the appointment, which Grinnell attributed to "a mistake or forgetfulness" on the part of the president.[25]

Roosevelt's explanation was that "in the multitude of matters I have to attend to this slipped my mind."[26] Early in 1904 Roosevelt did have other concerns. The revolution in the Isthmus of Panama and the U.S–Panama treaty that resulted had demanded much of his time. And he had been following closely a four-month-long Senate fight over his nomination of his friend Leonard Wood to the rank of major general.[27] Roosevelt also was intently tracking the Russo-Japanese War, which had gotten underway—he favored the Japanese—and he had to fend off those insisting that the United States intervene in Santo Domingo. Last but not least, the upcoming presidential campaign was never far from Roosevelt's thoughts as he tried to measure the strength of what he saw as a Wall Street–Mark Hanna alliance against him.

As usual, Roosevelt's intellectual interests and physical activity were maintained at a daunting pace. With French Ambassador Jean Jules Jusserand, he corresponded about reading *Chanson de Roland* in both old and modern French and determining whether the Venetian or the English manuscript was more authentic. When Jusserand had been presented to him, the president recognized that he was a welcome change from the "awful bore" he found most diplomats to be. The routine meeting had quickly turned into an absorbing discussion of the relative merits of Shakespeare and Voltaire.[28] On the physical side he was having trouble keeping his horses healthy, so he was reduced to "scrambles" along Rock Creek and working out with two Japanese wrestlers three times a week. Roosevelt marveled at their ability to throw him to the mat without inflicting major damage.

Grinnell was prepared to accept that Roosevelt was preoccupied by other matters, although he clearly was annoyed with the president's efforts to extenuate his error by citing the support of Monteath by Montana's Senator Paris Gibson and Representative Joseph M. Dixon. With some asperity Grinnell retorted that the two legislators were unfamiliar with Monteath's performance as an agent, and added: "I transmitted to you last summer a bunch of affidavits [against Monteath] . . . which you proposed at one time to have investigated by Mr. W. D. Foulke, but . . . presumably the affidavits have been pigeon holed somewhere."[29]

To bring more pressure to bear on Roosevelt, Grinnell already had turned to Matthew Sniffen of the IRA, and he also sought help from his old friend Hart Merriam, who promptly wrote the president. Roosevelt's response was to query him as to his knowledge of Monteath, and again to cite Congressman Dixon's and Senator Gibson's endorsements of the agent.[30]

Grinnell's efforts were too late. The same day that the IRA dispatched letters to senators on the Monteath issue, the Senate approved the reappointment of the agent. Brosius noted that Commissioner Jones had backed Monteath and that "it looks like a turn-down for Mr. Grinnell."[31] Five months earlier Jones had categorically assured Monteath of his backing, although he admitted cryptically, "There are influences that are at work with parties that are above me in authority." The commissioner also had suggested to the agent that even Secretary Hitchcock was "somewhat timid" about intervening in Blackfoot matters because of unnamed forces—obviously Grinnell.[32] As had been the case with Agent Burton, whom Jones had backed against Lummis, it appeared that the commissioner again had thwarted a friend of the Indians, this time one close to the president.

Jones's success was short-lived. Monteath had hardly been confirmed before Grinnell spelled out for Roosevelt one reason he had opposed the agent. He charged that Monteath favored the Montana Stock Association at the expense of the Indians "who occupy and by law have the use of the land."[33] And he described the Blackfoot range as badly overgrazed as a result of trespassing by white ranchers. The president forwarded the letter to Secretary Hitchcock and asked him "to look into the matter at once."[34] This would result in Roosevelt's requesting Leupp to investigate conditions on the reservation.

Now it was Jones's time to lose. Grinnell learned from Leupp that he would be investigating conditions at Monteath's agency and promptly briefed him on conditions there. Grinnell portrayed Monteath as, among other things, in league with local traders who charged 40 or 50 percent more than traders in nearby towns, while the agent refused Indians permission to leave the reservation to shop.[35] He also supplied Leupp with a list of possible informants, both white and Indian. When in November 1904 Leupp reported on his investigation, he permitted Grinnell to be present for the briefing. "You sized up Major Monteath just about as I said," was Grinnell's post mortem.[36] Within three months Monteath had been replaced by a retired army officer.

Grinnell would enjoy another success in the competition to win the ear of President Roosevelt and advance his Indian agenda. This would involve finding a place in the Indian Service for Frank Mead, an eccentric New York architect whose original sponsor was Mrs. Doubleday, who had helped launch the New York City chapter of the Sequoya League. In the spring of 1903 Meade gave up his practice and went West to learn more about Indians and how he might help them. He did this with the permission of Jones, with whom Mrs. Doubleday had interceded.

Mead's initial recommendations for improving the situation for Indians involved an irrigation project for a Yavapai band. To further this he returned East in August accompanied by an elderly chief, Yuma Frank. By this time he also had acquired a new advocate, Natalie Curtis, described by Hamlin Garland as "an intense little person" who went west for her health and became interested in Hopi music and art.[37] She had managed to get the president's attention and shared with him her knowledge of Hopi songs. This led to Roosevelt's providing her with a letter of introduction that guaranteed her entry to any reservation and the cooperation of agency personnel: "I desire that every opportunity be given Miss Natalie Curtis to travel through all Indian reservations, and to fully investigate and report on, to me or any official under me, all matters pertaining to the wellbeing, the education, the artistic development and industries of the Indians."[38]

A grateful Curtis described what it meant to have such backing: "Though you say that your power is not unlimited, the incisive force, clarity of purposeness and promptness of action with which you have met each issue . . . make us feel that any movement receives an enormous impetus by your championship."[39] She also would have been pleased to know that Roosevelt had urged Grinnell and Garland to talk to her about her ideas on "developing along its own lines their [the southwestern Indians'] marked artistic talent."[40]

Roosevelt, in addition, provided Curtis with a letter of introduction to Secretary Hitchcock that disturbed that curmudgeon, who did not appreciate private citizens' intruding on his bailiwick. The president spoke highly of Curtis and

her objectives: "Her desire is to see the exceptionally interesting artistic side of the life of these Indians preserved, and
to see their artistic efforts, both musical and manual, developed instead of suppressed. She feels—and I think she is entirely right—that the one side in which American life is weak
is the artistic, and that we ought not to throw away anything
which will give us a chance to develop artistically in any way
along original lines."[41] He concluded by asking Hitchcock to
tell Commissioner Jones to confer with Hamlin Garland and
George Bird Grinnell about Curtis's proposals and then report to him. That order was guaranteed to occasion some
commiserating between the secretary and the commissioner,
both fed up by now with their boss's willingness to listen to do-
gooders. The secretary's response was to indicate his willingness to comply, but he could not refrain from adding that
there was some "danger" in ideas such as Curtis's being "carried to extremes" when it was his "firm belief" that the greater
current Indian need was not artistic expression but industrial
development.[42]

It would not have relieved Hitchcock to learn that Natalie
Curtis was pushing Roosevelt to appoint Frank Mead to a position from which he could "start the Indians industrially"
while at the same time caring for their "artistic and ethnological side without any talk or fuss or antagonism of missionaries."[43] She proposed that he be made supervisor of all pueblos, plus the agencies in Arizona. Meanwhile, Roosevelt had
granted an audience to Mead and Chief Yuma Frank. Subsequently in a letter to the commissioner he described himself
as "really touched" by the elderly chief, and asked Jones if it
were not possible to find a position in the Indian Service for
Mead. "I think he could do good work for these strange, semi-
civilized tribes, not a few of whose manners and customs are
well worth preserving," declared the president. "In fact," he
continued, "it would be a distinct addition to our national

life to develop and make our own something of the art, industry and music of the tribes."[44]

Jones quickly agreed that Mead could be useful and put him in charge of settling Yuma Frank's Yavapai tribe, then referred to as the Mohave-Apaches, at Camp McDowell, an abandoned military post in Arizona. Within ten days Roosevelt, moving with customary dispatch, had set aside the nearly 25,000 acres for the Yavapais. It would be several years, however, before the government was able to rid the land of non-Indian squatters.

Grinnell also had urged the president to act on the Camp McDowell situation and, like Curtis, he would press him to appoint Mead as a supervisor of agencies in the Southwest to help move the region's Indians toward self-sufficiency. One of those to whom Grinnell turned for help in this project was Hart Merriam. Merriam then inquired of Charles Lummis about his knowledge of Mead, raising a question about the architect's "mental ballast."[45] Lummis replied with a reference to Meade's "Oscar Wilde estheticism," a curious comment given Lummis's own flamboyant dress and language. The Californian was of the opinion that Mead was "a good deal saner than he looks, and I am inclined to trust him; but still would hardly *vouch* for his balance."[46]

Mead got his appointment in the Indian Service, but within a few months Grinnell heard reports that he was at odds with Hitchcock and Jones. He then asked Leupp if he would join him and Mead if they could get an audience with the president. At this point Grinnell was unaware that Samuel Brosius had launched an investigation of a rumor that Mead had had an affair with a woman that had wrecked her marriage. This also had been called to the attention of the secretary, who delayed Mead's appointment.

Brosius, hypersensitive to charges of sexual indiscretion, was ready to mobilize the IRA's resources to track down clues about Mead's private life. "I am sorry to learn that Geo. Bird Grinnell is very friendly to this man Mead," Brosius confided to Matthew Sniffen, "but he probably does not know him."[47] Obviously a concerted IRA campaign against Mead—and that would come—could only further stress the six friends' fragile alliance.

Mead's initial appointment to resettle the Yavapais had been a temporary one. At the request of Grinnell and Mrs. Doubleday, Roosevelt directed the Interior Department to find a larger role for him. The one created was given the title of General Supervisor—someone to whom agents and superintendents in four states and two territories were ordered to report monthly regarding industry on their reservations. But Hitchcock continued to drag his feet on the appointment. Roosevelt finally pointed out that the charges against Mead related to "incidents" two years old and that Mead had "very emphatic backing" from Grinnell and Mrs. Doubleday. "I direct that my request be carried out," ordered Roosevelt.[48] Meade at last had his new position, although Brosius would continue to scavenge in the detritus of Mead's personal life.

Grinnell and Mrs. Doubleday could credit their success to Roosevelt's willingness to flout convention and to insist that the bureaucracy respond to his wishes. His handling of the Mead and Curtis affairs had demonstrated how a president willing to intervene could help preserve elements of Indian cultures and force the bureaucracy to consider unorthodox measures to improve the Indians' condition.

Hart Merriam, to whom Grinnell had turned for support of Mead, was based in Washington and had excellent contacts. Certainly Roosevelt thought highly of him as a scholar. He once advised Merriam to avoid falling into the pattern of German scholars who squandered their talent by collecting facts and publishing a stream of brief papers. The president believed Merriam should do the work of which he was capable, "the great monumental work on the mammals of North America." Roosevelt was urging Merriam to practice biology as he himself practiced history. Let others do the fact collection; his role and that of Merriam was to "do the work of generalization and condensation—that is, to build a structure out of a heap of bricks."[49]

The president valued Merriam's knowledge of Indians sufficiently to give him a letter of introduction to Indian Service personnel whom he encountered as a field biologist. He also requested that the scientist provide him information about the condition of Indians encountered and their "treatment by Government agents"—a phrase guaranteed to alert any official checking Merriam's credentials.[50]

In December 1903 Merriam had enough influence with Roosevelt that his proposal that landless California Indians be located in national forests was forwarded to Commissioner Jones. In his letter of transmittal Roosevelt described the plight of many California Indians as "a really heart-breaking story" and expressed his "very deep concern" that something be done.[51] Jones promptly took up the matter with Chief Forester Gifford Pinchot, who agreed to attempt to find a place in future forest reserves for homeless tribesmen.[52]

Merriam, however, overestimated his influence when he wrote to the president early in 1904 protesting the retention in service of agents Bingenheimer and Burton. Roosevelt forwarded the letters to the Interior Department for comment. Weeks later when he had in hand the responses of Jones and Hitchcock, he heard from Merriam, who at the instigation of Grinnell made the mistake of complaining about Agent Monteath. Roosevelt's reply was scathing: "I like frankness and I do not mind unconventionality. But when these two qualities change shape a little the result can be justified only by an accuracy which your last letter lacks." He went on to discuss each of the agents about whom Merriam had complained and concluded, "If your knowledge of Monteath is as inaccurate as your knowledge of what has happened in the Bingenheimer and Burton cases, I shall be almost sorry of having directed an investigation of him by the Interior Department." Roosevelt dismissed one bit of evidence Merriam cited, the testimony of Col. W. F. Sanders that he had seen Monteath intoxicated, on the grounds that the last two times Sanders had obtained interviews with him Roosevelt had had to cut them short because the colonel himself was drunk.[53]

Merriam was dismayed at the response he had elicited:

It is a long time since any act of mine has brought down on my head such a blow as your recent letter. I am mortified that I said what I had to say in such a blundering way that it was susceptible of the interpretation you gave it, and hurt that you do not know me better than to think me capable of implying that I do not believe in you. The fact that you are the only man in the world having the power to help the Indian situation is my excuse for troubling you. If I annoy you too much, tell me to quit, but don't charge me with unfaithfulness.[54]

The groveling letter reflected Merriam's deep personal regard for Roosevelt, and also the reason the friends of the Indian clung to any personal connection they had with him. Merriam could have found comfort in the knowledge that, despite his outburst, Roosevelt had forwarded his letter to Secretary Hitchcock with the request that he consider investigating Monteath's administration of the Blackfeet. Nor did the incident disrupt the exchange of information about wildlife that had characterized the Roosevelt-Merriam relationship. The president continued to send specimens to the head of the biological survey, who sent pelts of rare animals for Roosevelt's edification.

Unlike Merriam and other friends of the Indian, Hamlin Garland made few efforts to intervene in affairs at particular reservations. He tended to use his access to the president to recommend broad policies that were less politically sensitive than Indian Service personnel matters. Roosevelt once introduced Garland as his "Indian expert," and the writer delighted in this White House connection.[55] He did not abuse the privilege of access and prided himself on asking few favors regarding personnel.

Garland was deeply gratified to see one of his programmatic ideas adopted by Roosevelt. In April 1902 the onetime homesteader had published an article in the *North American Review*. One of his recommendations related to locating Indians on their allotments. Garland emphasized that the failure of the policy was inevitable because it ignored the fact that the Native American was a "sociable animal," incapable of living the "lonely life of the poor Western rancher, cut off from daily association with his fellows." He described the Indian as "a villager [who] . . . dreads solitude," and referred to a traditional tribal punishment, expulsion from the camp. To ease the conversion to the new life, Garland proposed that families be clustered in small settlements along streams, instead of isolating them on their allotments. He reached this conclusion not only because he believed Indians to be by custom village people, but because he remembered his own youth: "As a boy, I hated the solitary labor of the Western farm, and I would not condemn even a convict to such life as involved in a lonely cabin on the plains."[56]

Garland reported to Charles Lummis that Roosevelt had approved his article and "made [him] free for a week of the Executive Chambers in order to hear as much talk as possible."[57] Roosevelt indeed was impressed by Garland's proposal, forwarding it to Commissioner Jones and including a variation in his 1902 State of the Union message: "On the arid prairielands the effort should be to induce the Indians to lead pastoral rather than agricultural lives, and to permit them to settle in villages rather than force them into isolation."[58] However, this was a proposal that despite its wisdom was too radical given the historical commitment of the United States to individual homesteads. The plan also assumed the Indians' retaining substantially larger allotments than 160 acres if they were to live by raising cattle, and that would have been unpalatable to western members of Congress.

Garland had more success with a scheme for devising Indian family names. He got this idea as a result of a conversation with an Oneida Indian on the Cheyenne and Arapaho Reservation.[59] An attorney, the Oneida had complained of the problems of allotment, and particularly those stemming from the lack of family names. As the allotments came under territory and state inheritance laws, all of which were based on Euro-American family relationships, the inevitable result was confusion when an allottee died intestate and local officials tried to determine the heirs.

In April 1902 Garland broached the subject to Roosevelt. For support he brought Hart Merriam to the session, but he was not needed. When Garland spoke of the need for developing family names to reduce the legal squabbles over land, Roosevelt heard him out and gave him a note to take to Secretary Hitchcock.

The naming project had merit; indeed the Indian Office had recognized the need for something like this as early as 1890 when it issued a circular on the subject. In late 1902 Commissioner Jones, after consultation with Garland and Grinnell, issued a revised version. Agency officials were directed to use the name of the father as the family name and to stop the practice of assigning English names, as frequently "the Indian word is as short and as euphonious as the English." If not, the preference was for "dropping repetitious syllables and spelling phonetically." Care was to be taken to avoid translations of Indian names that might subject the individual to derision; parental consent should be obtained "wherever possible."[60]

Garland had suggested creation of a three-person committee to supervise the program but Jones demurred, citing the expense. He did agree, however, to employ Dr. Eastman, Captain Brown's old opponent and now physician at Crow Creek Agency, to undertake the task among the Sioux. Garland did not intend to participate in the project himself, describing his role as advisory, and Commissioner Jones made clear that he was delegating oversight to a subordinate. This was not to be a high-priority item and, as usual, the way the task at each agency would be addressed would depend upon the vagaries of local administration.

Garland had attempted to involve others in the project, consulting ethnologists Frederick Hodge and James Mooney as well as Grinnell, Merriam, and Charles Lummis. Grinnell agreed to help with work on Northern Cheyenne and Blackfoot rolls, although there is no evidence that he did anything. Lummis discouraged extending the project to the Pueblo and Mission Indians if it meant interfering with the Spanish baptismal names they already carried, and Commissioner Jones agreed.

The naming project inspired some amused comments in the press, and Jones wrote the editor of *Leslie's Weekly* regarding one of its articles. He denied that the intention was to eliminate only Indian names that embodied "obscene thoughts and vulgar ideas." Those that were "euphonious and proper" would be retained. Above all, he maintained, the objective was to provide family names that would simplify record-keeping and minimize error in the settlement of Indian estates.[61]

Roosevelt had responded promptly to Garland's request for assistance in selling the idea to the Interior Department. He also had attempted, when asked by Garland, to enable Dr.

Eastman to secure allotments for himself and his five children. In this case, however, even the president's intervention could not avail, the law allotting the Sioux reservations not permitting what Eastman sought.

During the period that Garland was pushing the naming project, he had one exchange with Roosevelt in which he disagreed heatedly with him. Normally, Garland verged on sycophancy in his approach to the president. For example, when Roosevelt took a public stand against the intrusions of what Garland called "the cattle barons" on public land, it inspired the author to laud his stand against special interests: "We are glorying in your youth and strength."[62] When Mrs. Garland had their first child, however, the father spoke up to challenge one of Roosevelt's most deeply held views, the virtue of large families.

The president had reacted enthusiastically to the news of the impending birth: "Three cheers for you, and especially Mrs. Garland! I am so pleased."[63] After the child's arrival, a shaken Garland reported it to Roosevelt. "Every woman who passes through the maternity battle should be sainted," he declared. "After seeing Zaleme in her agony . . . I am not prepared to follow you in your advocacy of large families."[64] Roosevelt replied with a strong letter comparing women to soldiers, both performing "a great and indispensable service which involves pain and discomfort, self-abnegation, and the incurring of risk of life." While he did not wish to see women die from too much childbearing, "the woman who flinches from childbirth stands on a par with the soldier who drops his rifle and runs in battle."[65] But even that strained parallel did not alienate the disciple. Garland accepted the "perfect consistency" of Roosevelt's logic, while admitting that he did not have his optimism and could not live under the pressure of his responsibilities. "I bow down before your marvellous endurance, your equanimity, your resolution," Garland gushed.

He depicted Roosevelt as being akin to Grant in his "purity of speech" and refusal to jest about maternity, unlike Lincoln, whose "obscenity" Garland found repellent. "Your letter increased my admiration of you," he assured the president.[66] Within a few weeks Garland again was invited to lunch at the White House, his presidential connection intact.

Francis Leupp was made of sterner stuff, although in his way he was as loyal to Roosevelt. Leupp's ties with him ran back over a decade. By 1902 the journalist had developed a relationship with Roosevelt unique for the friends, that of political confidant and adviser. Although Leupp did not brag of his connection with the most powerful American as Garland was tempted to do, his role was becoming known. Booker T. Washington continued to use him as a way to approach the president confidentially, and T. Thomas Fortune, an African-American newspaper publisher with ties to Washington, sought a federal appointment through Leupp.[67]

Although Leupp had been an employee of the IRA for two years and on occasion was contacted by Merriam, Grinnell, and Garland on Indian issues, he was very much his own man. The IRA people had no hold on him and he was never a member of the Sequoya League, much less part of the inner circle of that organization. Even Roosevelt was reluctant to approach him on some subjects, observing that Leupp, "though an exceedingly honest and fearless man . . . is very prejudiced when he makes up his mind."[68]

Roosevelt, however, came to trust Leupp, particularly in that most politically sensitive of all issues—race. The president had come under fire, in addition to the uproar over the dinner Booker T. Washington had attended, for his appointment of African Americans and his statements deploring lynching. And he did feel deeply about the race issue, as demonstrated in a private letter to a literary friend: "There are problems much more intense at the present time than the

race problem . . . but there is none about which I feel so
gravely concerned as regards the distant future. I can not be
sure what the right solution is, but I am absolutely sure that
the wrong solution is inevitable if we fail to treat the individual negro just as we treat the individual white man—that is
give him a fair chance; give him a square deal."[69]

One of Roosevelt's most controversial appointments was
that of Dr. William D. Crum, an African American, to the post
of Collector of the Port of Charleston, South Carolina, a city
southern to the core. The nomination set off another storm
of protest in the South, and even Roosevelt supporter and influential editor Lyman Abbott cautioned him against the action, because it "would probably do more to arouse anti-negro
prejudice than it would to vanquish it."[70] Leupp, however,
steadfastly supported Crum, whose name had been suggested
by Booker T. Washington. At one point during the fight,
which lasted over two years, Leupp tried to strengthen Roosevelt's resolve by needling him: "They are making bets all
over on your 'backing down'."[71]

Leupp prided himself on telling the president what he
needed to know, not what he wanted to hear: "I am making
myself *persona non grata,* but I shall keep on, because I would
rather have your appreciation ten years hence, than your pleasure in my courtiership now."[72] Surrounded, as presidents
are, by those reluctant to be the bearers of bad tidings, Roosevelt appreciated Leupp's integrity.

Twice the president prevailed on his trusted adviser to
conduct investigations of reservation conditions. The first
was a difficult situation at the Kiowa Agency, which administered two reservations in Oklahoma. One housed the Kiowas,
Comanches, and Kiowa Apaches; the other was the home of
the Wichitas and six affiliated tribes. Presiding over this bureaucratic headache was retired Lt. Col. James F. Randlett.

A dissident Kiowa faction led by Lone Wolf and supported by a few Comanches charged Colonel Randlett with having colluded to defraud the Indians. The IRA's Samuel Brosius communicated this to Senator Quay, who proceeded in August 1902 to file charges. To ensure that he got action, the senator made them to the president, detailing Randlett's alleged crimes. Roosevelt forwarded the accusations to the Interior Department for prompt consideration and a report on action taken.[73]

Randlett was aware of the IRA connection to the charges and in his 1902 annual report denounced the association for being "the allies of grafting attorneys."[74] Brosius saw this before it was printed and tried unsuccessfully to have the offending passage deleted. Meanwhile, an inspector was dispatched from Secretary Hitchcock's office and he cleared Randlett of the most serious charges.

Yet the situation continued to fester and in March 1903 the president asked for Grinnell's opinion, as he was acquainted with the reservation as a result of many trips to the area. Grinnell had had only one brief meeting with Randlett and had found him "most disagreeable and cantankerous," although he believed him to be honest. He attributed the charges against the agent to the IRA's Brosius, whom he characterized as "a man of good intentions, absolutely square, but I do not think his judgement good."[75]

Grinnell's recommendation was that some impartial person be sent to conduct another investigation. Roosevelt forwarded Grinnell's letter, together with one from Lone Wolf's attorney, to Commissioner Jones and requested a suggestion for an individual to carry out the task. Jones nominated Leupp, whom he described as "eminently fair . . . of a judicial temperament, and . . . familiar with Indian affairs." He concluded with a statement of his "implicit confidence" in Colonel Randlett's character, although he acknowledged that the colonel could be "a little brusque."[76]

At Roosevelt's request, Leupp accepted the assignment. Jones prepared the way by a letter to the contentious agent, assuring him of the support of Secretary Hitchcock and himself against the charges brought by "these Indian Rights people and other cranks." He also portrayed Leupp as "a gentleman in every respect, absolutely honest and impartial." Of Randlett, Jones had only one request: "keep your temper."[77]

Leupp spent six weeks at the agency, and even before he prepared his formal report the commissioner was assuring Randlett that "Mr. Leupp in the most emphatic terms stated to me that he thought you were the best equipped and most conscientious agent he has ever seen."[78] Leupp did completely exonerate Randlett, declaring him an "admirable but much maligned public servant."[79]

Even before completing this task, Leupp was asked to take on a much more onerous assignment, investigating a complicated and malodorous mess in Indian Territory. Leupp declined on the grounds that he was exhausted mentally and physically by his exertions at Randlett's agency. In less than a year, however, Roosevelt had persuaded him to take on another assignment involving the Sisseton and Blackfoot reservations. His report, discussed earlier, helped confirm Grinnell's estimate of Agent Monteath and get him discharged.

After completing his investigation in Oklahoma, Leupp cautioned Roosevelt "to 'walk a crack' from this time forward," as he had signed a contract to write a biography of the president to be published in time for the 1904 campaign.[80] It appeared in February, and a few years later Roosevelt remarked to a sister that Leupp's biography was his pick of the efforts to portray him.[81] It certainly was laudatory, although Leupp stated that it was not an authorized biography and that none of it had been submitted for Roosevelt's approval.

By the time the book had been published Roosevelt was maneuvering to secure the Republican nomination and then go on to win the general election. He intended to wage an aggressive campaign and he had picked the men who would play major roles. Elihu Root was his choice to deliver the keynote address at the convention, and he supplied Root with a list of talking points. The one on Indians was designed to appease both special interest groups concerned: "Steady policy of safeguarding the Indian in his rights, securing to him land on which he can develop into a good citizen, while throwing open to actual homemakers for settlement the surplus land in the Indian reservations."[82] That was a neat summary of Roosevelt's Indian policy. He constantly strove to protect Indian interests, but at the same time satisfy the land hunger of western voters. It was a difficult balancing act, and when choices had to be made the citizens had the edge. Roosevelt's record looked good only relative to the performance of other presidents of his era.

By late 1904, as Roosevelt moved toward being inaugurated for a full term, it was apparent that he expected to enjoy a freer hand. It also was obvious that among the six friends of the Indian who had tried to exploit their connections with him, Grinnell and Garland, and especially Leupp, still retained influence, and Charles Lummis and Herbert Welsh were no longer players. Merriam had been so intimidated by Roosevelt's tongue-lashing that he had retired to the sidelines on Indian issues.

With the exception of Leupp, none of the six took an active role in the 1904 campaign. The Bureau of Catholic Indian Missions did, and Roosevelt would be properly appreciative.

8

The BCIM Operates

The six friends of the Indian could have taken lessons in lobbying from the Bureau of Catholic Indian Missions. From early 1902 through the election of 1904 the prime concern of the BCIM was securing federal support for their schools in the form of government rations and tuition payments for Indian pupils. As discussed in chapter 4, the BCIM's interest was understandable. With a much larger school system (in 1902, of a total enrollment of 3,376 in all mission schools, 2,583 enrollments were in Catholic schools), the Catholics had suffered more than the Protestants from the ban on rations and the phasing out of government contracts.[1] The Catholics, however, were better at orchestrating political influence, and the BCIM was more focused than Protestant organizations like the Indian Rights Association. The IRA addressed general policy issues and in addition tried to respond to a great assortment of problems on a wide range of reservations. Many of these were personnel matters, as the association came to be looked upon by many in the Indian Service as their ombudsman. Although the IRA routinely attempted to engage Protestant leaders and journals in its causes, the fragmented nature of the Protestant movement put it at a considerable disadvantage in contesting with the BCIM.

The abrogation of the Browning Ruling in January 1902 had been a real victory for the BCIM, and its director, Father Ketcham, recognized that it had been facilitated by Theodore Roosevelt's occupancy of the White House. As discussed earlier, the president was intent on reversing the pattern of discrimination from which Catholics had suffered. By the summer of 1902 he had placed members of that church on the Board of Indian Commissioners and was attempting to see that they were properly represented on other boards and commissions and also as chaplains for the armed services.

Ketcham was preoccupied with the rations issue for almost three years. The Catholic schools were in severe financial straits, and he was convinced that "Catholicity among the Indians depends on the schools."[2] In January 1902 Ketcham presented the problem for the president's consideration. In a four-page letter he sketched the history of government rations for mission-school students, stressing that they would have drawn them routinely if they had remained at home. Ketcham referred to Commissioner Jones's decision to terminate rations as a "decided injustice to the Indian children," and defended his approach to Roosevelt as necessary given the attitudes of Jones and Secretary Hitchcock. He concluded by suggesting that the president seek an opinion on the issue from the attorney general.[3] Roosevelt did, but the result was an affirmation of Jones's action.[4]

The attorney general's decision was no comfort to the president either, as he was laboring to win Catholic support. He appointed a bishop to the board created to mediate the major coal strike in 1902 and placed a layman of that church on the Philippine Commission in 1903, later elevating him to the governor generalship of the islands.[5] The secretary of the Catholic Club in Washington, which closely followed administration activities affecting the church, listed several other commendable actions. Included were Roosevelt's offer of an additional ten chaplaincies to an archbishop invited to dinner at the White House and his policy in the Philippines, which was deemed "enlightened."[6] At about the same time, however, the president was confiding to Gov. William Howard Taft of the Philippines his shock at "the violent attack made upon us by the Catholics" and their "very genuine bitterness," which he attributed to misrepresentations of the administration's policy on the Spanish friars and their estates in the Philippines.[7]

Father Ketcham was one American Catholic who felt strongly that his church's religious orders in the Philippines were suffering from "unjust attacks." In a letter to a church official in the islands, Ketcham spoke disdainfully of those "timid souls among us" who were "inclined too easily to listen to the charges made against their brothers" in the Philippines. He charged these erring Catholics as being "forgetful of the fact that whenever a heretic takes one side of a question, it is generally an argument that the opposite side is the right one for a Catholic to espouse." But even the priest had to acknowledge an improvement: "Those in authority here are disposed to do what is right and just."[8]

Ketcham regarded it as his responsibility to see that the Roosevelt administration did right by the Catholic schools, and that necessitated his educating church leaders and laymen about the gravity of the issue. Nor were all of them persuaded that Ketcham's tactics were best; some felt that his aggressiveness might be self-defeating. New York attorney and influential Catholic layman Eugene A. Philbin was a case in point.

Philbin was active in city and state affairs, and he and Roosevelt had been political allies on occasion. John J. Wynne, a Jesuit associated with a Catholic publication who was close to Philbin, described him as "loyal" to Roosevelt and an "experienced politician in the highest sense."[9] In contrast to the outspoken Ketcham, Philbin appeared almost devious with his elliptical references to controversial subjects. He was critical of Archbishop Ireland, for example, but he usually avoided identifying him by name, preferring such obscure designations as "a certain gentleman of the West."[10]

Roosevelt valued Philbin's opinion, discussing with him the complexities of the friars' issue and giving him advance notice of his intention to appoint the Catholic to the Philippine Commission.[11] Philbin was happy to reciprocate, passing on Father Wynne's conclusion that grateful Catholics had voted Republican in state elections in November 1902. Philbin also informed Roosevelt that he was held in high esteem in the church's American College in Rome.[12]

It was Father Ketcham, however, who carried the burden of the fight for rations for the mission schools while at the same time defending his turf. The BCIM was, in Ketcham's words, "the official representative of the Church to deal with the Government in behalf of Catholic Indian Missions and Schools."[13] Nevertheless, as he explained to James Cardinal Gibbons, archbishop of Baltimore, and Patrick J. Ryan, archbishop of Philadelphia, bishops had been known to ignore his organization and take independent action. Even Commissioner Jones had complained about the conflicting messages he was receiving from Catholics.

As 1902 ended, Father Ketcham was pessimistic about the possible restoration of rations and the presence of "the multitude of bigots and incompetents" in the Indian Service.[14] And he deplored the practice of the Interior Department's using tribal funds, without tribal consent, to underwrite government schools while denying Catholic parents tribal funds with which to educate their children in Catholic schools. Ketcham believed that the last hope of the BCIM was to get a provision for rations attached to the Indian appropriation bill. But when he was able to do this the maneuver was negated by Henry Cabot Lodge, who had it removed on a point of order.

Ketcham was outraged at the action of that "bigot of bigots."[15] In desperation he turned to Eugene Philbin, who earlier had expressed a willingness to approach the attorney general and try to resolve the issue quietly. He made clear to Philbin that he held Roosevelt to some degree culpable, describing him as "fair in religious matters" but in agreement with Lodge regarding Catholic schools. Ketcham reminded Philbin that Senator Hanna, then Roosevelt's most likely opponent for the Republican nomination in 1904, was a staunch friend of the BCIM. A failure to restore rations, maintained the priest, could cost Roosevelt votes, as the bureau had a "sacred duty . . . to correctly inform the public concerning the attitude of public men towards Catholic Indian interests." And he added, "If they will antagonize us, both the guilt and the odium must rest upon their own heads."[16]

That blast set the dove cotes to fluttering in New York City. Philbin, and Father Wynne, with whom he had shared Ketcham's letter, responded. Wynne's brief note arrived first and was basically a request for information for Philbin, to enable him to develop his approach to Roosevelt. Wynne cautioned Ketcham to publish nothing on the issue, expressly warning him against using the services of E. L. Scharf, who operated an independent Washington news bureau and purported to represent the Catholic viewpoint. Wynne described Scharf's operation as "not discreet, nor does it seem fair on all scores."[17]

Ketcham replied that there was no connection between

the BCIM and Scharf, who simply called at the Bureau for news items in the same way that he approached other Catholic organizations. The priest, nevertheless, defended Scharf as "a very able and good man," although he had some doubts about his "judgment and prudence." Nor did Ketcham back down on the tone of his letter to Philbin, which he said was calculated "to arouse" him to get to the president about the rations. He included information for Wynne to pass on to Philbin, and indicated that he would not speak publicly on the issue while the New Yorker was trying to use his influence with Roosevelt. If Philbin were unsuccessful, Ketcham would then feel free to enlighten the Catholic public on the president's attitude. "We like Mr. Roosevelt, but we like our Indian schools better," observed Ketcham, "and if he *will* continue his unfavorable mood, I do not see why we should not rather say a good word for Mr. Hanna, or for some other possible candidate."[18]

As was to be expected, Philbin urged forgoing further attacks on Lodge because the senator might use his influence with the president against the Catholics. In New York, the attorney observed, they strove to avoid "personal attacks on politicians." Before he approached Roosevelt, Philbin wanted information on the position taken by Lodge, Hitchcock, and the attorney general on the rations issue.[19] Like the good lawyer he was, Philbin wanted to be on sound ground when he wrote his brief.

Despite the pleas of Philbin and Wynne, Ketcham wrote an editorial for a BCIM publication denouncing Lodge by name. He did so, however, only after submitting it for approval to Cardinal Gibbons. "My personal opinion is that we wrong the cause of our Indian schools by fawning upon such men and kissing the hand which is ever raised to strike us," Ketcham advised the cardinal, who apparently agreed.[20]

The same day that he composed the letter to the cardinal, Ketcham replied to one from Father Ganss warning against BCIM involvement with Scharf. Ketcham again denied any connection with the journalist, although he did defend the accuracy of a letter attacking Senator Lodge that Scharf had circulated widely. Moreover, the priest declared that he personally had been the source behind an assault on Lodge in a Baltimore Catholic publication. He maintained that Lodge could not be won over, and that "I would consider myself unfaithful to my trust were I to attempt to delude the Catholic public, or were I tamely to submit to such bigotry and injustice."[21]

Meanwhile, Roosevelt was accepting congratulations from a North Dakota bishop for appointing the Catholic Carrigan as agent at Standing Rock. And he thought it wise to remind Archbishop Ryan that another Catholic prelate was pleased with his choice. Later he would assure Cardinal Gibbons that he would find employment for a man the cardinal had recommended. The president was not missing an opportunity to conciliate Catholic prelates.[22]

But Ketcham was not interested in patronage; he was focused on rations and he would get valuable assistance from Charles Bonaparte. As president of the Civil Service Reform Association, Bonaparte had standing with a class of reformers that frequently sniped at President Roosevelt for being insufficiently aggressive when dealing with politicians and special interests. This, plus his reputation for integrity and his prominence as a Catholic layman, made Bonaparte someone whom Roosevelt was happy to have in his corner. In the spring of 1904 the president chose him to investigate a nasty situation in the Post Office Department.

During this assignment Bonaparte also took the opportunity to discuss with Roosevelt the rations issue, about which he had been briefed by Philbin and Ketcham. Bonaparte informed him that the Board of Indian Commissioners had passed a resolution criticizing the Interior Department for its termination of rations. He suggested that this might explain Secretary Hitchcock's refusal to continue to publish the board's annual report.[23] Hitchcock changed his mind after the resolution was modified, but he then declined to print the proceedings of the Lake Mohonk Conference. Roosevelt reacted quickly, directing the secretary to publish the Mohonk report, observing, "The Mohonk people are not always wise, but then few people are, and they are genuine in their zeal and devotion for what they conceive to be the rights of the Indians."[24]

That same day Roosevelt informed the attorney general that Bonaparte had persuaded him that the Justice Department might have rendered its opinion on rations without having been adequately briefed. Therefore the president directed the Justice Department to reopen the issue and obtain information from Bonaparte or Archbishop Ryan. He was then to share his findings with Roosevelt.[25]

Bonaparte's brief for the attorney general was developed in consultation with Philbin, Ketcham, and Archbishop Ryan. It was not submitted until February 1904 because in the interim Bonaparte had undertaken still another mission at Roosevelt's request, the investigation of affairs in Indian Territory that Francis Leupp had declined to do.

During the long delay, Ketcham kept the issue alive and worried Philbin and Father Wynne that his strident views might alienate the president. The head of the BCIM could not forget that the ban on rations "means money to us every day— it is a case of administrative robbery." And he suggested to Wynne that Roosevelt could learn from recent state elections "that a little of Mr. Hanna's spirit to do Catholic home enterprise justice would do no harm even to a Presidential candidate."[26] In contrast, Philbin's tactics emphasized the positive. In anticipation of a federation of Catholic societies issuing a resolution relative to the attitude of the government toward the church, he assured Roosevelt that it would be "moderate, even in praise . . . for it is felt to be entirely your due."[27]

In early January 1904 Father Ketcham still believed that a revised ruling by the attorney general was a more likely way than congressional action to get rations restored. Nevertheless, after a conference with James S. Sherman, chairman of the House Indian Committee, he concluded that the chances of getting a bill through Congress had improved. Roosevelt, with whom Ketcham had "a lengthy and agreeable interview," lent support by pressuring the chairs of both House and Senate committees to expedite legislation returning rations to mission schoolchildren.[28] Ketcham himself strenuously lobbied members of both houses. He was most successful with Sen. Nelson W. Aldrich, who persuaded the president to rein in his friend Henry Cabot Lodge, and the bill became law. A grateful Ketcham asked Bishop Matthew Harkins of Providence, Rhode Island, to do what he could to help Aldrich return to the Senate.[29] Archbishop Ryan chose to credit the president, whose "silent action has [done] much to secure the final success."[30]

Contributing to Father Ketcham's elation was still another triumph for the BCIM. At the encouraging interview with the president early in January 1904, Ketcham had raised the question of using not congressional appropriations, but tribal funds held in the Treasury, to pay mission school tuition costs. Roosevelt responded favorably, although he did insist that the policy should be applied gradually. He also asked Ketcham to provide him a memorandum justifying the procedure. A key point would be that in 1898 the Interior Department had accepted the suggestion of the BCIM that the Osage be permitted to continue spending tribal funds to support two contract schools on their reservation. Ketcham now proposed that this practice be extended to three other groups with funds held in trust by the United States—the Menominee, Chippewa, and Sioux.[31]

By January 11 the president was prodding his attorney general on the matter: "I think the sooner we arrive at a conclusion the better."[32] But it took a January 22 meeting at the White House of the attorney general and four other cabinet ministers to finally resolve the issue.[33] It resulted in contracts with eight Catholic schools and one Lutheran. Ketcham was delighted and willing to share the credit. He praised Charles Bonaparte: "What a tower of strength you have been to Our Church."[34] And he called on Catholic bishops to mobilize support for Senator Aldrich, through whom "we can get favorable bills . . . or, in case an adverse bill should slip through we can secure through his influence a veto from the President."[35]

Four months later Ketcham informed Archbishop John M. Farley of New York that government contracts would provide a total support of $97,960 from tribal funds and that "if your Grace can by any prudent means turn a hand for Senator Aldrich in the present contest in Rhode Island, it seems to me that it ought to be done." Ketcham also made a plea for political support of Roosevelt, pointing out that his decision to free tribal funds for mission schools "places us under many obligations to the Administration, particularly the President, whose fairmindedness and courage have made a reality of our fondest and (apparently) wildest dream."[36]

During the struggle to get rations returned and to get access to tribal funds, Father Ketcham had stressed the need to do it as quietly as possible. Unless the press alerted the opposition, "the Administration will give us everything that it can," he confided to Mother Katharine Drexel.[37] This Pennsylvania heiress was donating about $100,000 a year to Catholic mission schools, roughly two-thirds of the entire BCIM budget for schools.[38]

Father Ketcham's efforts to keep the general public un-aware of the new contracts providing tuition payments for BCIM-affiliated schools were surprisingly successful. Not until the fall of 1904 did the contracts become known to Epis-copal bishop Hare and his ardent IRA supporters. When the bishop protested to Commissioner Jones, that sly official ac-knowledged that when purely tribal funds were available and tribal members petitioned for their use to support their stu-dents at mission schools, he was happy to oblige them. In-deed, he assured Hare, "There is no objection whatever to entering into the same arrangement with you, if you care to do so."[39] Jones hoped thus to avoid a fight with the bishop and his supporters. The secrecy at which he had connived, however, only postponed the struggle until after the election of 1904. The burden then would fall on a new commissioner of Indian affairs.

The contest over rations and contracts for mission schools had demonstrated that while individuals like Grinnell and Garland could exploit personal contacts with Roosevelt to win occasional battles on specific topics, he was even more amenable to an institution like the BCIM that could mobilize thousands of voters. It is little wonder that at a time that he was so diligently wooing Catholic prelates the president also sought from Sen. Charles W. Fairbanks, a prominent Method-ist layman, "the best way of getting at the Methodist bishops and clergymen, and the hundreds and thousands of lay-men."[40] There is no evidence that Roosevelt had success in appealing to Methodists comparable to that achieved in his campaign for Catholic support.

Throughout the spring and summer of 1904 Roosevelt was preoccupied with the upcoming election. To his friend Henry Adams, who preferred to ignore the practical side of politics, it seemed that he "talks of nothing, and lives for noth-ing but his political interests." Adams, the descendant of two presidents who demonstrated that they were insufficiently concerned with politics to win reelection, observed caustically, "If you remark to [Roosevelt] that God is Great, he asks naively at once how that will affect his election."[41]

In the last weeks of the 1904 campaign, Roosevelt was sensitive to charges that he was favoring the Catholics for political reasons. In correspondence with Philbin he argued that he was motivated only by a desire to treat Catholics and Protestants alike, and that this was reflected in his social relations. According to Roosevelt, that his friend Grant La Farge was Catholic "never enters my head."[42] As the election drew nearer, he was sufficiently concerned to ask Philbin to refute a New York paper's claim "that the Catholics are supporting me because they expect unfair discrimination in their favor."[43] The record, of course, suggests that in 1904 the Catholics were responding as would any special interest group to the record of a politician seeking their support. For them the results were gratifying; the Catholics had backed a winner. Roosevelt defeated Democratic candidate Alton B. Parker by a wide margin, carrying thirty-three of the forty-five states and 336 of 470 electoral votes.

9

More Friends Fall by the Wayside

The 1904 election gave Theodore Roosevelt the mandate he sought to be president in his own right. As he described it to his son Kermit, he was "stunned by the overwhelming victory." He had "thought it probable we should win, but was quite prepared to be defeated, and of course had not the slightest idea that there was such a tidal wave."[1] In his elation Roosevelt did not forget those who had contributed to his victory. One was a Catholic priest who had published a flattering statement about the Republican candidate in a religious publication that "went all over" and "helped us in many ways." For this act he had been "exiled" to Canada at the behest of Tammany operatives with influence with the hierarchy in New York City. Roosevelt proposed to take surplus campaign funds to underwrite a year's study for the priest in Rome to prepare him for a teaching position.[2]

Roosevelt probably learned of the priest's plight from Father Ketcham, with whom he talked the same day that he sought help for Tammany's scapegoat. Ketcham described himself as being "overjoyed at the election," particularly since Roosevelt told him, "By George! I am going to keep on doing things for you."[3] And the president in a letter to humorist Finley Peter Dunne spoke of his support from Irish Catholics and cited his appointment of them to posts in his administration as evidence of his intention "to give everybody a square deal."[4]

But to a group that had opposed him, he was not prepared to be charitable. This was the "*Evening Post,* Carl Schurz, Francis Adams, Moorfield Story, and that set."[5] Roosevelt described them as "hypocritical and insincere when they oppose me," because he was convinced that he was providing the type of government they professed to advocate.[6] He did not include in his indictment Francis Leupp, a reporter for the *Evening Post.* Indeed, he credited Leupp with having been one of his key advisors at a critical stage of his campaign, urging him to respond publicly to charges of the Democratic candidate, a tactic Roosevelt found successful.[7]

It surprised few insiders that Indian Commissioner William Jones announced in November 1904 that he intended to retire. Nor could many acquainted with the Washington scene have been taken aback that the president quickly nominated Leupp as his successor. Jones explained his resignation as required by the exigencies of the family business back in Wisconsin. However, he was rushed into announcing his departure by inadvertently informing Secretary Hitchcock, who promptly shared the news. Within twenty-four hours Roosevelt had offered the position to Leupp, leading Jones to conclude that the president had only been awaiting his resignation to nominate a friend and advisor.[8] A month later when he got around to formally accepting Jones's resignation, Roosevelt graciously thanked him for his "fidelity to duty and entire disinterestedness" in "one of the most thankless and difficult positions in the Government."[9] That this was not all rhetoric was evidenced in another context, by his describing the post of ambassador to England as having not one-twentieth the importance of the commissionership of Indian affairs.[10]

The six friends warmly greeted the news of Leupp's appointment. IRA officials naturally applauded, given his history as the organization's Washington agent. Samuel Brosius was assured by the new commissioner that "the latch string would always hang out for him."[11] George Bird Grinnell had actually recommended Leupp to Roosevelt, and, after he learned that Leupp would be commissioner, Grinnell described him as "one of the very best men in the country for this job."[12] Later he would brag, "My man was appointed Indian Commissioner," although it seems clear that Roosevelt, as Jones recognized, had picked Leupp without consulting anyone.[13]

Commissioner Jones knew that his successor would be operating from a position of strength he had not enjoyed: "His close personal relation with the President is of such a character that he will practically have his own way in the conduct of affairs."[14] Charles Bonaparte said essentially the same thing to Father Ketcham, advising him not to try to get to Roosevelt with his recommendations on Indian Service matters but rather to work through Leupp, "a strong personal friend of the President."[15] And that was the way it was. Leupp often bypassed the regular channels that ran through the office of Secretary Hitchcock. It helped that Roosevelt was becoming increasingly unhappy with that irascible and chronically suspicious individual's handling of the Interior Department.

Leupp was definitely a hands-on administrator and unlike Jones had come to the office well versed in Indian affairs. He quickly put his own stamp on the Indian Service, and politicians learned that he did not have his predecessor's eagerness to please. Jones had tolerated as head of the Indian Service's Chicago warehouse a man he knew to be incompetent, the brother of Wisconsin's Senator John Spooner, to whom Jones owed his own job. Leupp persuaded the president to tell the senator that he must get his brother to resign.[16]

The new commissioner had not been in his office five months before he was reminding agents and superintendents that Roosevelt had ordered that no member of the Indian Service should seek intercession by members of Congress in job-related matters, the penalty for noncompliance being dismissal.[17] Leupp also spent three to five months in the field, personally checking on reservation trouble spots. Nor, unlike William Jones, did he have mining properties to distract him from his duties and create conflicts of interest.

In mid-April 1905 Leupp published "Outlines of an Indian Policy" in *Outlook*. It had taken Jones six years in the Indian Office to formulate his ideas for general readers, but Leupp was a journalist and had assumed the office knowing what he thought should be accomplished. Much of it was familiar to anyone who attended the conferences at Lake Mohonk. Like those people, he believed that the effort should be concentrated on the youth and that they should be prepared to survive on a ranch or farm. Leupp advocated treating them as individuals and severing their ties to both the federal government and their tribes as soon as they became self-sufficient. To that end, he endorsed the bill before Congress to divide tribally owned funds among the members. And to speed them along the road to independence, the commissioner already had created a new employment bureau for Indians of the Southwest and placed it under Charles E. Dagenett, an energetic Peoria mixed-blood.[18]

As for education, Leupp believed that "the mass of Indian children, like the corresponding mass of white children, are not prepared for conveyance beyond the elementary studies." He pledged, however, that while he was commissioner, "no young Indian with the talent to deserve and the ambition to ask for the best there is in American education will be refused."[19] He made clear to subordinates that he preferred day schools to boarding schools. Leupp argued that "the day-school system far outstrips any other in stimulating interest among the . . . parents as well as children—and in presenting our civilization to them in the most natural and attractive way." Moreover, he directed that parental preferences should be the determining factor, hoping that this would obviate the need to use "harsh measures to enforce attendance at the boarding schools."[20]

In his 1907 annual report Leupp reviewed his stance on boarding schools in a section labeled, "A Wasteful School System." He denounced such schools as "educational almshouses" that undermined the character of the students by encouraging them "to accept unearned privileges"—indeed, to come "to demand them." "The result," Leupp maintained, "is that in certain parts of the West the only conception his white neighbors entertain of an Indian is that of a beggar as aggressive as he is shameless."[21] Nor could he refrain from pointing out the difficulty of closing schools in communities that had come to depend on the dollars they generated.[22]

In other areas also, Leupp's conduct of his office revealed his intention to make a difference. Like Roosevelt, who took time to advise the army on the length of its spurs and the navy on the height of its ships' funnels, Leupp had an eye for detail. He had observed that Indian children, accustomed to the softer moccasins, when forced to wear shoes issued them at school frequently developed sore feet. To correct this he proposed to issue lighter footwear until they could adjust to the stiffer leather.[23]

To facilitate the Indians employed on reservations in learning thrift and avoiding "the clutches of the usurer,"

Leupp ordered them paid weekly rather than quarterly. This was in line with his policy "to assimilate, in every practicable way, the status and treatment of the Indian with the status and treatment of the white man."[24] Another approach was to permit the number of trading establishments on a reservation to be determined, as elsewhere, by the law of supply and demand. This was designed to expose the Native Americans to the same economic conditions they would encounter off the reservation.[25]

Leupp, like Roosevelt, was interested in preserving elements of Indian culture. Only six months in office, he successfully proposed to Secretary Hitchcock that a supervisor of native music be appointed, arguing that foreign musicians were astounded at our failure to investigate the "beautiful themes derivable from certain native songs and dances, which are now rapidly passing into oblivion." Not only did he urge the preservation of the "finest in the arts of this vanishing race," but he also deplored "the mistaken zeal of many teachers to crush or smother anything distinctly aboriginal in the young." Warming to his task, he declared, "The last thing that ought to be done with the youth . . . whom we are trying to indoctrinate with . . . self-respect, is to teach them to be ashamed of their ancestry."[26] Within months the superintendent of Indian schools was directing that the curriculum of all reservation schools be responsive to children's needs, including knowledge of their tribal histories.[27]

Leupp found another avenue for fostering Indian art. Josephine Foard, a Pennsylvanian with experience at Laguna Pueblo, devised a plan to teach potters to glaze their product to improve its sale in the non-Indian market. Although he was aware "that little faith in the scheme exists in the Pueblo country," Leupp assured Foard, "I am myself much interested in the preservation and development of native Indian art and I wish that Pueblo pottery, of the best sort, might be put upon a paying basis of manufacture and sale." He suggested that she visit Carlisle to meet Angel Decora, a Winnebago woman whom Leupp had appointed drawing instructor at the school. His hope was "that [Decora] will be able to call out the native talent . . . and get them to produce decorative work on lines distinctively Indian . . . and fill its own place in the world's great art mosaic."[28] That fall Foard, now on the government payroll as a field matron, was instructing Pueblo women in ways to glaze their pottery to make it more durable and attractive.[29]

Leupp was troubled by another related problem, the "despoliation of old Indian ruins" by tribal members encouraged by traders to bring in artifacts. Early in his administration he issued a directive to southwestern traders declaring such commerce contraband.[30] But with no way to reward the Indian finder or to systematically pack the valuable relics and send them on to a public museum, not much headway was made on this problem.

Leupp was constantly on the alert for ways to make education more practical. He arranged to have printing for the Indian Service, normally done at the Government Printing Office, handled by printing shops at the larger Indian schools. In the same fashion he sought to furnish his office with items crafted by Indians. After a year as commissioner he had a desk made at Chilocco, a table and bookshelves from Hampton, chairs from Carlisle, a Pueblo saucer for his paper clips, Navajo carpets, and an oil painting by a Winnebago—possibly Angel Decora.

We do know that Leupp selected Decora to head an art department at Carlisle that featured a "Leupp Art Studio." The new department's mission, in the words of a Philadelphia reporter, was "to foster the artistic instincts of the Indian instead of blotting out all his tendencies and civilizing him too completely."[31]

President Roosevelt shared Leupp's interest in encouraging Native American art and music. More important, in Indian matters he trusted Leupp implicitly and permitted him a much freer rein than commissioners were normally accorded, only occasionally intervening personally. There was a corresponding decline in the influence of Secretary Hitchcock, Leupp's nominal superior.

A month after his inaugural parade, in which five chiefs including the Comanche Quanah Parker rode, the president left Washington on a five-week western tour. At San Antonio he joined Spanish-American War comrades in a reunion, and he then headed for Colorado and a bear hunt. En route, he paused for a few days to hunt coyotes (prairie wolves). This involved riding cow ponies at breakneck speed through prairie-dog towns and over other rough terrain, a type of challenge in which Roosevelt delighted.[32] It took place on the "Big Pasture," a tract of over 400,000 acres that the Kiowas, Comanches, and Kiowa Apaches continued to hold in common.

When Roosevelt arrived at Frederick, Oklahoma Territory, he was received by an honor guard that included Quanah Parker, the son of white captive Cynthia Ann Parker and Comanche warrior Peta Nocona. In an article about the hunt Roosevelt wrote for *Scribner's Magazine,* he described Quanah as "in his youth a bitter foe of the whites, now painfully teaching his people to travel the white man's stony road."[33] At Frederick the president had Quanah join him on the speaker's stand and took that opportunity to stress one of his favorite themes, the Square Deal: "Give the red man the same chance as the white. This country is founded on a doctrine of giving each man a fair show to see what there is in him."[34]

Later, at the Big Pasture, Quanah presented members of his family to Roosevelt and briefed him on some of the problems the Comanches faced. The president was sufficiently impressed to write Commissioner Leupp: "My sympathies have been much excited and I have been aroused by what I have seen here, and I am concerned at the condition of these Indians and the seeming hopelessness of their future."[35] He suggested that perhaps clauses could be written into the cattlemen's Big Pasture leases specifying that they employ Indian cowboys. That, however, could only be a palliative, given the pressure from white settlers to have the government purchase that tract from the tribes. Indeed, Congressman James H. Stephens, whose Texas district lay just south of the Big Pasture, had discussed this with Roosevelt during his layover in Frederick. Reconciling the needs of his white constituents with those of his Indian charges would prove as difficult for this president as for his predecessors.

At least Roosevelt had some comprehension of the plight of Quanah's people when the following year Congress submitted for his signature a bill introduced by Stephens calling for the purchase of the Big Pasture and three smaller ones, a total of 480,000 acres. The bill ignored the desires of the Indians to use the 480,000 acres to supplement their original allotments, or at least to provide homesteads for the children born since the division of the reservation. The president, at the urging of Leupp, declined to sign the bill, resulting in Congress's revising it to permit the children born since 1900 to receive allotments. The changes included raising the price the United States would pay for the surplus acres from $1.50 an acre to $5.00, a figure suggested by the Indians' agent. But among the revisions was one permitting settlers who had leased tracts on the pasture with the best farmland to have preference over the Indians in acquiring those tracts.[36]

Roosevelt could sweeten the pill for the Indians, but they still had to take it. As he phrased it in another situation: "I am trying to get a result that will give the Indians as much as possible for their lands, and at the same time will result in actual homesteaders coming upon them instead of having them turned over in great tracts to huge corporations."[37]

In the summer of 1905 another chief who had ridden in Roosevelt's inaugural parade was brought to his attention. A famous warrior of the Chiricahua Apaches, Geronimo, and other members of that tribe had been held as prisoners of war since 1886, most recently at Fort Sill. S. M. Barrett, a local school superintendent, had struck up an acquaintance with Geronimo, and the chief agreed to permit Barrett to record his autobiography. The officer in charge of the prisoners refused to sanction this, and Barrett appealed directly to the president on the grounds that the old Apache should be able to tell his story. Roosevelt agreed, and when Barrett completed his manuscript he sent it to Roosevelt for his consideration.

In March 1906 the president had important issues to contend with. Congress was in session, and he was conferring constantly over such matters as railroad rate legislation and a statehood bill for Oklahoma. Nevertheless, he took time from a crowded schedule to give Barrett a little editorial advice and also sent the manuscript to two publishers whom he contacted personally. Both rejected the manuscript, although one, Century, would have taken it had the president written an introduction for the book. That he would not do, citing other commitments, including an essay on "old Erse sagas" for which he already was committed to *Century Magazine.* Although Barrett was unable to get it published in the East, Roosevelt's pressure on the army had made possible the preparation of the manuscript and Barrett did get it printed locally. This was one Indian matter on which Roosevelt did not consult Francis Leupp.[38]

The close personal relationship between Roosevelt and Leupp militated against others' effectively using their personal access to Roosevelt to influence Indian Service administration. Nevertheless, of the six friends, George Bird Grinnell had had the longest relationship with him and would continue to intercede for those tribes he knew best. Fortunately, Grinnell enjoyed a good relationship with Leupp, whom he described to Hart Merriam as "an eminently practical man."[39] On occasion each offered the other the hospitality of his home, and there seemed to be genuine mutual respect. When Leupp accepted the commissionership, Grinnell dropped him a note of congratulation and commiseration for receiving a post "full of grief and perplexity," yet giving him the opportunity to "be of great benefit to several hundred thousand people, whom the other eighty millions of the country are jumping on most of the time."[40]

One of Grinnell's hopes for Roosevelt's second term was to promote allotments of 640 acres on those reservations not suitable for agriculture. Leupp did not encourage him, however. As Grinnell explained it to Frank Mead, "His view . . . is that it is hopeless to oppose the sentiment in Congress for the opening of the lands, and that it is better to . . . try to guide them rather than to oppose, and then be swept away by the current."[41] Grinnell had gotten a better reception from the president, who agreed to include something on 640–acre allotments in his 1905 State of the Union message. But when Grinnell waited until late November to provide the proposal, it was too late. Roosevelt responded with a note fondly chiding his old friend:

Oh Grinnell, Grinnell—

I am prepared for the ordinary man not thinking about how a President writes his message; but surely, my dear fellow, you must know that . . . it had to be in the hands of the press associations at least ten days before Congress met. I . . . had it distributed over a week ago.[42]

Grinnell's interest in increasing the size of allotments grew out of his concern for the Blackfeet. Early in 1906 those

Indians were confronted by a move in Congress to open their reservation by allotment, as usual with the surplus land to be purchased by the government. And also as usual, some tribesmen could be found to espouse the opening that was being demanded by Montana citizens. In a letter to Rides At The Door, a Blackfoot, Grinnell described the move to allot that tribe as unstoppable. On the floor of the House, Joseph M. Dixon claimed, with a straight face, that open land was so scarce in Montana that ten thousand men from counties adjoining the Blackfeet had had to migrate to Canada to find farms. Leupp believed that Congress could not be prevented from acting and contented himself with drafting a bill that would at least protect Indian access to reservation water.[43]

A petition to the commissioner signed by 248 Blackfeet had protested the threat to their water and also asked for larger allotments than the 320 acres for adults authorized in the bill before Congress. The IRA took up the cause and Grinnell joined in with a letter to Congressman Dixon. He argued that it took 30 to 40 acres of the Blackfoot Reservation to support one cow, and that only if each Indian received 640 acres could families put together ranches large enough to support them. He could not refrain from adding: "The persons who drew the allotment act were ignorant of Indians, and ignorant of the west; they supposed that one law would answer for all tribes."[44] He stated that the Flathead Reservation might have enough arable land, but the Blackfoot definitely did not, as the soil was of poor quality and frosts were possible throughout the year. Grinnell communicated similar sentiments to Commissioner Leupp and helped a Blackfoot delegation make its case in Washington, but in vain.

Given western congressmen's hostility to large allotments, Leupp declined to fight for 640 acres for each Blackfoot. Nevertheless, he did react promptly when the Senate removed from the bill the provision he had drafted to protect

Blackfoot access to water. At his urgent request the president vetoed the bill. Only when the water clause had been reinserted did Roosevelt permit the bill to become law.[45]

As with the battle over the Big Pasture on the Kiowa, Comanche, and Kiowa Apache Reservation, Roosevelt's intervention in behalf of the Blackfeet only made the terms imposed on the Indians a little less painful. The Supreme Court's 1903 *Lone Wolf* decision had stressed the plenary power of Congress, and its members were in no mood to negotiate with tribes. As Leupp had advised Grinnell, members of the executive branch now found it wiser to try to work with Congress than to take a rigid stand and risk losing all.

Grinnell had undertaken other Indian causes in the first two years of Roosevelt's second term, and sometimes he had won. He tried to encourage the Blackfeet and Northern Cheyennes to get more cattle, which he believed to offer their only hope for self-sufficiency. Drawing on his own ranching experience he advised Leupp that the Blackfeet agency staff had failed to instruct Indians that they must wean the calves, because a cow would not live through the winter with a large suckling calf.[46] When the Northern Cheyennes were to get an issue of cattle, Grinnell told Leupp what kind of cattle to get and when: "in the spring, good cows with calves running by their sides." Moreover, he cautioned against purchasing the cattle beyond easy driving distance of the reservation because loss of calves in shipping was prohibitive.[47] Grinnell also was able to persuade Leupp to cancel a tax on government-issued cattle because it was discouraging Blackfeet from attempting to build herds.[48]

One of Grinnell's greatest disappointments had been the relief of Northern Cheyenne agent James C. Clifford, although it was a victory for the IRA's Washington agent. Operating in typical fashion, Samuel Brosius had filed charges against Clifford based on a complaint from a resident of the reservation. When an inspector from Secretary Hitchcock's office reached the agency to investigate the charges, Grinnell was there, and the inspector permitted him to be present when witnesses testified. The New Yorker was convinced that Clifford could not get justice because the inspector earlier had been criticized by Brosius for being too lenient, and therefore this time the official was being overly strict. Grinnell complained directly to Brosius, stating flatly, "I have known Major Clifford . . . for nearly seven years and consider him about the best Indian agent that I ever saw." Moreover, had he known Brosius was concerned about the agency he could have helped him by providing background on those bringing the charges, which "certainly would have spared the agent and also have spared me a lot of worry and annoyance."[49]

Brosius already was antagonistic to Grinnell for his role in getting Frank Mead into the Indian Service. He now chose to explain Grinnell's defense of Agent Clifford as understandable given favors accorded Grinnell when he visited Tongue River.[50] Brosius had deliberately not informed the New Yorker that he was bringing charges against Clifford, as the Mead affair had rendered Grinnell suspect in Brosius's eyes. He was happy to report to IRA headquarters at Philadelphia: "The Dept. has no use for Mr. Grinnell, no more than I have, so far as his judgment in the [Clifford] case is concerned."[51] Brosius also was sure that he had an ally in Secretary Hitchcock in uncovering dirt on Mead, the outsider whose elevation over veteran agents and superintendents in the Southwest had antagonized many in the Indian Service.

The Clifford investigation dragged on for nearly two years. It culminated in a visit to the agency by Leupp, who then decided to transfer Clifford to a less important post. He assured Grinnell that "I have held this case in abeyance for months on your account alone. It hurts me to go contrary to your judgment, but I do not see my way clear to do anything else."[52]

Grinnell was having his problems, and Lummis, Welsh, Merriam, and Garland were no longer influencing President Roosevelt's conduct of Indian affairs. When Lummis did seek action on one issue, the president backed Leupp's negative reaction: "Lummis is a wild coot. There are lots of things you can not do for him, and I guess this is one."[53] Merriam and Roosevelt, however, continued to correspond on topics such as animal species; the president still regarded him as "the greatest mammalologist" but did not turn to him for advice on Indians.[54]

Garland still had infrequent contact with Roosevelt, although the only presidential letter to him of which there is record in 1906 was an invitation to stop by the White House to discuss lynching. Garland was one of a large group that lunched with the president in early January that year, but he had only a few minutes' private conversation with Roosevelt. The author's fondest recollection of that lunch was his opportunity to become acquainted with Finley Peter Dunne. The visit to Washington also had permitted him to meet with Commissioner Leupp, with whom he was "delighted."[55]

Apparently Garland's interest in Indian affairs was waning. The New York chapter of the Sequoya League was moribund, and his interest in the naming project he had launched was fading. Now that he was a parent with two small children, domestic affairs demanded more of his attention. Moreover, the frontier he had experienced was rapidly disappearing. At a convocation at the University of Chicago in 1905 he lectured on the theme, "Vanishing Trails," concluding nostalgically: "The trail with all it subtends is fading from the earth and the white trailers, like the red, are dying."[56] There also seemed to be a corresponding decline in his creative skills. Psychic experimentation had interested him for many years, but the novel in which he attempted to develop the theme was poorly received. Garland was increasingly devoting his time to organizations of those prominent in literature and the arts, like the Players and the American Academy of Arts and Letters, both in New York. In 1907 he also took the lead in launching the Cliff Dwellers, a Chicago counterpart of the Players.[57]

The six friends' impact on Indian affairs was fading fast. In large part that was because they themselves were less involved. Attendance at the Lake Mohonk conferences continued to be good, although the participants were spending more of their time discussing the plight of the Filipinos and "Other Dependent Peoples." The reformers believed that with the extension of the merit system to the Indian Service, the creation of an ambitious school system, and the introduction of Native Americans to private property in land, that assimilation was inevitable.

For both Garland and Grinnell the West was losing its magic. Grinnell had actually accompanied Indians in buffalo hunts and observed their efforts to defend their territory against intruders. These warriors had been a link with the past that he cherished. Now Grinnell was recording the last time that he saw a dog travois and was confiding to a friend that the Indians "are becoming so civilized that the younger generation are not at all interesting." He did get satisfaction from seeing them becoming more independent economically, "but after all it is not for that that I go to the West."[58] As early as 1903 he had communicated to Dr. Eastman, the Sioux, that the Blackfoot medicine lodge ceremony had changed to the point that it was "only a Fourth of July celebration," and "I shall probably never go there again."[59] Nevertheless, Grinnell did not sever his relationship with the Blackfeet, although trying to mediate a strike called by Indians digging an irrigation ditch was a far cry from his buffalo-hunting experience with the Pawnees in 1872. Times were a-changin'.

10

 And Then There Was One

Francis Leupp may have attended meetings as an IRA employee and later as Indian commissioner, but he never felt himself a real member of the group that gathered at Lake Mohonk each fall to ruminate about the plight of the Native Americans. As commissioner, however, he was forced to deal with them because President Roosevelt routinely referred their queries and complaints to him, bypassing Secretary Hitchcock. Indeed, the confidence that he had in Leupp was unparalleled in the relations of presidents with the heads of the Indian Office. In his autobiography Roosevelt described him as "a capital Indian Commissioner. . . . I found that I could rely on his judgment not to get me into fights that were unnecessary, and therefore I always backed him to the limit when he told me a fight was necessary."[1]

In contrast, the president found Secretary Hitchcock chronically suspicious and prone to unsubstantiated charges against Indian Service personnel who were then defended by members of Congress whom Roosevelt could not afford to alienate. To Charles Bonaparte he once described him as "our beloved Hitchcock, who, I think, at the bottom of his heart would like me to shut up all the offices in Oklahoma and Indian Territory and stop all business in the future State of Oklahoma until we could arrange to have the entire population investigated for say from six to ten years."[2]

Earlier Roosevelt had reacted strongly to a Hitchcock observation that could be interpreted as meaning that they were guilty of appointing political hacks to office. In a calculated rebuff, he offered Hitchcock's subordinate Leupp as an example of how it should be done: "Under Mr. Leupp I am getting a pretty good type of Indian Agent; better men than we could obtain by any kind of competitive examination which has yet been developed."[3] That would have daunted a man less confident of his rectitude, but the secretary battled on.

The charges that Hitchcock brought against Gov. Frank Frantz of Oklahoma Territory further eroded his influence with the president. Frantz had commanded a Rough Rider company and had profited from Roosevelt's notorious partiality for those who had served under him in Cuba. Roosevelt himself could jest about it, once justifying an appointment on the grounds that "there seems to be no Rough Rider available and every individual in the Southern District of the Indian Territory (including each Rough Rider) seems to be either under indictment, convicted, or . . . should be indicted."[4] Frantz must have impressed his colonel, because Roosevelt appointed him Osage agent and then governor of Indian Territory.

It was charges of malfeasance related to oil leases that led Hitchcock to warn the president that he might find it necessary to ask him to remove Governor Frantz.[5] Leupp, however, had a different reading of the affair, arguing that the charges were a political ploy by Democrats to thwart Republican Frantz's ambition to be elected the first governor of the State of Oklahoma. A relieved Roosevelt wrote Leupp: "Upon my word I can never sufficiently thank my stars for having round me men like Root, Taft, Moody and yourself. . . . I am almost ashamed to say that your letter in Frantz's case gives me a clearer idea than I had from my own independent investigations."[6] In a letter to Hitchcock, he alluded to "a deliberate intrigue against Governor Frantz" and concluded bitingly: "This incident gives me the gravest concern for it shows that I must myself exercise constant personal vigilance lest in similar cases in your Department irreparable injury may be done honest public servants."[7] Coupled with his unhappiness with that department's handling of his correspondence with the secretary, the Frantz affair guaranteed that when he reshuffled his cabinet in March 1907, Hitchcock would be relieved of his post.

On several occasions the president did voice his concern with the quality of appointments to the Indian Service. When a Republican senator from Kansas proposed a constituent for a position in Indian Territory, Roosevelt rejected him, stating that the candidate did not have the necessary experience to protect Indians, who had "critical times ahead . . . and I do not feel that I ought to consider anything but their interests."[8] He also disappointed a South Dakota senator interested in patronage. The president approved his suggestions for district attorneys, but he drew the line at Indian agents: "I do not wish to treat them as standing upon a footing with the other positions, because of the peculiar needs of the service."[9] These were principled stands for a president whose party had enshrined home rule as the basis for filling positions in the Indian Service.

In a variety of other ways Roosevelt continued to demonstrate a concern for Indians that was rare for presidents. At Leupp's request, he stopped "until . . . the needs of the Indians have been met" an irrigation project on the Uintah Reservation that threatened to divert reservation water to settlers. The president declared that "we must be particularly careful . . . that our great desire to benefit the white settlers shall not lead us into forgetting the honorable obligation imposed upon the Government to keep faith with the Indians."[10] He also recognized this special relationship when he instructed Hitchcock, regarding oil and gas leases in Oklahoma, "to exercise a rigid and effective control over them in the interest of the public, and of course doubly in the interest of the Indians, who are the special wards of the Government."[11]

Seldom, however, did Roosevelt give Indian affairs the ranking that he did in September 1906, when he excused his inability to respond to a correspondent's wish by citing "the Cuban revolt and the trusts . . . corporations and labor, the Panama Canal, Indian matters, the Congressional election and a good many other things needing my constant and practical attention."[12]

Roosevelt's support of those interested in preserving Indian culture never faltered. He recommended Natalie Curtis to Edward S. Curtis, the celebrated photographer of Native Americans, as someone he should consult on their music. He also provided her a statement, part of which she used to introduce *The Indians' Book:* "These songs cast a wholly new light on the depth and dignity of Indian thought, the simple beauty and strange charm—the charm of a vanished elder world—of Indian poetry."[13] And when he heard selections from an Indian opera composed by Arthur F. Nevin, Roosevelt congratulated him on his subject matter: "It seems to me to be a peculiarly good thing to try to preserve the old Indian songs and music in this fashion; and it is one of those characteristically American bits of work which appeals to me very strongly."[14]

The president also remembered Native Americans when

he embarked on a project to redesign the nation's gold coins. For the task he was able to recruit the country's leading sculptor, Augustus Saint-Gaudens. He then, unabashedly, insisted that Saint-Gaudens substitute, for the Phrygian cap he had placed atop the figure representing liberty on one coin, a Plains warrior's feathered war bonnet. "[A]fter all," Roosevelt declared, "it is *our* Liberty—not what the ancient Greeks and Romans miscalled by that title—and we are entitled to a typically American head-dress for the lady."[15]

Roosevelt did not consult Leupp about that project, but they communicated often on strictly Indian issues. Nor did his choice of James R. Garfield, son of the president, to replace Secretary Hitchcock diminish Leupp's access. This is rather remarkable given Roosevelt's high opinion of Garfield, whom he had first appointed to the Civil Service Commission and then to head the Bureau of Corporations. Moreover, Garfield was a member of what the president termed his Tennis Cabinet, a group of men who joined him in vigorous exercise, including hiking and medicine ball. The new secretary frequently recorded in his journal these physical activities— and the opportunity it gave him to discuss Indians and other matters relating to his department.

It is surprising that neither Leupp nor Garfield seems to have resented the other's access to the president. They worked well together, and one evidence of this was the quiet demise of the Indian Division of the secretary's office, which reformers had cited for years as exercising power that should reside with the commissioner. William Jones had warned his successor that "in practice if not in theory" clerks in the Indian Division were "superior to the Commissioner of Indian Affairs."[16] Leupp needed the backing of an understanding secretary as he found himself at odds with two institutions as active as the Indian Rights Association and the Bureau of Catholic Indian Missions.

With Garland, Merriam, and Lummis on the sidelines and Grinnell less active than before, it was the BCIM and the IRA that best represented public efforts to influence the Indian policy of the Roosevelt administration. Father Ketcham remained the driving force in the BCIM, but Herbert Welsh no longer dominated the IRA, as his physicians continued to prescribe periods of rest and foreign travel to help him overcome his nervous condition. As early as 1903 Leupp had described Welsh to Roosevelt as "mentally unsound," an evaluation to which the president was likely to give credence given his resentment of Welsh's strident criticism of American conduct in the Philippines.[17]

Both the IRA and the BCIM were optimistic about prospects stemming from the 1904 election. Father Ketcham was confident because "our Republican friends are under great obligation to us."[18] For their part, IRA leaders took comfort that former associate Francis Leupp was now running the Indian Office. He did not have William Jones's desire to please, however, and he would ultimately alienate both the BCIM and the IRA as he strove to implement his idea of a proper Indian policy.

Weeks before officially replacing Jones, Leupp began helping the president respond to letters on Indian issues, particularly those relating to the sensitive subject of government contracts with sectarian schools. Leupp had, according to Matthew Sniffen, with whom he discussed it, "told [Roosevelt] that he was wrong" to have agreed to the new contracts with the Catholics and "strongly argued the case with him." The president responded that he was confident he had acted correctly and would not back down unless told to do so by either Congress or the courts. Leupp, a practitioner of "tough love" before that term had been coined, then predicted that Roosevelt would face legal action and that as the new commissioner he would help bring that about. The president did not fire his subordinate, only reiterating his willingness to abide by whatever decision the courts might reach.[19]

After conversations with Brosius and Roosevelt, Leupp advocated two remedies for the situation. The first was a lawsuit such as Bishop Hare had first suggested, which could produce a court determination as to how far the government could go in subsidizing the education of Indian children in church schools. The other was to get Congress to do for tribal funds held in trust by the government what it had already done for tribal lands—allot them. The 1887 Dawes Act had, according to Leupp, "snapped one of two demoralizing bonds of tribal communism, and as soon as the trust funds are individualized the second will be broken also."[20]

Individualizing tribal funds was not a new idea. Roosevelt had included it in his first annual message to Congress, probably at the suggestion of Merrill Gates of the Board of Indian Commissioners, who had strongly urged it at Lake Mohonk that October.[21] Commissioner Jones also had referred to individualization in annual reports and in a memorandum he prepared for Leupp on some of the problems he would face.

Leupp proposed to take no chances and followed a conservative policy in dealing with Catholic requests for contracts, but even that would be resisted by Protestants invoking separation of church and state. Once he had learned in the fall of 1904 of the Catholics' securing contracts for some of their schools, Herbert Welsh briefly abandoned his semiretired status to launch a movement to get the contracts revoked, directing Matthew Sniffen to "act with promptness and vigor."[22]

Within three months the IRA had a full-blown campaign underway. Brosius was responsible for lobbying members of Congress, while Sniffen sought support from editors, Protestant missionary groups, the Board of Indian Commissioners, the Boston Indian Citizenship Committee, and individuals known for their anti-Catholic views. By letter and personal visits to their offices in New York City, Sniffen alerted Protestant leaders to the existence of the contracts and what he described as the "surreptitious and illegal manner" by which they had been negotiated. He urged the missionary boards to "protest to the President and Secretary of the Interior against this perversion of trust funds for sectarian purposes." He also indicated that financial assistance would be welcome should the IRA seek an injunction blocking the implementation of the contracts, although that tactic would not be resorted to until 1906.[23]

Sniffen got a good response from Baptists, Presbyterians, Congregationalists, and Episcopalians. Even the spokesman for the Society of Friends indicated a willingness to broach the issue with authorities, while ruling out participation in a suit: "We have always thought it unwise to assume an attitude of hostility or antagonism to the Government."[24] But protests from other sects began to appear on the desk of the president. To one Protestant prelate Roosevelt suggested that he communicate with Leupp, who "has the right idea for its permanent solution in his desire that all those funds held for the tribes should be allotted to individuals."[25] Later, he would strenuously object to Lyman Abbott, editor of *Outlook* and normally an ally of Roosevelt's, about one of his pieces. Abbott had cited a report that the contracts had been made in return for Catholic support at the polls. This, Roosevelt declared, was "a lie pure and simple."[26] Nevertheless, there is abundant evidence that he had sought Catholic political support and was motivated in his distribution of jobs and contracts by more than his commitment to a "square deal."

The IRA pressed charges of a corrupt alliance with crusading fervor. As Sniffen phrased it, "Our work is conducted on the theory that God is on the side of right. We aim to do our part to the best of our ability and leave the result to Him, believing that sooner or later right will prevail."[27] He larded his correspondence with references to "Romanists," "fine Italian hand," and other terms that reflected an anti-Catholic bias and a susceptibility to conspiracy theories.

Samuel Brosius was, if anything, narrower still in his religious views. Reared as a member of the Society of Friends, he revealed a dogmatism early in his association with the IRA that worried Herbert Welsh: "That Mr. Brosius should have assumed that we could take up such a question as that of heterodoxy [of a superintendent of Indian schools], surprises and raised in my mind a doubt as to his . . . largeness of view, and sense of propriety of things."[28]

But even Brosius appeared moderate when compared with Dewitt C. Morrell, with whom Sniffen was prepared to cooperate against the Catholics. Morrell was also of Quaker extraction, and Sniffen described him as "a most ardent" advocate of the views of the American Protective Association, which Welsh had denounced a decade earlier as "dangerous follies" of "ignorant and unscrupulous people."[29] Sniffen, while recognizing him as an "extremist" who believed that "the Roman Church is striving to secure temporal power in the affairs of this country," nevertheless was willing to work with Morrell to get the contracts voided.[30] His contribution was to circulate attacks on James S. Sherman in his New York district, Sherman being the pro-Catholic chairman of the House Indian Committee.

The fervor of Protestants like Sniffen and Brosuis was matched by the zeal of Catholics like Father Ketcham. In the battle that waged into 1908 he had the aid of the Marquette League and other Catholic societies, plus the continued backing of prominent Catholic laymen like Eugene Philbin and Charles Bonaparte, whom Roosevelt had made secretary of the navy in the spring of 1905. Father John Wynne still was supportive, and E. L. Scharf's assistance remained a mixed blessing.

Attention shifted to Congress in December 1904 when Texas representative Stephens, one of the most anti-Catholic members of the House, attempted to ban the use of tribal trust funds for educating children in church schools. In support of Stephens the IRA distributed a pamphlet that Ketcham denounced as a "tissue of inaccuracies and misrepresentations."[31] Sniffen sent copies to church boards and members of Congress, but Ketcham ally James Sherman was able to block Stephens's attempt to attach his motion to the Indian appropriation bill.

Catholic interests would suffer in the Senate, however. Thomas R. Bard of California, a member of the Sequoya League, sponsored an amendment similar to the Stephens effort in the House. At hearings on the Indian appropriation bill, Senator Bard introduced letters from the Boston Indian Citizenship Committee, the Board of Indian Commissioners, Baptists, and Presbyterians, all opposing contracts. Commissioner Leupp, Father Ketcham, and Brosius testified before the committee. The IRA's agent took the opportunity to raise the issue of the lobbying tactics of Catholic publicist Scharf and was supported by Senator Bard. On the basis of information supplied him by Bard, Brosius charged Scharf with promising sufficient Catholic votes to elect Republicans in twenty nominally Democratic congressional districts. In return the Republicans were to support continued funding for the church's Indian schools.[32]

When Father Ketcham appeared before the committee he held that Scharf was "in no sense of the word an agent of the Catholic Church or the bureau of Catholic Indian Missions."[33] In addition he presented a statement—one he had drafted for Cardinal Gibbons's signature—denying any connection between Scharf and the church. But the damage had been done. Newspapers began to publish stories on Scharf and the contracts, agitating more Protestants. With obvious pleasure, Sniffen observed to Brosius: "We are making Rome howl!"[34] Bonaparte, then parked in the Navy Department until Roosevelt could make him attorney general, agreed that the situation had deteriorated for the Catholics: "I fear we must count upon decided hostility from Mr. Leupp and that the Scharf incident has done us more injury than was at first apparent."[35]

As the debate between the IRA and BCIM intensified, Commissioner Leupp tried to maintain a public posture of neutrality. Before the Senate committee he had maintained that there was no law authorizing or forbidding the use of treaty funds—as opposed to tribal funds that were on deposit in the Treasury and did not need to be appropriated. To clarify the issue, Leupp assured the senators that he had asked Secretary Hitchcock to submit it to the attorney general for opinion. The IRA continued to think of Leupp as an ally—and the BCIM to regard him with deep suspicion, with good cause.

When the Catholics sought a renewal of their contracts for the fiscal year ending June 30, 1906, they were told that no action could be taken until the attorney general had given his opinion. Then they learned that Hitchcock had not even forwarded the matter to the Justice Department for resolution. This produced a flurry of activity. The BCIM called upon Philbin, Bonaparte, Cardinal Gibbons, and Senator Aldrich for help. A letter from Philbin to Roosevelt got a quick response, a telegram to the Interior Department demanding that the Justice Department be queried "instantly."[36] When that did not produce results, Cardinal Gibbons contacted the president, who again directed Hitchcock to get the contracts issue before the attorney general "immediately."[37] But the bureaucracy was still in the summer doldrums. Come September it was Aldrich's turn. He went to the vacation White House at Oyster Bay and returned satisfied that the BCIM contracts would finally be authorized.[38]

This resort to lobbying disturbed one of Ketcham's allies, Father Wynne. The Jesuit confided to Ketcham his "misgivings" about the contracts being obtained "by what must always seem to be political connivance on the part of the President as much as the merits of the principle involved."[39] He could have relaxed; it was not yet accomplished fact.

Even after the Justice Department addressed the problem, staff disagreements were so serious that the attorney general would not render an opinion.[40] Not until the following May, eleven months into the fiscal year, did Roosevelt finally order Hitchcock to implement the contracts: "It is not fair that the money should be held up any longer than necessary."[41]

During the intervening months the issue had continued to simmer. In October 1905 the Lake Mohonk Conference, to no one's surprise, came out against tribal funds being used for financing sectarian schools. In December the president held two meetings on the subject, both of which Bonaparte and the attorney general attended. Others involved were Senator Aldrich at the first meeting and Commissioner Leupp at the second. Leupp had devised strict procedures governing the allotment of funds to individual schools. Roosevelt, however, required Leupp to make modifications that favored the Catholics. Nevertheless, Ketcham was still concerned that the amount authorized would be so small as to be "disastrous," and for that he blamed Leupp's slavish adherence to regulations.[42]

Both sides continued to seek support in Congress. Matthew Sniffen solicited lobbying help from Protestant leaders for a new version of the Stephens bill and sent mailings to members of the House Indian Committee. Brosius actually worked with Stephens on tactics and helped him draft remarks for the *Congressional Record*.[43] For his part, Ketcham continued to press Representative Sherman and Senator Aldrich to advance the contracts' cause. On one occasion Ketcham described Aldrich to Archbishop Ryan as "the only really faithful friend we have," while blaming Leupp for having "blocked the way as much as he can."[44]

Aldrich certainly did what he could to represent the Catholic position. On one occasion he overdid it, and Roosevelt responded with some heat that he was "very indignant at the talk Father Ketcham has seemingly indulged in about an alleged bargain on our part." That, Roosevelt continued, "is not merely a falsehood but a ridiculous falsehood." As was so often the case, he supported his position by citing Leupp, quoting his description of the accusation as "grotesque."[45]

Leupp's hope of individualizing the Indian trust funds, as not only a major step in eliminating tribes but also a way of putting contracts on a sounder basis, received support from Iowa Congressman John F. Lacey. In December 1904 he introduced a bill to divide tribal trust funds among the members on a per capita basis. The president informed Hitchcock that it was "greatly to be desired," because "each individual Indian would be then left free to use the money to which he is entitled outright on his own initiative."[46] The IRA supported the bill in its initial form and urged Sherman to expedite its passage through the House Indian Committee. In contrast, Ketcham opposed it on the grounds that "many of [the Indians] are little capable of using money judiciously, and would probably squander it as soon as they received it."[47] That would mean little would be left for a Catholic education.

The IRA had lost its enthusiasm for the bill when it was amended in committee to exclude tribal assets other than funds held by the government. As Brosuis observed, no "sane member with good business judgment would withdraw from the tribe and lose his pro-rata share of the million of assets that had not been reduced to cash."[48] As usual he blamed the Catholics for the committee's action. When the bill reached the floor of the House it was passed with a minimum of discussion. The Senate, however, took no action in that first session of the 59th Congress. In the second session the bill underwent additional refinements, although not to the taste of the IRA, as it had been so altered as to leave tribal funds intact.

While the battle over the Lacey bill was being fought in Congress, the IRA had turned to the courts, the move Bishop Hare had recommended when the contracts issue first arose. Brosuis had recently become an attorney and was attracted to the idea of litigation. He was aided in convincing the IRA leadership by Rev. Aaron B. Clark, an Episcopal missionary at the Sioux Rosebud Reservation in South Dakota and a long-time ally of the IRA. President Roosevelt described him to a Catholic bishop as "Mr. Leupp's most violent opponent . . . in this contract school business." And he defended his own record: "If you will see Mr. Bonaparte he will tell you that my object has been to go as far as under the law I could go in supporting the so-called contract schools." Roosevelt made clear to the bishop that he looked forward to a judicial determination: "We can then simply follow the decree of the court."[49]

Early in 1906 Reverend Clark spent a month in the East agitating about the issue. He conferred with both Sniffen and Brosuis. Sniffen described him as "loaded to the muzzle" and predicted he would get action.[50] Roosevelt, whom Clark had been showering with letters on the issue, described him as "the type of Protestant clergyman who has his analog among certain Catholic priests . . . each loudly complaining that I am discriminating against his creed."[51] He routinely turned over Clark's letters to Leupp; nevertheless, he did grant the missionary an audience when he was in Washington.

By early May the IRA had determined to go ahead with injunction proceedings to stop payment on contracts. Sniffen attributed it to frustration with Congress's inaction, which he blamed on "the influence of certain ecclesiastics." As the IRA did not wish to appear as the principal mover, it sought power of attorney to represent Indians on the Rosebud Reservation.[52] The result was that Reuben Quick Bear and two other Sioux filed suit against Leupp. This was the same Quick Bear who had appealed in 1904 for help in blocking the agreement. He was a former chairman of the Rosebud council, had been educated in the East, and had actually been a member of the IRA and a subscriber to Welsh's *City and State*—not exactly your average Sioux.

As Roosevelt had already stated that the arrangement he approved in May 1906 for that fiscal year would not be continued, the IRA was gambling in seeking a court decision. As he pointed out, a decision in *Quick Bear* could "cause us to continue for the future the very practices which [Brosius] protests against."[53]

To try the case, the IRA drew upon members who were attorneys and also obtained assistance from Hampton L. Carson, a leading member of the Philadelphia bar who had participated in the *Lone Wolf* litigation. Bonaparte persuaded Father Ketcham that the BCIM should employ an able Baltimore attorney, Edgar H. Gans, to aid the government staff defending Leupp. The Marquette League took care of his retainer.[54] In the first trial the supreme court of the District of Columbia handed down a split decision, approving the use of trust but not treaty funds. Both parties appealed that decision, and the district court endorsed the use of treaty as well as tribal funds, which pleased the BCIM and dismayed the IRA. A final recourse for the IRA was the U.S. Supreme Court, but in May 1908 the justices dismissed the suit of Quick Bear and his fellow Sioux. The reaction of the IRA was surprisingly muted. Their defeat in the litigation that had absorbed energies and scarce funds elicited only the statement in the IRA's 1908 annual report that the "general belief" that Congress had ruled out all contracts with sectarian schools had proved to be "without legal basis."[55]

Father Ketcham was not completely at ease with the fund situation. When he learned that the Board of Indian Commissioners, to which Roosevelt had appointed Archbishop Ryan and another Catholic, had endorsed individualization of the funds, Ketcham was distressed. "I feel pretty sure that the Archbishop and the other Catholic member of the Board . . . are in the hands of the Philistines," he complained to Mother Katherine Drexel.[56] To Ryan himself, Ketcham protested that discontinuance of the funds would be the first step in termination of the schools that could not survive on donations of the faithful alone.[57]

By 1906 the IRA had other concerns than contract schools, being on a collision course with its former employee, Commissioner Francis Leupp. Several things had contributed to the growing rift between him and the leadership of the IRA. One was his reluctance to accept advice or criticism. Once when a member of the Indian Service whom Leupp had discharged threatened to go over his head to the president, he made his case to Roosevelt: "But you know me well enough to know that I will not be bulldozed into anything under the blue sky." Leupp proposed that he be left to handle the matter himself, the president to tell the man "that you have always refused to interfere with my decisions and do not care to begin now."[58] Roosevelt may have had this in mind when he described Leupp's bullheadedness to a friend: "Though an exceedingly honest and fearless man, he is very prejudiced when he makes up his mind."[59] This time the president was content to let his headstrong subordinate deal with the problem.

Leupp was also responsible for important legislation that the IRA did not approve, as it felt that he was removing restrictions on Indian land while keeping tribal funds intact. In 1906 Congress passed the Burke Act, which the commissioner had initiated as a serious modification of the Dawes

Severalty Act of 1887. The latter had provided that while the government would hold in trust for twenty-five years the land of allotted Indians, they would hold citizenship from the date of allotment. Leupp had two objections to granting citizenship in this fashion. One was "the practice, among a certain class of political bandits, of herding Indian voters like cattle and 'voting them' in a mass,"[60] something Roosevelt had heard boasted of during his tour of the reservations in 1893.

Leupp was also disturbed at a recent court decision. In *Matter of Heff*, 1905, the Supreme Court had held that it was legal to sell liquor to an Indian who had become a citizen. The Burke Act addressed these problems by specifying that after May 8, 1906, citizenship would not be granted the allottees until the end of their wardship. It also provided that wardship could be terminated at any time the secretary of the interior was convinced that Indians were competent to handle their affairs. Leupp was also responsible for getting added to the Indian appropriation bill of 1906 a provision authorizing the president to extend wardship beyond the twenty-five-year period for those still needing its protection.

The IRA ignored the authorization for the extension of wardship and focused on the Burke Act's denial of citizenship to newly allotted Indians while their land was held in trust. Samuel Brosius protested that it would be unconstitutional to expose Indians' land to taxation if they had not solicited the end of their wardship. The Board of Indian Commissioners agreed with the IRA and referred to the Burke Act as "a long step backward."[61]

The IRA could not have been happy with another law that Leupp fostered. This was the Noncompetent Indian Act, which in 1907 passed Congress attached to the Indian appropriation bill. Leupp devised this legislation to ameliorate the plight of allotted Indians who, because of the lack of stock or equipment, were unable to make their land productive.

The commissioner proposed that they be permitted to sell a portion of their allotment in order to be able to better exploit the rest. He said this would also open more land for settlers and aid local governments by adding to the tax rolls. Leupp's rationalization was an excellent example of how he was able to reconcile the government's role of guardian with furthering the loss of the Native Americans' landed estate. The Noncompetent Indian Act did not inspire any organized opposition from friends of the Indian, although they would strongly object to another piece of legislation sought by Leupp.

In the spring of 1908 the commissioner, with the backing of Secretary Garfield, began to seek legislation to punish Indians who refused to cooperate with efforts to educate their children and to eliminate "the evil of drunkenness."[62] Leupp proposed that these erring Indians lose their tax exemptions by being issued a fee-simple title to their allotments. Senator Robert Owen of Oklahoma, himself a mixed-blood Cherokee and a former agent for the Five Civilized Tribes, introduced the bill, and Brosius led the fight against it. The IRA lobbyist pointed out that it would contribute to the impoverishment of Indians most in need of protection, as they would be likely to sell any land to which they obtained fee-simple title. In a circular addressed to members of Congress, the IRA forcefully summed up its opposition to forcing "control of their allotments upon *incompetent* and *incapable* Indians as a *punishment, a penalty,* to be inflicted upon lawbreakers and drunkards."[63] The Boston Indian Citizenship Committee also joined the fight, and together they were able to block the proposed legislation. That time Leupp had overextended himself.

The commissioner was happy to call on the IRA to help raise scholarship funds for Indian students or to suggest an attorney who might help allot a reservation, but he did not appreciate the friends' challenging his mode of disciplining Indians. Leupp resorted to armed force to suppress Indian resistance to government policies, and the IRA, with help from other friends of the Indian, rallied to the defense of the objects of his wrath. Four episodes illustrate the clash between them over what the IRA regarded as his growing reliance on harshly autocratic methods. In the order in which they arose, the episodes involved Navajos who had attacked the local superintendent, Hopis on one mesa who refused to send their children to school, a band of White Water Utes who fled their reservation, and Navajos who followed the lead of a local medicine man in resisting government policies.

Early in November 1905, Leupp heard disturbing news from Reuben Perry, superintendent of the Navajo Agency. Perry reported that he had been seized and roughed up by Indians trying to protect an alleged rapist he had intended to arrest. Perry requested that troops be sent to arrest the ringleaders and imprison them at a military post. Leupp concurred, and Captain H. O. Willard and a troop of cavalry from Fort Wingate helped take the suspects into custody. Leupp then recommended that the prisoners be held at a military prison, although he insisted that he did so regretfully because he preferred to rely on civil authorities. In this situation, however, he believed recourse to the army was the only possibility, because "the offending Indians are not only noncitizens, but among the most ignorant and lawless people with whom the Office has to deal." He was clearly aware that he was without specific warrant to imprison Indians without trial, in this case at Alcatraz. Nevertheless, Leupp rationalized that "from a strictly technical point of view such treatment of offenders is anomalous; but, for that matter, so is the Reservation system under which the Navajos have been brought up to the present time." He justified his actions as being "but a logical evolution from the existing situation."[64]

Seven Navajos were imprisoned at Alcatraz, and Brosius brought it to the attention of the IRA's executive committee.

The committee authorized him to register a complaint with the Indian Office, which he did, emphasizing not only the lack of due process but also the risk of imprisoning Indians from the arid Southwest in the dangerously damp facility in San Francisco Bay. In the summer of 1906 he attempted to see the prisoners but was refused access.

Leupp had responded to Brosius's original complaint by requesting that the War Department investigate conditions at Alcatraz. That produced a recommendation from the prison's surgeon that the Navajos be transferred to a drier climate. The commissioner himself stopped at the island in July, confirming that conditions were indeed unhealthful, and within weeks the Navajo prisoners were en route to Fort Huachuca in southeastern Arizona.[65] By that time Leupp was busy defending himself against IRA charges that he was abusing Hopis.

The Indians involved were residents of Oraibi on Second Mesa. They had been divided for several years into what came to be known in government circles as "Hostiles" and "Friendlies," based on the extent to which they chose to accept government policy, particularly with regard to sending their children to school. Leupp visited Oraibi and left it convinced that the time would soon come when the government would have to intervene "in order to prevent such a spread of the spirit of defiance of, and contempt for, the Federal authority as might breed violence and possibly bloodshed."[66]

Violence did erupt at Oraibi in September 1906. The two factions clashed and settled their differences the Hopi way, by a shoving match that resulted in the hostiles being forced out. They did not waver in their refusal to send their children to school, however. With authority from Leupp, Reuben Perry, now Indian school supervisor and aided by Indian police and a few soldiers, seized eighty-two of the children and enrolled them in the school at Keams Canyon. Leupp got

Secretary Garfield to approve the incarceration of fifteen Indian men at Fort Huachuca "on prison fare and at hard labor" for at least a year. Leupp had talked to one Oraibi Hopi who had been jailed and whose treatment had been so lax as to inspire no fear of repeating the experience, so the commissioner wanted to be sure the Indians would take seriously the threat of imprisonment.[67]

Leupp did try to avoid appearing autocratic. In his instructions to Supervisor Perry he made clear that he was not dictating where the hostiles might locate their new village. Nor did he approve Perry's suggestion that the new dwellings have chimneys and fireplaces. "I am not *forcing* these things on anybody," Leupp wrote. "I should rather have such improvements come as *the product of natural evolutionary forces* than arbitrarily to compel their adoption."[68] Subsequently he repeated his insistence that the Indians be left some latitude for personal expression. "Civilization is something which must proceed from the inside out, if it is to be a real and not a merely specious change," he observed. He also noted that one of his first acts on taking office had been to cancel the collecting of statistics on dress: "I should not ask what an Indian wears, any more than I should ask what a white man wears, as long as he keeps within the limits of decency and behaves himself."[69]

The leaders of the IRA, however, judged the commissioner on his handling of the Hopi prisoners. Matthew Sniffen deemed their being held at Fort Huachuca "unnecessarily harsh treatment."[70] Brosius suggested that in the absence of a trial committing the Indians to prison perhaps the IRA should seek writs of habeas corpus.[71] Meanwhile, the plight of the White Water Utes was coming to the attention of the IRA.

These Utes belonged to the Uintah and Ouray Agency and were distinctly unhappy with the 1905 allotment of their reservation. The following year about four hundred determined to relocate to South Dakota and settle among the Sioux, where they fantasized that they could continue to live by hunting and gathering. In July the migration got underway and alarmed whites aware that one of the Ute leaders was Red Cap, reputed to have killed Agent Nathan Meeker in 1879 by driving a barrel stave down his throat.[72] The governor of Wyoming had troops called out, although an armed confrontation was avoided.[73]

The IRA early on expressed some concern about the situation and was assured by Leupp that the department's best troubleshooter, Inspector McLaughlin, already had persuaded a few Utes to return to their reservation. The rest of the band, however, persisted in its quest for a new home. Refusing to return to Utah, they were housed for the winter at Fort Meade in southwestern South Dakota.

President Roosevelt, who received a Ute delegation from Fort Meade, commented to his son Kermit on the refugees, using some of the DeQuincey imagery Senator Quay had applied to Delawares:

> The poor Tartar tribe! Such a shabby, pathetic, hopelessly inefficient and wrong-headed Tartar tribe, quite unable to profit by kindness; and such easy victims of tyranny! I have done the best I could do for them. I put them in special charge of Captain Johnson (who is the hero of Remington's story . . . 'Massai's Crooked Trails;') who will do all that can be done for them. The pathetic geese had nothing to suggest for themselves excepting that I should allow them to live on one of the Sioux reservations, where I should supply them with food, clothing, etc.[74]

The temporary agent, Capt. Carter P. Johnson, was permitted to arrange a Ute lease of a portion of the Cheyenne River Sioux Reservation, but within a year the government's policy of reducing rations for able-bodied Indians precipitated another crisis with the refugees. Leupp had coupled the ration reduction with a campaign to find employment for the Indians. For the Utes it was grading railroad lines through South Dakota, and most of them refused to work. Leupp then sharply reduced their rations, ignoring their protests. Roosevelt assured him that "I am with you in any necessary sternness of measures." He believed that "we have made fair allowances and they have shown themselves ungrateful," and that now the Utes should "suffer the hardships which their own fault brings."[75]

Roosevelt could respond harshly to what he regarded as a threat to law and order, whether it was by cowboys, as in the attack on the Few Tails party in 1891, or the alleged Brownsville riot of African-American soldiers in 1906. In race relations, as in other areas, Roosevelt's record was uneven. Nor was the public always aware of his actions behind the scenes. In October 1908, for example, in a note marked "Private," he directed that seating for a play to be presented on the White House grounds be arranged so "that the seats in the section for the colored people are just as good as the seats for the white people."[76] In the context of the times, that was evidence of remarkable presidential sensitivity.

But neither Roosevelt nor Leupp had much give in him when challenged. In October 1907 at Lake Mohonk, the Indian commissioner made his case against the Utes. He described them as having insisted that, "we are government people, not like the Sioux—the Sioux have to work, but the government will feed *us*." Leupp told his audience that the Utes "must either go to work or go hungry," and that if they resisted they would be "suppressed, and, if necessary, with an iron hand." The audience applauded when he went on to say, "If they persist in that course they will be made to understand what the word 'must' means."[77]

One of his listeners, Samuel Brosius, did not agree, and within a week would propose that the IRA take up the Ute cause. Welsh, just back from Europe, did draft a statement in which he acknowledged that Leupp "has done much good work for Indians," while denouncing his threat to use an "iron hand."[78] But Leupp had the backing of the president, who met with him and Secretary Garfield to discuss the Ute problem. Two days later Roosevelt informed Garfield that he was in total agreement with Leupp's recommendations, including, if necessary, the use of force.[79]

Matthew Sniffen went down to Washington and for an hour heard Leupp explain the government's position. Sniffen shared this with Brosius, who was not convinced, and drafted a circular in which he defended the Utes. He stated that the government had taken for national forest over two million acres of the Utes' land remaining after allotment without paying them a cent. If they had been paid the more than $7 million the land was worth, Brosius maintained, the Utes could have been living off the interest. Moreover, he insisted, if "they desire to avoid hard labor, they are entitled to do so in like manner with their white neighbors, however strongly we may believe that honest labor is ennobling."[80] This novel idea was unheard of at Mohonk, most of whose attendees knew hard labor only secondhand.

A pressing reason for the Indians' returning to their allotments in Utah related to water. These had been carefully selected to ensure that in that parched country they could be irrigated, and Utah law specified that water had to be used within five years of its being claimed or that right would be forfeited. With no viable future in South Dakota, the Utes had to reclaim their allotments and the government supplied wagons and teams for a well-organized return trip with Captain Johnson in charge.

Once again Leupp had succeeded because of his influence with the president and his own persistence. As he told Matthew Sniffen at the height of the crisis: "I am sorry this issue has been raised, but I am as certain of my position in the matter as I am in the rising of the sun. I am perfectly willing to stand by everything I have done, and it will not matter whether it makes or breaks me."[81] Everyone else was learning what Roosevelt already knew; once Leupp made up his mind, he was hard to move.

Leupp's self-assurance, bordering on arrogance, was also apparent in his handling of another Navajo problem. This one occurred at the San Juan Agency, which had been split off from the Navajo Agency in 1903. The superintendent in 1907, with headquarters at Shiprock, New Mexico, was William T. Shelton. In late March he reported a potentially dangerous situation with a band of Navajos led by By-a-lil-le (The Rainmaker), a medicine man who opposed Shelton's efforts to prevent the Indians' selling their sheep-breeding stock, refusing to enroll children in school, and practicing polygamy. An Indian Office special agent conducted his own investigation and proposed that cavalry be sent to arrest By-a-lil-le, whom he described as beyond control by the agency staff and a menace to both them and San Juan's progressive Navajos.[82]

Nothing was done at the time, but in September the superintendent, who had only eight police (and they were intimidated by the medicine man's claims of supernatural power), renewed his plea for soldiers.[83] With prompting from Leupp, Secretary Garfield persuaded the War Department to send two troops of cavalry from Fort Wingate under the command of Captain Willard, whom Leupp suggested because of his able performance on the 1905 assignment. After conferring with Shelton and traders in the area, one of whom described By-a-lil-le's band as "vicious, bad Indians of the worst type," the captain decided to arrest the Navajos.[84]

Accompanied by the superintendent and his Indian police, Willard surprised the band at dawn on October 28. There was no resistance until one Navajo opened fire on the cavalry. Their return volley killed two Indians and wounded one. Captain Willard's only regret was that he "did not succeed in killing the balance that fired upon us and then escaped." He also informed Leupp that a Catholic missionary had told him of a letter he had received from "the head of the Catholic missions in the United States [Ketcham?], saying that the Indian Rights Association was endeavoring to stir up a good deal of trouble for you and Superintendent Shelton on account of 'the poor defenseless peace loving blanket wearing Navajoes having been shot down in cold blood by the soldiers.'" For this the captain blamed Reverend Harold R. Antes, who had written several newspapers and organizations, including the IRA, his version of what had occurred, featuring brutal soldiers shooting innocent Indians in the back.[85] Superintendent Shelton had expelled Reverend Antes from the reservation, and some believed that the missionary sought revenge.

Antes inspired enough protests that Leupp concluded that an outside investigator should be sent to Shiprock. He declined to suggest anyone to Roosevelt, who decided upon Col. Hugh L. Scott, the superintendent of West Point who earlier in his career had commanded a unit of Indian soldiers at Fort Sill. The president thought highly enough of Scott to have proposed jumping him from major to brigadier general.[86] Presented late in April 1908, the colonel's report rejected Reverend Antes's charges and included a written retraction from Antes himself. This simply confirmed Roosevelt's judgment, at least as far as Captain Willard's conduct was concerned. When Willard expressed a desire to attend the army's service school at Fort Leavenworth, the president supported him in a letter describing him as "the young captain who did so well with the Navajos a year ago."[87] But the issue refused to go away because of the attention given it by the IRA.

The news of the killing of two Navajos and the wounding

of another, together with the imprisonment at Fort Huachuca without trial of nine other Indians, including By-a-lil-le, got a reaction from the IRA leaders. They already were smoldering over a dispute with the Interior Department concerning their failure to get a satisfactory investigation of charges of wrong-doing at the Crow Reservation.[88] Indeed, Samuel Brosius had been ordered off the reservation, and when Matthew Sniffen had insisted on visiting it in one of his rare absences from the IRA headquarters, an inspector from the secretary's office arrested and expelled him. Within the IRA there was much criticism of Brosius for not returning to the reservation even at the risk of arrest, and at one point he tendered his resig-nation, which was declined after an embarrassingly long con-sideration by the IRA's executive committee.

Perhaps the need to redeem himself was a factor in Bro-sius's concluding that the By-a-lil-le affair "is the golden op-portunity to teach the Indian Commr. a lesson, and the Supt. of the Ship Rock school also. Shelton is an arrogant fellow, conceited, and living upon injustice and deception."[89] Bro-sius's choice of instructional method was to file writs of habeas corpus for the Navajos held at Fort Huachuca. First, however, he would need the approval of the association's ex-ecutive committee.

It took several months for the IRA to accept the tactic suggested by its Washington agent. The principal opponent of the plan was its president, Charles C. Binney. He, according to Brosius, Sniffen, and Welsh, had fallen under Leupp's spell, or, as Sniffen put it, "We should not be hypnotized by Mr. Leupp through one of our own members."[90] Not until the an-nual meeting in December 1908, however, was Binney voted out of office. Then the campaign to free By-a-lil-le and the other remaining Navajo prisoners finally got underway.

Meanwhile, President Roosevelt came to the defense of his Indian commissioner in reaction to IRA-inspired letters protesting detention of the Indians. Responding to one from the Boston Indian Citizenship Committee, he was extravagant in his support of Leupp: "I cannot speak too strongly of his courage and efficiency, and utter disregard of everything except the interests of the Indians."[91]

Roosevelt must have been happy when Leupp's actions were sustained by a district court in Tombstone in January 1909. The IRA, however, appealed the case to the Arizona Territory Supreme Court, which ordered the release of the only two Navajos still in custody, By-a-lil-le and his chief lieutenant. At that point the new administration of President William Howard Taft declined to appeal the case to the U.S. Supreme Court, and Leupp had lost the last battle. By that time he also had severed all but strictly official relations with his former employer, the IRA.

What had remained of any friendship between Francis Leupp and IRA personnel was a casualty of the ongoing Crow Reservation controversy. Once the IRA had leveled charges that impugned his reputation, Leupp had taken the position that he could not comment on the issue while it was being investigated by Secretary Garfield. Nevertheless, IRA members continued to try to communicate with the commissioner on the subject. Finally, Leupp curtly directed Welsh "to confine [his] further correspondence . . . to strictly official channels."[92] Welsh retorted that his letter had been "conceived in an entirely friendly spirit" and that he had nothing further to say except that "I shall endeavor . . . to stand up for the interest and right treatment of the Indians, as I have always done."[93] Two months later Leupp had to write a similar letter to Samuel Brosius. It is little wonder that he was not among the IRA's list of acceptable candidates for the post of Indian commissioner in the Taft administration.

Roosevelt had gone all out to assist Taft in getting the nomination and winning the election. Although he had sought to avoid any act that might prejudice Taft's chances, he no longer felt it necessary to cater to pressure groups to the same degree. For example, there was a new tone in his responses to Catholics seeking favors. When Eugene Philbin chided him about "complaints that are frequently made that the administration is not disposed to be fair to the Church," Roosevelt shot back that for every Catholic complaint of that nature he had "twenty from Protestant missionaries that [he] was over-favorable to the Catholic Church." And he added, "I receive more requests for special favors for Catholics . . . than is the case with any other religious organization."[94]

Within a month Roosevelt was expressing his unhappiness with Cardinal Gibbons for trying to bring "ecclesiastical pressure" to bear on behalf of a naval officer.[95] He even had occasion to complain about an artist who used her Catholic connections to get commissions to "paint frightful daubs of prominent men," including himself. A bishop who interceded for her was told bluntly that there was no correlation between artistic ability and religious fervor.[96] Yet Roosevelt made one last contribution to the Catholic cause, introducing Father Ketcham to Taft as "a good friend of mine and one of your staunchest and most effective supporters," as well as a "high-minded, zealous and reasonable friend of the Indians."[97]

The president was leaving office under the illusion that he had handpicked a successor who agreed with him on all major issues. Moreover, he was confident that he had passed the baton to one likely to respond favorably to officeholders such as Secretary Garfield and Commissioner Leupp who wished to continue.

Leupp's retention was strongly endorsed by at least one of those who had so enthusiastically welcomed him to the commissionership in 1905, George Bird Grinnell. He dropped a note to Leupp regretting reports of his ill health, at the same time expressing the hope that the commissioner would be able to continue under Taft. Leupp replied at length, admitting to being temporarily "impaired" due to the "continuous nervous strain" that he had been under. He also unburdened himself on the failings of reformers, obviously having in mind the IRA people with whom he had been feuding. He was prepared to recognize their "benevolent intentions," although he regarded many of them as "painfully uninformed concerning the Indian and his traits, and the condition obtaining in the frontier country." Leupp was particularly critical of the willingness of the "philanthropists" to accept the word of any obscure missionary over that of the "man [himself] who has lived in the public eye for a long generation, and spent half that time studying the Indian problem at large instead of one little corner of it." He obviously was nettled by the IRA's willingness to make charges based on reports from its missionary contacts. Leupp held that these "fanatics" were more of a problem than the grafter whose crimes could be exposed or the professional politician who could be dealt with, "as long as you have a firm, steady-headed and courageous President behind you."[98]

Despite painting such a gloomy picture of the office, Leupp indicated his willingness to continue if Taft chose a secretary of the interior as competent as Garfield, whom he praised as "the best man I have ever seen in that place." Leupp would also require some indication from the new president that he would enjoy "the same unqualified and unshakable personal confidence in me that I have enjoyed for the better part of twenty years from Mr. Roosevelt."[99]

Grinnell was appreciative of Leupp's problems with the eastern reformers, whom he himself had often ridiculed as impractical theorists: "I sympathize with you entirely on the difficulties that you meet with the good and worthy people who know nothing about the Indians, and yet who are quite ready to take up any startling story that may be brought to them. These are the hardest people to deal with, because they are so honest and sincere, and in many cases—so foolish."[100] When he learned that Leupp had accepted an invitation from Taft to remain at the Indian Office for a few months, Grinnell expressed his happiness, recalling his "joy" on hearing from Roosevelt in late 1904 of his intention to appoint Leupp.[101]

Leupp not only was not the IRA's nominee for Indian commissioner in the new administration, neither was he backed by the Boston Indian Citizenship Committee, the BCIM, or the Board of Indian Commissioners. The board's secretary, Merrill Gates, speculated that Garfield's policy of ignoring the board could be attributed to advice he had received from Leupp, who claimed to have been promised a "free hand" by the president. He also blamed Leupp for Roosevelt's turning less and less to the board for advice.[102] For his part, Father Ketcham was most intent on defeating the candidacy of the superintendent of Haskell Institute, whom he denounced for permitting hundreds of Catholic students to be seduced from their faith.[103]

The Boston Indian Citizenship Committee proposed one of its own members to be commissioner. Its president communicated to Brosius's receptive ear his disillusionment with the current administration: "The President continues this endless chain of admiration for all Indian employees—as Shelton, who fools Leupp; 2nd: Leupp who fixes the President; 3rd: the President swallows everything and thinks that all of us who are friends to the Indians know nothing about the Indian Service, all of which is rather hard on us and the poor Indian."[104]

Thus Roosevelt's administration came to an end on a discordant note for the six friends of the Indian. Their buoyant optimism inspired by his ascension to the presidency had produced a coalition that proved too fragile to reconcile their individual and organizational differences. And in 1905 Roosevelt, tired of their bickering, had been happy to place control of Indian affairs in the hands of Leupp, whose mode of operation left the other friends with little voice.

Epilogue

By December 1908 Roosevelt had become uneasy about his relations with William Howard Taft. The president-elect had informed him privately that there would be a general cabinet turnover, despite having assured his patron at the beginning of the campaign that this would not be the case. Roosevelt refrained from leaking this to his cabinet officers, including those like Garfield who hoped to be continued. For three more weeks Garfield was left twisting in the wind before finally hearing the bad news from Taft. Meanwhile, Roosevelt had confided to the secretary and a few others his distress at what Garfield referred to in his diary as "hostile influences . . . at work and estranging [Taft] from the President."[1]

Francis Leupp's prospects were better than those of his superior. George Bird Grinnell did what he could, praising Leupp to Taft as "the most practical and earnest commissioner of Indian affairs that I have known." Grinnell strongly endorsed Leupp's emphasis on "cultivating in the Indian a sense of individual responsibility." He also moved to counteract criticism of Leupp by "New England philanthropists . . . people who know little or nothing about the Indian. These good people believe, I am told, that Mr. Leupp is too severe with the Indians, but they do not understand that under many circumstances the Indian requires severity."[2]

The inauguration came and went and Leupp remained in office. Early in April, President Taft informed Cardinal Gibbons, who was pushing a BCIM candidate, that "Mr. Leupp has kindly consented to continue indefinitely as Commissioner."[3] Nevertheless, it was generally understood that Leupp would stay only a few months, meanwhile grooming his protégé Robert G. Valentine for the post.

In June Leupp did step down and President Taft appointed Valentine. Herbert Welsh and Matthew Sniffen had originally opposed him as Leupp's creation, but Sniffen concluded after a lengthy interview with Valentine that as commissioner "he would be far ahead of Leupp."[4] Sniffen then sold Valentine to Welsh, and just in time because the IRA's founder was corresponding with none other than former commissioner William Jones, who was signaling a willingness to return to Washington. With his usual unctuousness he had confided in Welsh: "It would be in bad taste on my part to criticise or discuss [Leupp's] policies, although I confess to you personally that I think he is wrong, and that some things that he has done have been quite injurious to the Indians."[5] Welsh praised the former commissioner for his "broad-minded integrity," documenting his own gullibility.[6]

After departing the Indian Office, Leupp continued speaking out on Indian affairs. His publications included two books, *The Indian and His Problem* (1910), and *In Red Man's Land* (1914). The first was dedicated to Roosevelt, who had provided him "unwavering confidence and support." Letters to the former president revealed additional evidence of the remarkable latitude that Roosevelt had entrusted to Leupp, making him, as the commissioner saw it, the "guardian of [the president's] Indian conscience."[7]

In May 1911, Leupp called Roosevelt's attention to a recent decision of the Supreme Court that had reminded him of how well they had worked together. The court had rejected a Sac and Fox of Iowa claim to about $450,000, which then went to members of the tribe who had submitted to removal to Oklahoma. The Iowa congressional delegation had pushed a bill through Congress to give the money to the Indians in their state, but Roosevelt had vetoed it on the advice of Leupp. The commissioner had argued that to give the money to the Indians in Iowa would be rewarding "recusancy and backwardness, and giving a black eye to Indian progress toward citizenship, for which we had been working so long and hard." The president had told the Iowa governor, the state's congressional delegation, and the two Iowans in his cabinet—all of whom had protested the veto—to take it up with his Indian commissioner. With solid backing from Roosevelt, Leupp held firm.[8]

As was the case with several other issues, Leupp was willing to have this one settled in the courts. He saw to it that the Oklahoma Indians were well represented, and he could now congratulate Roosevelt for refusing "to be badgered into helping rob" them. "It is that sort of thing that makes me look back on your administration with a thrill of pride," Leupp wrote.[9] Roosevelt said he was so pleased with the letter that he would "keep it permanently," and referred to a "feeling of satisfaction in dealing with you that I had with only a few others of the very best men under me."[10]

Despite their close relationship it would appear that in 1912 Leupp did not support Roosevelt when he broke ranks with the Republicans to head the Bull Moose Party. Nevertheless, their relationship based on shared views of Indian policy survived. On the few occasions that the former commissioner called Roosevelt's attention to something that had occurred in his administration, Roosevelt always answered with a warm endorsement of Leupp's conduct of the office. And in 1917 when Roosevelt sought permission to raise a volunteer division and lead it to France, Leupp heartily endorsed the quixotic proposal and detailed his own family's contributions to the war effort. Roosevelt's response was typically cordial: "It is exactly what I should have expected of the family!"[11]

Of the other five individuals who had applauded Roosevelt's occupancy of the White House in 1901, only Grinnell had continued to use personal contacts to seek to influence the administration of Indian affairs. Even he did so on a declining scale and through Leupp, not Roosevelt. Well acquainted with conditions facing tribes, Grinnell remained severely practical. He believed wholeheartedly, as he assured Commissioner Valentine, "that to shelter, protect and generally coddle the Indian does him no permanent good." Grinnell, however, was always concerned to "protect him from being run over by selfish people" and to ensure that Indian Service personnel were honest and efficient.[12]

The other four friends had their own problems. As early as 1904 Herbert Welsh had given up trying to influence Indian affairs through Roosevelt. Four years later he no longer had access to Leupp, having exhausted the commissioner's patience in the running battle over the Crow Reservation. Meanwhile, Charles Lummis's interest remained focused on Indians of the Southwest, although after the fiascoes involving the Cupeños and the Hopis he gave up trying to influence what happened in Washington. He, however, did not completely cease trying to correspond with Roosevelt, although he got little response to his letters. In 1912 he dropped the failed candidate a vintage Lummis note: "We went up [to vote] in a solid phalanx and loaded Right," he informed Roosevelt. "The Machine had too many thoughtless cogs. We are bitterly disappointed."[13]

C. Hart Merriam also remained in contact with Roosevelt, although only in regard to non-Indian matters. In 1909 Samuel Brosius reported to Sniffen that he had seen Merriam for the first time in four or five years and that Merriam seemed unaware of controversial Leupp policies.[14] The scientist, however, had preserved enough relationship with Roosevelt to be invited to lunch at Oyster Bay in March 1912, despite the presidential primary's absorbing most of the candidate's time and energies.[15]

Hamlin Garland's efforts to affect Indian policy may have declined, but he also retained ties with the former president he so admired. Like Lummis, Garland made certain in 1912 that Roosevelt was aware of his support. And like Merriam, he was on sufficiently good terms to be invited to lunch at Oyster Bay.[16] When Roosevelt died in 1919, Garland became a staunch supporter of the memorial association created to honor the man he described as "a dominating figure in my world for over a quarter of a century."[17]

Institutions are less sentimental. In the 1912 campaign the Catholic hierarchy did not support the man who had done so much to advance the cause of Catholic participation in the government process. Roosevelt had appointed Catholics to positions they either had not previously held or in which they had been underrepresented. His initiatives helped set the stage for a Catholic presence at Lake Mohonk as early as 1902, and even Father Ketcham appeared at this Protestant stronghold in 1908.

That had not signaled an end to Catholic-Protestant rivalry in Indian matters. Father Ganss had already resigned his membership in the IRA after vigorously protesting what he regarded as the anti-Catholic tone of one of its pamphlets.[18]

In 1909 Father Ketcham reacted to what he viewed as the same failing in the annual report of the IRA for 1908. In an address to the Marquette League of New York City, printed as "The Indian Rights Association *vs* The Rights of the Indians," Ketcham accused the IRA of misleading statements. He declared that while it was willing to cooperate with the association, the BCIM "finds itself somewhat in the predicament of a man who would refuse to clasp the right hand in fellowship with one who experience had proved had ever clutched in his left hand a dagger for his 'brother's' back."[19]

Herbert Welsh drafted a response to remarks attributed to Ketcham and damned them in a phrase: "The source and animus of these statements can be made manifest by one word—Jesuits." He concluded: "Let us suggest that Dr. Ketcham or other critics be careful to keep to the truth, the whole truth and nothing but the truth."[20] The tone of the dialogue of these Christians did not promise much of a future for cooperation. Compared with them, Roosevelt's tolerance seemed admirable indeed.

For a man often portrayed as racist and anti-Indian, Roosevelt had compiled a formidable record of interventions in behalf of Native Americans. These usually were occasioned by information from interested private citizens who went to Roosevelt because they knew he would take action. Occasionally some of the six friends would join forces to promote an objective, although on occasion they offered conflicting advice, particularly on personnel matters. In January 1905 Roosevelt must have breathed a sigh of relief at being able to turn the Indian Office over to Leupp, a strong-willed individual accepted by the reformers, at least initially, as one of their own. The new commissioner's ways, however, soon alienated many supporters. Nevertheless, the president's consistent backing gave Leupp a degree of control of Indian administration not enjoyed by any previous commissioner.

As an appointed official, Leupp had to answer only to
the president, but Roosevelt could not ignore politicians with
constituents seeking preference in the Indian Service or access to Indian land, timber, water, and minerals.

A talk he gave in 1908 to a delegation from the Tulsa
Commercial Club suggests the fine line he trod throughout
his White House years when trying to protect Indian rights
and property from a clamorous electorate. The Oklahomans
arrived at the White House literally with a brass band and ban-
ners and accompanied by two members of Congress. Their
objective was the removal of all restrictions on Indian land in
the new state. Roosevelt agreed that it was not to the Indian's
"advantage or to yours that there should be large tracts of
non-taxable and non-improved land," and advocated removing restrictions on any amount over a forty-acre homestead.
He balanced that with a plea that the Tulsans recognize that
many of the tribesmen were incapable of protecting their own
interests: "He is the oldest American of all of us, so give him
a fair show; give him a chance."[21] Unfortunately, the record
does not suggest that appeals to their better nature ever diminished Americans' lust for Indian property.

The six friends—even Leupp—must often have ruefully
reflected on their buoyant optimism when Roosevelt had succeeded to the presidency. It had seemed to them a God-given
opportunity to change the course of Indian affairs. Even at
their best, however, they had only ameliorated the universally
bad conditions afflicting Indians. Nor could organizations
like the BCIM and the IRA, even if they so desired, stay the car
of juggernaut that was destroying the cultures of the tribes
while stripping them of their property and the vestiges of
their autonomy. Father Ketcham once remarked to Mother
Katharine Drexel, relative to the inability of the Five Civilized
Tribes to defend themselves against intruders, "Right or
wrong, you could as easily remove the Atlantic from our east-

ern coast as you could remove the hundreds of thousands of white people from the Indian Territory."[22]

Nevertheless the six friends had had their modest successes, and they usually owed them to Roosevelt. While Indians ranked low in the hierarchy of interests of this wide-ranging intellect, no other president in modern times intervened as often in their behalf or worked harder to improve the caliber of Indian Service personnel. Civil service was then thought to be the key, and by 1908 all but two agents had been replaced by superintendents under the merit system.

Roosevelt had also demonstrated a strong interest in preserving aspects of Indian cultures. This was apparent even after he left office, as when in 1913 he toured Arizona and reported on its Indians in articles for *Outlook*. His accounts are suffused with appreciation for the culture of the Native Americans he encountered. He singled out for particular notice a Hopi grandmother who "entirely unhelped from without and with no incentive of material reward, but purely to gratify her own innate artistic feeling . . . had developed the art of pottery-making to a most unusual degree: it was really beautiful pottery."[23] Roosevelt also provided a detailed description of a Hopi snake dance he attended and stated categorically, "It is mere tyranny . . . to stop all dances."[24] He then found space to praise Hopi architecture and the efforts of Frank Mead, now back to practicing architecture, to incorporate Native American themes in houses he was designing in California.

While in Arizona, Roosevelt had encountered Natalie Curtis, who had helped educate him on the beauty of the arts and music of southwestern Indians. For his readers he identified her as one "who has done so very much to give to Indian culture its proper position."[25] After his death she wrote of that encounter, praising him for recognizing "what the American Indian might mean to our Nation."[26] He indeed had used the "bully pulpit" to help his fellow Americans appreciate possible Indian contributions to a common culture.

The six friends had not been any more united on the necessity of salvaging Indian cultures than they had been on any other issue. But despite their differences, there had been occasions when some of them cooperated. The Sequoya League had appeared briefly to offer real possibilities of collaboration, but Lummis was too much of an eccentric to provide effective leadership. And the others had their own goals as well as personality flaws.

In the final analysis the only thing the six friends had in common was their access to the president and their hope of employing it to advance their Indian agendas. While never as successful as they had hoped, the six had made a difference, helping Roosevelt to at least approximate the role of the Indians' Great Father.

 Notes

Abbreviations

BCIMR   Bureau of Catholic Indian Missions Records
GBGP   George Bird Grinnell Papers
HGC   Hamlin Garland Collection
IRAP R   Indian Rights Association Papers, Microfilm Reel
JP   William A. Jones Papers
LP   Charles Lummis Papers
ML   Elting E. Morison, *The Letters of Theodore Roosevelt*
NARG   National Archives Record Group
OIA-LR   Office of Indian Affairs—Letters Received
TRPR   Theodore Roosevelt Papers, Microfilm Reel
TWTR   *The Works of Theodore Roosevelt, National Edition*

Chapter 1. An Education in Indian Advocacy

1. Herman Hagedorn, *Roosevelt in the Bad Lands,* 355.
2. Robert M. LaFollette, *LaFollette's Autobiography,* 479.

234   Notes to Pages 5–14

3. TR to Mrs. Lodge, January 11, 1907, Papers of Henry Cabot Lodge, III. To Mrs. Henry Cabot Lodge, with whom he enjoyed intellectual discourse, he wrote that he saw a strong resemblance "between the Japanese spirit and the Greek spirit of the Periclean age."

4. TWTR 1:375.

5. TR to Cecil Arthur Spring Rice, July 3, 1901, ML 3:107.

6. TWTR 1:279.

7. TWTR 11:15.

8. This appeared in Jackson's first annual message. James D. Richardson, *Compilation of Messages and Papers of the Presidents* 2:459.

9. TWTR 1:79.

10. TWTR 1:72–73.

11. TWTR 1:65.

12. TWTR 1:77.

13. TWTR 1:63, n. 1.

14. TWTR 1:168.

15. TWTR 1:171.

16. TR to Anna Roosevelt, October 13, 1879, ML 1:41.

17. TR to Theodore Roosevelt, Jr., February 24, 1903, TRPR 330.

18. TR to Anna Roosevelt, August 22, 1880, ML 1:74.

19. TR to Eugene Hale, May 13, 1901, ML 3:77.

20. Grinnell to TR, May 8, 1889, GBGP.

21. Grinnell's introduction to TR's *Hunting Trips of a Ranchman,* TWTR 1:xv.

22. TWTR 1:371–73.

23. George Bird Grinnell, *The Passing of the Great West,* 124.

24. John F. Regier, *American Sportsmen and the Origins of Conservation,* 120.

25. Herbert Welsh to George William Curtis, March 15, 1886, IRAP R68.

26. Welsh to Benjamin Harrison, November 17, 1886, IRAP R68.

27. Grinnell to TR, May 14, 1889, GBGP.

28. Painter to Welsh, May 23, 1889, IRAP R24.

29. TR to Welsh, July 12, 1889, IRAP R5.

30. Frederick Jackson Turner, "The Winning of the West," 73.

31. William Hard, quoted in William Davison Johnston, *TR: Champion of the Strenuous Life,* 109.

32. TR to Welsh, March 15, and April 1, 1890, TRPR 5.

33. Welsh to TR, December 22, 1890, IRAP R70.

34. Welsh to TR, December 31, 1890, IRAP R70.

35. Copy of TR to Charles Collins, January 21, 1891, IRAP R6.

36. TR to Welsh, January 24, 1891, IRAP R6.

37. TR, "Indians Who Deserve Pensions," *The Century Magazine* 46 (May 1893), 155.

38. TR to Welsh, January 24, 1891, IRAP R6.

39. TR to Welsh, February 13, 1891, IRAP R7.

40. Ibid.

41. TR to Welsh, March 26, 1893, IRAP R10.

42. Herbert Welsh, "Civilization among the Sioux Indians," 6, IRAP R102.

43. Brown to Welsh, September 7, 1892, IRAP R9.

44. TR to Peabody, September 15, 1892, Endicott Peabody Papers.

45. Grinnell to TR, September 12, 1892, GBGP.

46. "Report of Hon. Theodore Roosevelt: Made to the United States Civil Service Commission . . ." 16, IRAP R102.

47. Herbert Welsh, "Civilization among the Sioux Indians," 6, IRAP R102.

48. For Roosevelt's comments, see 1892 Proceedings of the Lake Mohonk Conference, 80, 86, 93, 108, and 127.

49. Painter to Welsh, October 17, 1892, IRAP R9.

50. Anna Dawes to Welsh, October 31, 1892, IRAP R9.

51. Philadelphia, *Times,* December 17, 1892, IRA scrapbook, Historical Society of Pennsylvania.

52. Welsh to Mrs. James E. Fisk, December 30, 1892, IRAP R72.

53. TR to Endicott Peabody, September 15, 1892, Endicott Peabody Papers.

54. 1892 Proceedings of the Lake Mohonk Conference, 81.

55. "Report of Hon. Theodore Roosevelt," 15, IRAP R102.

56. Ibid., 14.

57. 1892 Proceedings of the Lake Mohonk Conference, 83.

58. "Report of Hon. Theodore Roosevelt," 8, IRAP R102.

59. Ibid., 9.

60. Ibid., 8.

61. Ibid., 10.
62. Ibid., 13.
63. Ibid., 8.
64. Ibid., 21.
65. 1892 Proceedings of the Lake Mohonk Conference, 108.
66. 1893 Annual Report of the Board of Indian Commissioners, 128.
67. TR to Welsh, October 10, 1892, IRAP R9.
68. TR to Welsh, December 21, 1892, IRAP R9.
69. TR to Welsh, February 24, 1892, IRAP R9.
70. Welsh to TR, February 15, 1893, IRAP R72.
71. Welsh to TR, February 2, 1893, IRAP R72.
72. TR to Welsh, February 4, 1893, IRAP R72.
73. Welsh to TR, February 6, 1893, IRAP R72.
74. TR to Richard Henry Dana, December 28, 1891, ML 1:269.
75. TR to Bonaparte, January 4, 1892, TR Correspondence Photostats, Houghton Library.
76. TR to Welsh, January 23, 1895, IRAP R12.
77. Pratt to Merrill E. Gates, October 9, 1894, Pratt Papers.
78. Charles Lyman and TR to the president, June 19, 1893, TR Correspondence Photostats, Houghton Library.
79. TR to Welsh, June 28, 1893, IRAP R10.
80. Pratt to Merrill E. Gates, October 9, 1894, Pratt Papers.
81. TR to Welsh, July 1, 1893, IRAP R10.
82. Grinnell to Welsh, February 13, 1889, IRAP R10.
83. Grinnell to Welsh, March 1, 1890, GBGP.
84. TR to Welsh, March 11, 1893, IRAP R10.
85. TR to Welsh, March 18, 1893, IRAP R10.
86. Grinnell to Welsh, May 9, 1893, IRAP R10.
87. Welsh to Grinnell, October 19, 1893, IRAP R72; IRA Office Report, November 7, 1893, IRAP R100.

Chapter 2. A Heartbeat from the Presidency

1. TR to Anna Roosevelt Cowles, August 16, 1893, TR, *Letters from Theodore Roosevelt to Anna Roosevelt Cowles*, 130.
2. TR to Frederic Remington, November 29, 1892, ML 1:497.

3. TR to Matthews, May 21, 1894, ML 1:379.

4. TR to Matthews, June 29, 1894, ML 1:389.

5. TR to Matthews, December 7, 1894, ML 1:410.

6. Garland, *A Daughter of the Middle Border*, 29.

7. Grinnell to Garland, September 1, 1897, HGC.

8. *City and State*, October 3, 1895, 2.

9. TR to Dear Sir, November 23, 1895, TR Scrapbook, TR Collection, Widener Library.

10. Hana Samek, *The Blackfoot Confederacy*, 108.

11. Grinnell to William Jackson, November 6, 1895, GBGP.

12. Grinnell to Welsh, August 15, 1896, IRAP R13.

13. "A Review of the Spotted Hawk Case," 2, IRAP R102.

14. Grinnell to the IRA, November 18, 1898, IRAP R14.

15. Grinnell to Mooney, January 14, 1896, GBGP.

16. TR to William Frederick Poole, November 8, 1889, ML 1:201.

17. TR to Henry Cabot Lodge, June 7, 1886, ML 1:102.

18. TR to Frederick Jackson Turner, November 4, 1896, ML 1:564.

19. Welsh to L. Edwin Dudley, February 12, 1897, IRAP R74.

20. Leupp to Welsh, March 10, 1897, IRAP R13.

21. TR to Anna Roosevelt Cowles, March 8, 1897, ML 1:583.

22. TR to Maria Longworth Storer, December 5, 1896, ML 1:568.

23. TR to Henry White, March 8, 1897, ML 1:583.

24. TR to Anna Roosevelt Cowles, January 2, 1897, ML 1:573.

25. Garland, *Daughter of the Middle Border*, 56.

26. Garland, "My Neighbor, Theodore Roosevelt," 12.

27. Lonnie E. Underhill and Daniel F. Littlefield, Jr., *Hamlin Garland's Observations on the American Indian 1895–1905*, 23.

28. TR to Henry Cabot Lodge, August 10, 1886, ML 1:108.

29. TR to William Sheffield Cowles, December 22, 1895, ML 1:501.

30. TR to William Sturgis Bigelow, March 29, 1898, ML 2:801.

31. Grinnell to TR, April 23, 1898, GBGP.

32. *City and State*, April 15, 1897, 2.

33. TR to Leupp, January 29, 1898, TRPR 315.

34. *City and State*, June 23, 1898, 671.

35. *City and State*, June 30, 1898, 689.

36. Grinnell to TR, September 14, 1898, GBGP.

37. TR to James Bryce, November 25, 1898, ML 2:889.

38. William D. Foulke, *A Hoosier Autobiography*, 112–13.

39. TR to Welsh, January 5, 1899, ML 2:900.

40. *Boston Evening Transcript*, November 19, 1898, photostat in TR Collection, Widener Library.

41. TR to James Bryce, November 25, 1898, ML 2:889.

42. Welsh to Foulke, January 18, 1899, IRAP R74.

43. TR to Welsh, January 18, 1899, IRAP R133.

44. TR to Welsh, February 10, 1900, IRAP R133.

45. TR to Lodge, April 9, 1900, ML 2:1252.

46. Edmund Morris, *The Rise of Theodore Roosevelt*, 730.

47. For a detailed study of the workings of the committee, see Laurence M. Hauptman, "Governor Theodore Roosevelt and the Indians of New York State."

48. Matthew Sniffen to TR, February 21, 1900, IRAP R133.

49. TR to Garrett, May 26, 1900, ML 2:1311.

50. TR to Welsh, June 13, 1900, IRAP R133.

51. 1900 Report of the Board of Indian Commissioners, 7–8.

52. Ibid., 20–22.

53. Garrett to Merrill E. Gates, December 28, 1900, Records of the Board of Indian Commissioners.

54. TR to Arthur Hamilton Lee, November 23, 1900, ML 2:1439.

55. TR to John Proctor Clarke, March 29, 1901, ML 3:34; TR to Hugh S. Thompson, May 16, 1901, TRPR 326.

56. TR to Bellamy and Maria Stover, April 17, 1901, ML 3:58.

57. Welsh to TR, January 3, 1901, IRAP R75.

58. TR to Jones, March 18, 1901, OIA-LR 15306–1901.

59. Jones to TR, March 20, 1901, Jones's personal letterbook, NARG 75.

60. Charles Lummis, *Letters from the Southwest*, xii.

61. Turbesé Lummis Fiske and Keith Lummis, *Charles F. Lummis*, 49–51.

62. Morgan to Secretary of the Interior, Nov. 30, 1892, Copy, IRAP R9.

63. *The Land of Sunshine*, July 1900, 115–16.

64. *The Land of Sunshine*, 5, August 1896, 171.

65. *The Land of Sunshine,* November 1896, 248–49.
66. Grinnell to Lummis, December 24, 1901, GBGP.
67. TR to Henry Fairchild Osborn, May 18, 1897, ML 1:612.
68. Morris, *The Rise of Theodore Roosevelt,* 589.

Chapter 3. The Wards and Their Guardians

1. Draft of a Jones memorandum, [January 4, 1905], JP.
2. *Ecumenical Missionary Conference,* 1, 41.
3. Grinnell to Garland, April 2, 1902, GBGP.
4. TR to Charles Collins, January 21, 1891, copy, IRAP R6.
5. TR to Welsh, February 13, 1891, IRAP R7.
6. 1901 Annual Report of the Commissioner of Indian Affairs, 41.
7. W. David Baird, "William A. Jones 1897–1904;" WPA Notes, JP.
8. Jones to Deloria, September 25, 1902, JP.
9. Jones to Lodge, August 26, 1904, JP.
10. Jones to Hanna, January 13, 1902, JP.
11. Jones to J. B. Shoenfelt, July 10, 1903, JP.
12. Jones to George Beck, August 11, 1899, JP.
13. Grinnell to Welsh, July 13, 1897, GBGP.
14. Jones to C. J. Crandall, March 23, 1903, JP.
15. Jones to Welsh, October 26, 1897, JP.
16. Jones to Dawes, November 5, 1898, JP.
17. 1899 Proceedings of the Lake Mohonk Conference, 33.
18. Welsh to TR, January 3, 1901, IRAP R75.
19. Jones to all Indian agents, May 5, 1899, IRAP R14.
20. Jones to R. C. Spooner, February 10, 1904; Jones to J. V. Quarles, August 24, 1904; Jones to T. S. Rattle, August 24, 1904; all in JP.
21. Jones to W. B. Biddle, May 18, 1903, JP.
22. Jones to John C. Eden, August 25, 1904, JP
23. Jones to J. M. Stradling, December 24, 1904, JP.
24. Jones to Phil Allen, Jr., December 24, 1904; Jones to Allen, June 16, 1905; Jones to Allen, August 1, 1901; all in JP.
25. Jones to Allen, May 11, 1903; Jones to H. P. Myton, November 7, 1899; both in JP.
26. Welsh to S. M. Brosius, April 10, 1899, IRAP R74.

Chapter 4. The Honeymoon Period
for the Roosevelt Administration

1. 1901 Proceedings of the Lake Mohonk Conference, 3.
2. TR to McKinley, March 25, 1901, ML 3:27.
3. 1901 Proceedings of the Lake Mohonk Conference, 68.
4. Garland to TR, September 24, 1901, TRPR 19.
5. Garland, "My Neighbor, Theodore Roosevelt," 14.
6. Garland, *Daughter of the Middle Border,* 245.
7. Ibid., 246.
8. Grinnell to Major Clifford, October 4, 1901, GBGP.
9. 1901 IRA Annual Report, 3–4.
10. City and State, November 21, 1901, 325.
11. Welsh to Philip C. Garrett, October 14, 1901, IRAP R75.
12. Leupp to Welsh, October 7, 1901, IRAP R15.
13. Leupp to George B. Cortelyou, January 16, 1902, TRPR 24; Leupp to Cortelyou, May 14, 1902, TRPR 26; Booker T. Washington to Leupp, May 5, 1904, TRPR 334.
14. TR to Lodge, October 11, 1901, Papers of Henry Cabot Lodge.
15. S. M. Brosius to the IRA, October 7, 1901, IRAP R15.
16. Lummis to TR, October 8, 1901, TRPR 20.
17. TR to Lummis, October 16, 1901, TRPR 327.
18. Lummis to TR, TRPR 21.
19. *The Land of Sunshine* 14, no. 1 (May 1901): 420.
20. Lummis to Grinnell, December 12, 1901, LP.
21. Lummis to Garland, January 2, 1902, LP.
22. Lummis to Garland, February 13, 1902, HGC.
23. Lummis to Grinnell, [n.d.], LP.
24. *Out West* 16, no. 1 (January 1902); 66.
25. *The Land of Sunshine,* December 1901, 461.
26. 1901 Board of Indian Commissioners Annual Report, 3–4.
27. Welsh to Jones, November 21, 1899, IRAP R75.
28. TWTR 15:129.
29. 1900 Proceedings of the Lake Mohonk Conference, 16.
30. Jones to Welsh, July 7, 1899, IRAP R14.
31. Jones to Welsh, January 4, 1899, IRAP R14.

32. Jones to J. H. Monteith, October 23, 1901, JP.
33. 1901 Commissioner of Indian Affairs Annual Report, 6.
34. Grinnell to Merriam, February 1, 1902, GBGP.
35. Grinnell to Schultz, February 1, 1902, GBGP.
36. For a thorough and well-balanced discussion of this issue, see Francis Paul Prucha, *The Churches and the Indian Schools,* 1888–1912.
37. James F. Randlett to Commissioner of Indian Affairs, September 3, 1901, Kiowa Letterbook, Oklahoma Historical Society.
38. Copy of Hare to Secretary Hitchcock, November 15, 1901, IRAP R15.
39. Welsh to Mrs. John Markoe, December 3, 1901, IRAP R75.
40. Prucha, *The Churches and the Indian Schools,* 44–45.
41. Ketcham to Most Rev. dear Archbishop, October 10, 1901, BCIMR Box 41.
42. Ketcham to Charles S. Lusk, September 14, 1901, BCIMR Box 41.
43. TR to Ireland, September 27, 1901, TRPR 327.
44. Ketcham to Ireland, October 24, 1901, BCIMR Box 41.
45. Ketcham to Ryan, November 1, 1901, BCIMR Box 41.
46. Ketcham to James Gibbons, November 16, 1901, BCIMR Box 41.
47. Jones to Superintendent of Haskell Institute, November 30, 1901, BCIMR Box 41.
48. Welsh to Philip C. Garrett, March 18, 1901, IRAP R75.
49. Ibid.
50. Lewis L. Gould, *The Presidency of Theodore Roosevelt,* 58–60.
51. Ketcham to Ryan, November 30, 1901, BCIMR Box 41. Similar letters were sent to two other bishops and two priests.
52. Thiele to Ketcham, November 27, 1901, BCIMR Box 41.
53. Lusk to Thiele, December 11, BCIMR Box 41.
54. A. C. Tonner to J. Franklin House, April 12, 1902, Education Letterbook, NARG 75.
55. Education Circular No. 60, December 20, 1901, NARG 75.
56. A. C. Tonner to Superintendent of Chilocco Indian School, June 12, 1902, Education Letterbook, NARG 75.
57. Jones to Pine Ridge Agent, January 8, 1902, IRAP R16.
58. Garland, "The Red Man's Present Needs," 482–83.

59. Jones to Grinnell, March 6, 1902, JP; Grinnell to Mrs. W. C. Kohlenberg, March 22, 1902, GBGP.

Chapter 5. Land Problems

1. TR to Thomas William Symons, May 14, 1904, ML 4:798.
2. Jones to C. W. Crouse, Land Letterbook, NARG 75.
3. 1901 Proceedings of the Lake Mohonk Conference, 84.
4. Brosius Report, January 9, 1902, IRAP R134.
5. Garland to TR, January 21, 1902, Hitchcock Papers Box 1.
6. TR to Hitchcock, January 30, 1902, ML 3:223.
7. *City and State,* February 6, 1902, 85.
8. Grinnell to Merriam, February 11, 1902, GBGP.
9. Grinnell to Lummis, February 14, 1902, GBGP.
10. Grinnell to Merriam, February 19, 1902, GBGP.
11. Jones to John P. Roche, January 20, 1902, GBGP.
12. Jones to E. S. Kelley, February 7, 1902, JP. In this letter he inadvertently referred to the Standing Rock leases as "mining leases," a subject much on his mind.
13. Brosius to Welsh, April 11, 1902, IRAP R16.
14. Jones to Reuben G. Thwaites, June 3, 1902, JP. Jones shared with Thwaites of the Wisconsin Historical Society his indignation at Kennan's publicizing Wade's charge.
15. TR to Hitchcock, April 22, 1902, Hitchcock Papers Box 32; TR to Grinnell, April 28, 1902, TRPR 328.
16. Grinnell to E. Hough, May 2, 1902, GBGP.
17. Grinnell to Brosius, May 8, 1902, GBGP.
18. Grinnell to the Secretary of the Interior, May 29, 1902, NARG 48, 1902–10908.
19. Jones to J. A. Sullivan, June 12, 1902, JP.
20. TR to Grinnell, TRPR 328.
21. Jones to Keeley, July 24, 1903, JP.
22. TR to E. L. Bonner, April 22, 1902, ML 3:254.
23. TR to Grinnell, June 13, 1902, TRPR 328.
24. Grinnell to TR, July 18, 1902, GBGP.
25. *City and State,* June 12, 1902, 372.

26. TR to Lodge, July 30, 1902, *Selections from the Correspondence of Theodore Roosevelt and Henry Cabot Lodge,* 1:521.

27. TR to Taft, December 26, 1902, ML 3:398; TR to Elihu Root, May 23, 1903, Theodore Roosevelt Collection, Houghton Library, R 22–0.

28. TR to Elihu Root, July 17, 1903, ML 3:519.

29. Jones to Bingenheimer, January 31, 1903, JP.

30. Brosius to Sniffen, February 10, 1903, IRAP R16.

31. TR to Shanley, March 19, 1903; TR to Ryan, March 19, 1903. Both in TRPR 330.

32. Brosius to Sniffen, February 10, 1903, IRAP R16.

33. Donald J. Berthrong, *The Cheyenne and Arapaho Ordeal,* 280.

34. Jones to Secretary of the Interior, February 16, 1902, Land Letterbook, NARG 75.

35. Brosius, Report of the Washington Agency, April 5, 1902, IRAP R134.

36. Merrill Gates to James S. Sherman, April 8, 1902, Board of Indian Commissioners Papers.

37. Brosius to Sniffen, July 17, 1902, IRAP R16.

38. Jones to John M. V. Meulen, August 18, 1902, JP.

39. Jones to A. L. White, June 12, 1902, JP.

40. Quoted in Felix Cohen, *Handbook of Indian Law,* 233.

41. *City and State,* September 4, 1902, 233.

42. 1904 Proceedings of the Lake Mohonk Conference, 16.

43. For a full discussion of this landmark case, see Blue Clark, *Lone Wolf v. Hitchcock.*

44. 1903 IRA Annual Report, 24.

45. "Another 'Century of Dishonor'?" IRAP R102.

46. *Congressional Record,* 57th Congress, 1st Session, 4801.

47. Ibid., 4805.

48. "A New Indian Policy," 8, IRAP R102.

49. Jones to Secretary of the Interior, November 23, 1901, in Senate Report No. 651, 58th Congress, 2d Session, 12.

50. Jones to E. J. DeBell, September 1902, JP.

51. Senate Report No. 651, 58th Congress, 2d Session, 4.

52. Ibid., 5.

53. Reprinted in *Congressional Record,* 58th Congress, 2d Session, 2887.

54. *City and State,* January 28, 1904, 53.

55. Kennan to TR, February 12, 1904, Hitchcock Papers.

56. TR to Gamble, February 15, 1904, ML 4:729.

57. Jones to Kennan, February 20, 1904, JP.

58. "Another 'Century of Dishonor'?" 1, IRAP R102.

59. TR to M. S. Quay, April 21, 1904, TRPR 334.

60. 1903 IRA Annual Report, 50.

61. 1904 IRA Annual Report, 53.

62. Brosius to Sniffen, May 3, 1904, IRAP R17.

63. Brosius to IRA, November 1, 1901, IRAP R15; Brosius's Report for November 1904, IRAP R154.

64. *Theodore Roosevelt: An Autobiography,* 156.

65. Brosius to Sniffen, January 23, 1904, IRAP R16; H. Craig Miner, *The Corporation and the Indian,* 150–51.

66. *New York Times,* January 21, 1904, 6; William Loeb, Jr., to Hitchcock, March 14, 1904, Hitchcock Papers.

67. *Theodore Roosevelt: An Autobiography,* 157.

68. TR to Hitchcock, January 21, 1904, Hitchcock Papers.

69. Loretta Fowler, *Arapahoe Politics, 1851–1978,* 95–96,

70. TR to Frank B. Tracy, September 24, 1904, TRPR 335.

71. TR to Tracy, August 11, 1904, TRPR 335.

Chapter 6. A Friend Self-Destructs

1. Lummis to Grinnell, December 12, 1901, LP.

2. Jones to Secretary of the Interior, January 21, 1902, Land Letterbook, NARG 75.

3. Jones to Secretary of the Interior, January 29, 1902, JP.

4. Jones to Secretary of the Interior, March 6, 1902, Indian Division/Letters Received, 1902–2011, NARG 48.

5. Jones to Welsh, April 12, 1902, IRAP R16.

6. Lummis to TR, May 11, 1902, LP.

7. Grinnell to George H. Gould, April 8, 1902, GBGP.

8. Lummis to TR, May 11, 1902, LP.

9. TR to Lummis, May 20, 1902, TRPR 328.

10. Comment on a newspaper clipping, filed Indian Division/Letters Received, 1902–7735, NARG 48.

11. *Out West* 19, no. 3 (October 1903): 422.

12. Jones to Lummis, August 8, 1902, JP.

13. *Out West* 17, no. 2 (August 1902): 215.

14. *Out West* 17, no. 6 (December 1902): 732.

15. *Out West* 18, no. 6 (June 1903): 744.

16. Jones to George B. Cortelyou, November 6, 1902, JP.

17. Lummis to Grinnell, November 13, 1902, LP.

18. Grinnell to Lummis, November 22, 1902, GBGP.

19. Lummis to Merriam, April 25, 1903, LP.

20. Lummis to Jones, March 26, 1903, Indian Office/Letters Received, 1903–38274, NARG 75.

21. Hitchcock to Jenkins, April 10, 1903, TRPR 33.

22. Hitchcock to Lummis, April 14, 1903, TRPR 33.

23. Hitchcock to Lummis, April 22, 1903, TRPR 33.

24. Hitchcock to TR, April 24, 1903, TRPR 33.

25. *Los Angeles Times,* May 11, 1903, 8.

26. Ibid., May 13, 1903, section 2, 1.

27. Ibid., May 15, 1903, 4.

28. Ibid., May 7, 1903, 1.

29. Jones to Quinton, May 9, 1903, JP.

30. Brosius to Sniffen, June 24, 1903, IRAP R134.

31. Ibid.

32. *Out West* 16, no. 3 (March 1902): 301–2.

33. *Out West* 16, no. 2 (February 1902): 189.

34. Jones to Seaton, February 3, 1902, JP.

35. "Answers to questions asked by the Delegation from Standing Rock of the Commissioner," February 4, 1902, JP.

36. Jones to Hitchcock, February 19, 1902; *Out West* 18, no. 1 (January 1903): 103–5.

37. TR to Hitchcock, June 23, 1902, ML 3:280.

38. TR to Hitchcock, July 22, 1903, ML 3:523.

39. Report of Charles E. Burton, in 1902 Commissioner of Indian Affairs Annual Report, 153.

40. Jones to Burton, November 29, 1902, JP.
41. Copy of Lummis to Dorsey, November 29, 1902, JP.
42. Jones to Dorsey, December 16, 1902, JP.
43. *Out West* 18, no. 6 (June 1903): 686.
44. TR to Hitchcock, May 9, 1903, Hitchcock Papers.
45. Jones to Quinton, May 9, 1903, JP.
46. Burton to Jones, May 18, 1903, JP.
47. Jones to Ralph P. Collins, December 16, 1902, JP.
48. Jones to Dr. E. Snyder, June 18, 1903, JP.
49. Jones to George A. Buckstaff, June 23, 1903, JP.
50. Jones to Burton, July 9, 1903, JP.
51. *Out West* 19, no. 2 (August 1903): 171.
52. TR to Hitchcock, August 29, 1903, TRPR 331.
53. TR to Natalie Curtis, September 2, 1903, TRPR 332.
54. Lummis to TR, September 4, 1903, TRPR 36.
55. TR to Lummis, September 10, 1903, TRPR 332.
56. Lummis to Hitchcock, September 19, 1903, TRPR 37.
57. Lummis to TR, September 26, 1903, TRPR 37
58. TR to Lummis, October 5, 1903, TRPR 332.
59. Grinnell to Lummis, October 6, 1903, GBGP.
60. Jones to Jenkins, November 7, 1903, JP.
61. Brosius to Sniffen, December 3, 1903, IRAP R16.
62. Jones to Burton, November 18, 1904, JP.
63. Lummis to TR, December 30, 1903, TRPR 39.
64. TR to Lummis, January 4, 1904, ML 3:688.
65. Lummis to TR, January 15, 1904, TRPR 40.
66. TR to Lummis, January 21, 1904, TRPR 333.

Chapter 7. More Trouble for the Friends

1. January 26, 1903, Garland Diaries.
2. Grinnell to James Willard Schultz, July 16, 1902, GBGP.
3. Grinnell to Farrand Sayre, April 6, 1904, GBGP.
4. Grinnell to Schultz, March 1, 1902, GBGP.
5. Grinnell to TR, May 1, 1903, GBGP.
6. TR to Burroughs, July 6, 1903, ML 3:512.

7. TR to Henry Cabot Lodge, September 30, 1903, ML 3:606.

8. TWTR 15:163.

9. TWTR, 15:240.

10. Grinnell to Brosius, February 18, 1902, GBGP.

11. Grinnell to Lummis, November 6, 1902, GBGP.

12. Grinnell to Spotted Hawk, February 14, 1903, GBGP.

13. Grinnell to Spotted Hawk, February 18, 1904, GBGP.

14. Grinnell to Merriam, March 9, 1904, GBGP.

15. Jones to Grinnell, March 18, 1904, JP.

16. Jones to Leupp, August 25, 1903, JP.

17. James Willard Schultz, *Blackfeet and Buffalo*, 84.

18. TR to Jones, August 24, 1903, TRPR 331.

19. Jones to TR, August 26, 1903, JP.

20. Grinnell to Lummis, October 6, 1903, GBGP.

21. Grinnell to W. F. Sanders, March 17, 1904, GBGP.

22. TR to Hitchcock, January 23, 1904, Hitchcock Papers.

23. Grinnell to Monroe, January 29, 1904, GBGP.

24. Grinnell to TR, March 10, 1904, GBGP.

25. Grinnell to Quay, March 10, 1904, GBGP.

26. TR to Grinnell, March 11, 1904, TRPR 333.

27. Wood was a "playmate" with whom he worked out with single sticks. This required them to wear helmets and padding and "beat one another like carpets." TR to Kermit Roosevelt, December 4, 1902, ML 3:389.

28. TR to Kermit Roosevelt, February 8, 1903, ML 3:422.

29. Grinnell to TR, March 13, 1904, GBGP.

30. TR to Merriam, March 14, 1904, TRPR 333.

31. Brosius to Sniffen, March 22, 1904, IRAP R17.

32. Jones to Monteath, October 31, 1903, JP.

33. Grinnell to TR, March 23, 1904, GBGP.

34. William Loeb, Jr., to Hitchcock, March 24, 1904, Hitchcock Papers.

35. Grinnell to Leupp, June 14, 1904, GBGP.

36. Grinnell to Leupp, November 15, 1904, GBGP.

37. Garland's Diary, February 23, 1904.

38. TR to Indian Agents, July 22, 1903, TRPR 331. TR also enjoyed

Arthur Nevin's Indian opera and told the composer that he considered it "a peculiarly good thing to try to preserve the old Indian songs and music." TR to Nevin, May 1, 1907, TRPR 345.

39. Curtis to TR, July 29, 1903, TRPR 35.

40. TR to Grinnell and to Garland, July 22, 1903, TRPR 331.

41. TR to Hitchcock, July 22, 1903, ML 3:523.

42. Hitchcock to TR, August 7, 1903, TRPR 36.

43. Curtis to TR, August 31, 1903, TRPR 36.

44. TR to Jones, September 3, 1903, TRPR 332.

45. Merriam to Lummis, December 10, 1903, LP.

46. Lummis to Merriam, December 17, 1903, LP.

47. Brosius to Sniffen, September 17, 1904, IRAP R17.

48. TR to Hitchcock, October 18, 1904, Hitchcock Papers.

49. TR to Merriam, April 21, 1903, TRPR 330.

50. TR to Merriam, March 31, 1903, ML 3:460.

51. TR to Jones, December 12, 1903, TRPR 332.

52. Although another employee of the Bureau of Biological Survey took the lead, Merriam was part of the effort to save for Indian use the Blue Lake area adjoining Taos Pueblo. This was done by withdrawing the area from the public domain and including it in a new national forest. See R. C. Gordon-McCutchan, *The Taos Indians and the Battle for Blue Lake*, 10–14.

53. TR to Merriam, March 19, 1904, ML 4:756.

54. Merriam to TR, March 26, 1904, TRPR 43.

55. Garland Diaries, March 23, 1903.

56. Garland, "The Red Man's Present Needs," 480–81.

57. Garland to Lummis, [n.d.], LP.

58. TWTR 15:164.

59. Garland, *Companions on the Trail*, 23. For a good study of the naming project, see Daniel F. Littlefield, Jr., and Lonnie E. Underhill, "Renaming the American Indian: 1890–1913." For Garland's own view of how it should be done, see Garland to John H. Seger, November 26, 1902, HGC.

60. Jones to Agents, December 1, 1902, Miscellaneous Letterbook, NARG 75.

61. Jones to Editor of *Leslie's Weekly*, July 27, 1903, JP.

62. Garland to TR, May 1, 1902, TRPR 26.

63. TR to Garland, July 19, 1903, ML 3:521.

64. Garland to TR, July 22, 1903, TRPR 24.

65. TR to Garland, July 19, 1903, ML 3:520.

66. Garland to TR, July 22, 1903, TRPR 35.

67. Leupp to Cortelyou, January 16, 1902, TRPR 24; Leupp to Cortelyou, May 14, 1902, TRPR 26; TR to Washington, May 9, 1904, ML 4:793.

68. TR to Leonard Wood, June 16, 1903, ML 4:793.

69. TR to Brander Matthews, July 11, 1903, TRPR 331.

70. Abbott to TR, December 4, 1902, TRPR 31.

71. Leupp to TR, November 25, 1902, TRPR 31.

72. Leupp to TR, May 3, 1902, TRPR 26. Earlier he had informed Roosevelt that "[I have] no fondness for playing Brutus to Your Caesar" but that "[you will live] to thank me for my frankness." Leupp to TR, April 18, 1902, TRPR 31.

73. A. C. Tonner to Hitchcock, August 28, 1902, Land Letterbook, NARG 75.

74. 1902 Commissioner of Indian Affairs Annual Report, 289.

75. Grinnell to TR, March 12, 1903, GBGP.

76. Jones to TR, March 16, 1903, JP.

77. Jones to Randlett, April 18, 1903, JP.

78. Jones to Randlett, September 29, 1903, JP.

79. Senate Document, number 26, 58th Congress 2d Session, 1903, 497.

80. Leupp to TR, September 3, 1903, TRPR 36.

81. TR to Anna Roosevelt Cowles, July 19, 1908, Roosevelt Papers, Houghton Library, BMS, Am, 1834, (696).

82. TR to Root, June 2, 1904, ML 4:812.

Chapter 8. The BCIM Operates

1. Ketcham to J. M. Kassel, January 10, 1903, BCIMR Box 44.

2. Ketcham to Richard Phelan, January 8, 1902, BCIMR Box 33.

3. Ketcham to TR, January 25, 1902, Indian Division/Letters Received, 1902–1843, NARG 75.

4. Francis Paul Prucha, *The Churches and the Indian Schools 1888–1912,* 68.

5. Archbishop Ireland wrote, "In naming Bishop Spalding as one of the arbitrators you have shown to all Catholics favor, which they will gratefully remember." Ireland to TR, October 31, 1902, TRPR 30.

6. W. C. Nohe to Ketcham, June 15, 1902, BCIMR Box 43.

7. TR to Taft, July 31, 1902, ML 3:303.

8. Ketcham to Vincente Cavanna, December 1, 1902, BCIMR Box 43.

9. Wynne to Ketcham, March 16, 1903, BCIMR Box 44.

10. Philbin to TR, September 30, 1903, TRPR 37.

11. TR to Philbin, July 12, 1902, ML 3:295.

12. Philbin to TR, November 24, 1902, TRPR 31.

13. Philbin to James Gibbons and Patrick J. Ryan, November 8, 1902, BCIMR Box 43

14. Ketcham to J. M. Kasel, December 22, 1902, BCIMR Box 43.

15. Ketcham to Rev. dear Father, February 17, 1903, BCIMR Box 44.

16. Ketcham to Philbin, March 10, 1903, BCIMR Box 44.

17. Wynne to Ketcham, March 13, 1903, BCIMR Box 44.

18. Ketcham to Wynne, March 14, 1903, BCIMR Box 44.

19. Philbin to Ketcham, March 14, 1903, BCIMR Box 44.

20. Ketcham to Gibbons, March 16, 1903; Ketcham to Wynne, March 31, 1903, both in BCIMR Box 44.

21. Ketcham to Ganss, March 16, 1903, BCIMR Box 44.

22. TR to Ryan, March 19, 1903, TRPR 330; TR to Gibbons, June 25, 1903, TRPR 331.

23. Bonaparte to TR, July 22, 1903, TRPR 35.

24. TR to Hitchcock, July 25, 1903, Hitchcock Papers. After appearing at Mohonk in 1892, Roosevelt had described the conference to his friend Lodge as "an absurd, though useful, 'Indian' conference." TR to Lodge, ML 1:293.

25. TR to Attorney General, July 25, 1903, TRPR 331.

26. Ketcham to Wynne, November 10, 1903, BCIMR Box 44.

27. Philbin to TR, July 29, 1903, TRPR 35.

28. Ketcham to Ryan, January 6, 1904, BCIMR Box 46; Eric F. Goldman, *Charles J. Bonaparte,* 45.

29. Ketcham to Matthew Harkins, March 23, 1904, BCIMR Box 46.

30. Ryan to Ketcham, March 25, 1904, BCIMR Box 46.

31. Ketcham to TR, January 5, 1904, BCIMR Box 46.

32. TR to Attorney General, January 11, 1904, TRPR 333.

33. Goldman, *Bonaparte*, 47.

34. Ibid.

35. Ketcham to Harkins, March 23, 1904, BCIMR Box 46.

36. Ketcham to Farley, August 25, 1904, BCIMR Box 46.

37. Ketcham to Drexel, February 23, 1904, BCIMR Box 46.

38. Charles S. Lusk to Henry M. Teller, March 11, 1904, BCIMR Box 46.

39. Jones to Hare, October 12, 1904, JP.

40. TR to Fairbanks, August 13, 1904, TRPR 335. At the same time he urged George B. Cortelyou, chairman of the Republican National Committee, along the same lines. TR to Cortelyou, August 13, 1904, ML 4:892.

41. Patricia O'Toole, *The Five of Hearts,* 378.

42. TR to Philbin, September 20, 1904, TRPR 335.

43. TR to Philbin, October 4, 1904, TRPR 335.

Chapter 9. More Friends Fall by the Wayside

1. TR to Kermit Roosevelt, November 10, 1904, ML 4:1024.

2. TR to Cortelyou, November 10, 1904, ML 4:1022.

3. Ketcham to Rev. Mother M. Mercedes, November 11, 1904, BCIMR Box 46.

4. TR to Dunne, December 3, 1904, TRPR 336.

5. TR to Anna Lodge, November 10, 1904, ML 4:1025.

6. TR to Owen Wister, November 19, 1904, ML 4:1037.

7. TR to Donald M. Dickinson, November 7, 1904, ML 4:1016.

8. Jones to James E. Jenkins, December 27, 1904, JP.

9. TR to Jones, December 23, 1904, TRPR 336.

10. TR to J. B. Bishop, November 23, 1904, TRPR 336.

11. Sniffen to Charles E. McChesney, December 10, 1904, IRAP R76.

12. Grinnell to Charles Aubrey, November 21, 1904, GBGP.

13. Grinnell to John Pitcher, December 8, 1904, GBGP.

14. Jones to J. S. Perkins, December 28, 1904, JP
15. Bonaparte to Ketcham, December 23, 1904, BCIMR Box 46.
16. TR to Leupp, August 20, 1906, TRPR 342.
17. Leupp to Agents and Superintendents, April 10, 1905, in Instructions for Agents, Kiowa Agency Files, Oklahoma Historical Society.
18. Dagenett, "The Work of the Indian Employment Bureau," 1907 Lake Mohonk Conference Proceedings, 24–26.
19. Leupp, "Outlines of an Indian Policy," 949.
20. Education Circular, no. 161, July 1, 1907, NARG 75.
21. 1907 Commissioner of Indian Affairs Annual Report, 22.
22. Ibid., 28.
23. Leupp to Superintendents and Agents, January 30, 1906, in Instructions for Agents, Cheyenne and Arapaho Agency Files, Oklahoma Historical Society.
24. Leupp to Superintendents and Agents, March 29, 1905, in Instructions for Agents, Cheyenne and Arapaho Agency Files, Oklahoma Historical Society.
25. C. F. Larrabee to R. J. Gamble, May 26, 1905, Miscellaneous Letterbook, NARG 75.
26. Leupp to Secretary of the Interior, June 13, 1905, Education Letterbook, NARG 75.
27. Education Circular, no. 80, March 15, 1906, Kiowa Agency Files, Oklahoma Historical Society.
28. Leupp to Foard, February 12, 1906, Miscellaneous Letterbook, NARG 75.
29. C. F. Larrabee to Superintendent of Keams Canyon School, October 25, 1906, Miscellaneous Letterbook, NARG 75.
30. Leupp to O. T. Mason, March 29, 1906, Miscellaneous Letterbook, NARG 75. The Antiquities Act of 1906, relating to objects found on the public domain, also failed to curtail the pot-hunting.
31. "Indians to Foster Their Native Art," *The Indian Craftsman*, April 1909, 19.
32. TR to Kermit Roosevelt, April 14, 1905, ML 4:1160.
33. TR, "A Wolf Hunt in Oklahoma," 53.
34. Oklahoma City, *Daily Oklahoman*, April 9, 1905, 1. On one

occasion Roosevelt spoke to Frederic Remington of having found positions not only for Western types like Bat Masterson, but also for Indians, including one whom he appointed to West Point. TR to Remington, February 20, 1906, TRPR 340.

35. TR to Leupp, April 14, 1905, TRPR 337.

36. *Congressional Record,* 59th Congress, 1st Session, 4454 and 4739; TR, *Theodore Roosevelt,* 361–62; John P. Blackman to Leupp, February 26, 1906, Kiowa Agency Letterbook, Oklahoma Historical Society.

37. TR to Lyman Abbott, February 26, 1907, TRPR 345.

38. TR to Charles Scribner, March 20, 1906, TRPR 341; TR to R. W. Gilder, April 6, 1906, TRPR 341; TR to Barrett, April 6, 1906, TRPR 341.

39. Grinnell to Merriam, May 25, 1905, GBGP.

40. Grinnell to Leupp, November 21, 1904, GBGP.

41. Grinnell to Mead, June 23, 1905, GBGP.

42. TR to Grinnell, November 30, 1905, TRPR 339.

43. Grinnell to Rides At The Door, February 20, 1906, GBGP; *Congressional Record,* 59th Congress, 1st Session, 7818.

44. Grinnell to Dixon, February 19, 1906, GBGP.

45. Hitchcock to TR, June 25, 1906, Hitchcock Papers; Report of the Blackfeet agent in 1906 Commissioner of Indian Affairs Annual Report, 251.

46. Grinnell to Leupp, January 18, 1905, GBGP.

47. Grinnell to Leupp, December 12, 1906, GBGP.

48. Grinnell to Leupp, March 3, 1906, GBGP.

49. Grinnell to Brosius, November 16, 1904, GBGP.

50. Brosius to Sniffen, November 16, 1904, IRAP R17.

51. Brosius to Sniffen, December 21, 1904, IRAP R17.

52. Leupp to Grinnell, July 22, 1905, GBGP Box 25.

53. TR to Leupp, August 30, 1905, TRPR 338.

54. For example, Roosevelt sent twelve skins and skulls from animals killed in the Big Pasture in April 1905 to Merriam, who concluded that the eleven identifiable were coyotes. Roosevelt, "A Wolf Hunt in Oklahoma," 518.

55. Garland Diaries, January 4–5, 1906.

56. Jean Holloway, *Hamlin Garland,* 195.

57. Ibid., 187–88.
58. Grinnell to George H. Gould, October 17, 1907, GBGP.
59. Grinnell to Eastman, July 27, 1903, GBGP.

Chapter 10. And Then There Was One

1. *Theodore Roosevelt, An Autobiography,* 361.
2. TR to Bonaparte, July 5, 1906, ML 5:333.
3. TR to Hitchcock, October 9, 1905, ML 5:52.
4. TR to Attorney General, January 16, 1906, TRPR 340.
5. Hitchcock to TR, May 26, 1906, TRPR 65.
6. TR to Leupp, October 2, 1906, ML 5:438.
7. TR to Hitchcock, October 26, 1906, ML 5:472. H. Craig Miner argues that Hitchcock had a better grasp than Roosevelt of Frantz's performance. See Miner, *The Corporation and the Indian,* 177–84.
8. TR to Charles I. Long, December 22, 1905, TRPR 340.
9. TR to Alfred B. Kittredge, May 6, 1907, TRPR 345.
10. TR to Charles Walcott, March 28, 1906, TRPR 341.
11. TR to Hitchcock, August 18, 1906, ML 5:370.
12. TR to Samuel Alain Harper, September 12, 1906, ML 5:407.
13. Curtis, *The Indians' Book,* xxv.
14. TR to Nevin, May 1, 1907, TRPR 345.
15. TR to Saint-Gaudens, March 14, 1907, TRPR 345.
16. Jones Memorandum, [ca. Jan. 4, 1905], JP
17. Leupp to TR, September 3, 1903, TRPR 36.
18. Ketcham to Cardinal Gibbons, November 28, 1904, BCIMR Box 46.
19. Sniffen to A. S. Lloyd, January 7, 1905, IRAP R76.
20. Leupp to Hitchcock, January 5, 1905, Hitchcock Papers.
21. 1901 Lake Mohonk Conference Proceedings, 2.
22. Welsh to Sniffen, November 13, 1904, IRAP R17.
23. Sniffen to H. L. Morehouse, and to F. P. Woodbury, both December 3, 1904, IRAP R76.
24. J. J. Janney to Sniffen, December 15, 1904, IRAP R17.
25. TR to George Worthington, December 10, 1904, TRPR 336.
26. TR to Abbott, February 12, 1905, ML 4:1120.

27. Sniffen to Mary P. Lord, February 20, 1905, IRAP R76.

28. Welsh to Leupp, May 7, 1898, IRAP R74.

29. Welsh to Charles Collins, June 4, 1894, IRAP R73.

30. Sniffen to Brosius, April 21, 1905, IRAP R76.

31. Ketcham to Wynne, January 24, 1905, BCIMR Box 48.

32. Indian Appropriation Bill, 1905. Hearing before the Subcommittee of the Senate Committee on Indian Affairs, January 28–February 10, 1905, 17–19.

33. Ibid., 63.

34. Sniffen to Brosius, February 10, 1905, IRAP R76.

35. Bonaparte to Ketcham, February 22, 1905, BCIMR Box 48.

36. B. F. Barnes to Thomas Ryan, August 8, 1905, BCIMR Box 49.

37. TR to Secretary of the Interior, August 12, 1905, Indian Division/Letters Received, 1905, 8426, NARG 48.

38. Aldrich to Charles Lusk, September 15, 1905, BCIMR Box 49.

39. Wynne to Ketcham, September 7, 1905, BCIMR Box 49.

40. Bonaparte to Ketcham, December 22, 1905, BCIMR Box 49.

41. TR to Hitchcock, May 28, 1906, Hitchcock Papers.

42. Bonaparte to Ketcham, December 22, 1905, BCIMR Box 49; Ketcham to Aldrich, January 4, 1906, BCIMR Box 51.

43. Brosius to Sniffen, February 27, 1906, IRAP R18.

44. Ketcham to Ryan, January 31, 1906, BCIMR Box 51.

45. TR to Aldrich, January 23, 1906, TRPR 340.

46. TR to Hitchcock, February 3, 1905, TRPR 337.

47. Ketcham to Finton Kraemer, February 14, 1906, BCIMR Box 51.

48. Brosius to Sniffen, April 13, 1906, IRAP R16.

49. TR to Ignatius Frederick, August 10, 1906, TRPR 342.

50. Sniffen to Brosius, March 20, 1906, IRAP R77.

51. TR to W. N. McVickar, March 21, 1906, TRPR 341.

52. Sniffen to Charles Saunders, May 8, 1906, IRAP R77.

53. TR to W. H. Hare, June 4, 1906, TRPR R341.

54. Bonaparte to Ketcham, June 4, 1906; Lusk to Ketcham, June 25, 1906, both in BCIMR Box 52.

55. 1908 IRA Annual Report, 23.

56. Ketcham to Drexel, February 20, 1909, BCIMR Box 63.

57. Ketcham to Ryan, February 20, 1909, BCIMR Box 63.

58. Leupp to TR, May 15, 1905, TRPR 54.

59. TR to Leonard Wood, May 15, 1905, TRPR 54.

60. Leupp, "The Story of Four Strenuous Years," 329.

61. Brosius to Sniffen, April 13, 1906, IRAP R18; 1906 Board of Indian Commissioners Annual Report, 17.

62. Garfield to the Speaker of the House of Representatives, March 18, 1908, House Document 790, 60th Congress, 1st Session.

63. Brosius to Members of the Senate and the House, December 12, 1908, IRAP R102.

64. Leupp to Secretary of the Interior, December 13, 1905, Land Letterbook, NARG 75.

65. Brosius to Sniffen, May 8, 1906, IRAP R18; 1906 Commissioner of Indian Affairs Annual Report, 121–24.

66. Ibid., 125.

67. Leupp to Secretary of the Interior, November 8, 1906, Education Letterbook, NARG 75.

68. Leupp to Perry, December 5, 1906, Education Letterbook, NARG 75.

69. Leupp to Perry, December 28, 1906, Education Letterbook, NARG 75.

70. Sniffen to Brosius, October 14, 1907, IRAP R77.

71. Brosius to Sniffen, October 16, 1907, IRAP R19.

72. Louis L. Pfaller, *James McLaughlin*, 248; C. F. Larrabee to Secretary of the Interior, June 6, 1905, Land Letterbook, NARG 75.

73. 1907 Commissioner of Indian Affairs Annual Report, 125–31.

74. TR to Kermit Roosevelt, January 26, 1907, TRPR 344.

75. TR to Leupp, September 4, 1907, TRPR 346.

76. TR to James E. West, October 12, 1908, TRPR 351.

77. 1907 Proceedings of the Lake Mohonk Conference, 23.

78. Memorandum by Welsh, November 2, 1907, IRAP R19.

79. TR to Garfield, November 3, 1907, TRPR 337.

80. "The Claims of the Utes," November 11, 1907, IRAP R19.

81. Sniffen's report on an interview with Leupp, November 9, 1907, IRAP R77.

82. For a reliable overview of this issue, see Donald L. Parman, "The 'Big Stick' in Indian Affairs: The Bai-a-lil-le Incident in 1909."

83. One Navajo died convinced that By-a-lil-le had killed him by witchcraft. See Garfield to Secretary of War, November 22, 1907, in Senate Document 517, 60th Congress, 1st Session, 27.

84. Ibid., 26.

85. Willard to Leupp, November 29, 1907, TRPR 79.

86. TR to Senator John Kean, August 26, 1905, TRPR 338.

87. TR to Chief of Staff, May 15, 1908, TRPR 349.

88. For discussions of this affair, see Donald L. Parman, "A White Man's Fight: The Crow Scandal, 1906–1913" and Frederick E. Hoxie, "Building a Future on the Past: Crow Indian Leadership in an Era of Division and Reunion."

89. Brosius to Sniffen, June 15, 1908, IRAP R20.

90. Sniffen to Henry S. Pancoast, November 20, 1908, IRAP R78.

91. TR to John Davis Long et al., December 29, 1908, ML 6:1450.

92. Leupp to Welsh, October 15, 1907, IRAP R19.

93. Welsh to Leupp, October 17, 1907, IRAP R77.

94. TR to Philbin, April 15, 1908, TRPR 349.

95. TR to Secretary of the Navy, May 25, 1908, TRPR 349.

96. TR to Dennis Joseph O'Connell, December 7, 1908, ML 6:1413.

97. TR to Taft, November 4, 1908, ML 6:1327.

98. Copy of Leupp to Grinnell, December 26, 1908, Garfield Papers Box 88.

99. Ibid.

100. Grinnell to Leupp, December 31, 1908, GBGP.

101. Grinnell to Leupp, March 11, 1909, GBGP.

102. Gates to Andrew S. Draper, January 4, 1909, Records of the Board of Indian Commissioners, NARG 75.

103. Ketcham to Philbin, January 30, 1909, BCIMR Box 63.

104. John S. Lockwood to Brosius, January 4, 1909, IRAP R21.

Epilogue

1. Garfield Diaries, January 4, 1905, Garfield Papers.

2. Grinnell to Taft, January 22, 1909, GBGP.

3. Taft to Gibbons, April 3, 1909, BCIMR Box 63.

4. Sniffen to Elliott H. Goodwin, May 10, 1909, IRAP R78.

5. Jones to Welsh, June 7, 1909, IRAP R21.

6. Welsh to Jones, May 10, 1909, IRAP, R78.

7. Leupp to TR, January 22, 1912, TRPR 124.

8. Leupp to TR, May 1, 1911, TRPR 105.

9. Ibid.

10. TR to Leupp, May 9, 1911, TRPR 366.

11. Leupp to TR, May 13, 1917, TRPR 232; TR to Leupp, May 15, 1917, TRPR 391.

12. Grinnell to Valentine, March 17, 1910, GBGP.

13. Lummis to TR, November 8, 1912, TRPR 157.

14. Brosius to Sniffen, March 11, 1909, IRAP R21.

15. Merriam to TR, March 12, 1912, TRPR 133.

16. TR to Garland, November 6, 1916, HGC.

17. Holloway, *Hamlin Garland,* 245.

18. Ganss to Sniffen, January 8, 1908, IRAP R20.

19. "The Indian Rights Association *vs.* The Rights of the Indians," 16, IRAP R127.

20. Memorandum by Welsh, June 14, 1909, IRAP R78.

21. *New York Times* clipping dated April 18, 1905. Roosevelt Collection, Houghton Library.

22. Ketcham to Drexel, November 28, 1904, BCIMR Box 46.

23. TR, "The Hopi Snake Dance," 367.

24. Ibid., 368.

25. Ibid., 365.

26. Curtis, "Theodore Roosevelt in Hopi-Land," 93.

 Bibliography

Manuscripts

Harvard University
  Houghton Library
    Endicott Peabody Papers
    Theodore Roosevelt Collection
  Widener Library
    Theodore Roosevelt Collection
Historical Society of Pennsylvania
  Indian Rights Association Papers (microfilm edition by Micro-
    filming Corporation of America, Glen Rock, New Jersey, 1975,
    136 reels)
  Indian Rights Association Scrapbook
The Huntington Library
  Hamlin Garland Diaries
Library of Congress
  Charles J. Bonaparte Papers
  James R. Garfield Papers

Clinton Hart Merriam Papers
Theodore Roosevelt Papers (microfilm edition, 485 reels)
Marquette University
  Bureau of Catholic Indian Missions Records
Massachusetts Historical Society
  Henry Cabot Lodge Papers
  Henry Cabot Lodge III Papers
  Moorfield Storey Papers
National Archives
  Indian Division, Secretary of Interior's Office, Letters Sent and
    Received, Record Group 48
  Office of Indian Affairs, Letters Sent and Received, Record
    Group 75
  Private Papers of Ethan Allen Hitchcock, Record Group 200
  William A. Jones Personal Letterbook, Record Group 75
  Records of the Board of Indian Commissioners, Record Group
    75
Oklahoma Historical Society
  Cheyenne and Arapaho Agency Files
  Kiowa Agency Files
Southwest Museum (Los Angeles)
  Charles F. Lummis Collection
University of Southern California
  Doheny Library: Hamlin Garland Collection
Wisconsin Historical Society
  William A. Jones Papers
Yale University
  Beinecke Library: George Bird Grinnell Papers

Annual Reports

Commissioner of Indian Affairs
Secretary of the Interior
Board of Indian Commissioners
Proceedings of the Annual Meeting of the Lake Mohonk
  Conference

Secondary Works

Baird, W. David. "William A. Jones 1897–1904." In *The Commissioners of Indian Affairs, 1824–1977,* edited by Robert M. Kvasnicka and Herman J. Viola. Lincoln: University of Nebraska Press, 1979.

Berthrong, Donald J. *The Cheyenne and Arapaho Ordeal.* Norman: University of Oklahoma Press, 1976.

Bingham, Edward R. *Charles F. Lummis.* San Marino: Huntington Library, 1955.

Clark, Blue. *Lone Wolf v. Hitchcock.* Lincoln: University of Nebraska Press, 1994.

Clow, Richmond L. "Cattlemen and Tribal Rights." *North Dakota History* 54 (Spring 1987): 23–30.

Cohen, Felix S. *Handbook of Federal Indian Law.* Albuquerque: University of New Mexico Press, 1971.

Curtis, Natalie. *The Indians' Book.* New York: Bonanza Books, 1987.

———. "Mr. Roosevelt and Indian Music." *Outlook,* March 5, 1919, 399–400.

———. "Theodore Roosevelt in Hopi-Land." *Outlook,* September 17, 1919, 87–93.

Cutright, Paul Russell. *Theodore Roosevelt: The Making of a Conservationist.* Urbana: University of Illinois Press, 1985.

Dyer, Thomas G. *Theodore Roosevelt and the Idea of Race.* Baton Rouge: Louisiana State University Press, 1980.

Ecumenical Missionary Conference. 2 vols. New York: American Tract Society, 1900.

Ellis, John Tracy. *The Life of James Cardinal Gibbons, Archbishop of Baltimore 1834–1921.* 2 vols. Milwaukee: Bruce Publishing Company, 1952.

Fiske, Turbesé Lummis, and Keith Lummis. *Charles F. Lummis.* Norman: University of Oklahoma Press, 1975.

Foulke, William Dudley. *A Hoosier Autobiography.* New York: Oxford University Press, 1922.

Fowler, Loretta. *Arapahoe Politics, 1851–1978.* Lincoln: University of Nebraska Press, 1986.

Garland, Hamlin. *Companions on the Trail.* New York: Macmillan, 1931.

———. *A Daughter of the Middle Border.* New York: Macmillan, 1922.

———. *Hamlin Garland's Diaries.* Edited by Donald Pizer. San Marino: Huntington Library, 1968.

———. "My Neighbor, Theodore Roosevelt." *Everybody's Magazine* 41 (October 1919): 9–16.

———. "The Red Man's Present Needs." *North American Review* 174 (April 1902): 476–88.

Goldman, Eric F. *Charles J. Bonaparte.* Baltimore: Johns Hopkins Press, 1943.

Gordon-McCutchan, R. C. *The Taos Indians and the Battle for Blue Lake.* Santa Fe: Red Crane Books, 1991.

Gould, Lewis L. *The Presidency of Theodore Roosevelt.* Lawrence: University Press of Kansas, 1991.

Grinnell, George Bird. "The Indian on the Reservation." *Atlantic Monthly* 83 (February 1899): 255–67.

———. "The Indians and the Outing System." *Outlook* 75 (September 1903):167–73.

———. *The Passing of the Great West: Selected Papers of George Bird Grinnell.* Edited by John F. Regier. New York: Winchester Press, 1972.

———. "Tenure of Land among the Indians." *American Anthropologist* 9 (January 1907): 1–11.

Hagan, William T. "Civil Service Commissioner Theodore Roosevelt and the Indian Rights Association." *Pacific Historical Review* 44 (May 1975): 187–200.

———. *The Indian Rights Association.* Tucson: University of Arizona Press, 1985.

Hagedorn, Herman. *Roosevelt in the Badlands.* Boston: Houghton Mifflin Company, 1921.

Hauptman, Laurence M. "Governor Theodore Roosevelt and the Indians of New York." *Proceedings of the American Philosophical Society* 119 (February 1975): 1–7.

Holloway, Jean. *Hamlin Garland.* Austin: University of Texas Press, 1960.

Hoxie, Frederick E. "Building a Future on the Past: Crow Indian Leadership in an Era of Division and Reunion." In *Indian Leadership,* edited by Walter Williams. Manhattan, Kans. Sunflower University Press, 1984.

———. *A Final Promise.* Lincoln: University of Nebraska Press, 1984.

Jones, William A. "A New Indian Policy." *World's Work* 3 (March 1902): 1838–40.

Johnston, William Davison. *TR, Champion of the Strenuous Life.* New York: Farrar, Straus and Cudahy, 1958.

Kennan, George. "Have Reservation Indians Any Vested Rights?" *Outlook* 70 (March 29, 1902): 759–65.

———. "Have the Standing Rock Indians Been Fairly Treated?" *Outlook* 71 (May 3, 1902): 90–96.

Kroeber, A. L. "C. Hart Merriam as Anthropologist." In C. Hart Merriam, *Studies of California Indians.* Berkeley: University of California Press, 1955.

LaFollette, Robert M. *LaFollette's Autobiography.* Madison: Robert M. LaFollette Company, 1913.

Leupp, Francis E. "Back to Nature for the Indian." *Charities and the Commons* 20 (June 6, 1908): 336–40.

———. "The Failure of the Educated American Indian." *Appleton's Booklover's Magazine* 7 (May 1906): 594–602.

———. "A Fresh Phase of the Indian Problem." *Nation* 69 (November 16, 1897): 367–68.

———. *In Red Man's Land.* New York: Fleming H. Revell Company, 1914.

———. *The Indian and His Problem.* New York: Charles Scribner's Sons, 1910.

———. "Indian Funds and Mission Schools." *Outlook* 83 (June 9, 1906): 33–45.

———. "The Indian Land Troubles and How to Solve Them." *American Review of Reviews* 42 (October 1910): 468–72.

———. "Indian Lands." *Annals of the Academy of Political and Social Science* 33 (May 1909): 620–30.

———. "The Indian Territory Problem." *Harper's Weekly* 42 (January 1, 1898): 18.

————. "'Law or No Law' in Indian Administration." *Outlook* 91 (January 30, 1909): 261–63.

————. *The Man Roosevelt.* New York: D. Appleton and Company, 1904.

————. "Outlines of an Indian Policy." *Outlook* 79 (April 15, 1905): 946–50.

————. "The Pillager Indian Outbreak." *Harper's Weekly* 42 (October 22, 1898): 1031.

————. "The Protest of the Pillager Indians." *Forum* 26 (December 1898): 471–84.

————. "Roosevelt the Politician." *Atlantic Monthly* 109 (June 1912), 315.

————. "The Spoilsmen and the Indian Agencies." *Nation* 65 (October 28, 1897): 333–34.

————. "The Story of Four Strenuous Years." *Outlook* 92 (June 5, 1909): 328–31.

————. "Taft and Roosevelt." *Atlantic Monthly* 106 (November 1910): 648–53.

Littlefield, Daniel F., Jr., and Lonnie E. Underhill. "Renaming the American Indian: 1890–1913." *American Studies* 12 (Fall 1971): 33–45.

Lummis, Charles F. *Bullying the Moqui.* Edited by Robert Easton and Mackenzie Brown. Prescott, Ariz.: Prescott College Press, 1968.

————. *Letters from the Southwest.* Tucson: University of Arizona Press, 1989.

Miner, H. Craig. *The Corporation and the Indian.* Norman: University of Oklahoma Press, 1989.

Morris, Edmund. *The Rise of Theodore Roosevelt.* New York: Coward, McCann and Geohagan, 1979.

O'Neil, Floyd A., and John D. Sylvester, eds. *Ute People.* Salt Lake City: University of Utah, 1970.

O'Toole, Patricia. *The Five of Hearts: An Intimate Portrait of Henry Adams and His Friends.* New York: Ballantine Books, 1990.

Parman, Donald L. "The 'Big Stick' in Indian Affairs: The Bai-a-lil-le Incident in 1909." *Arizona and the West* 20 (Winter 1978): 343–60.

————. "Francis Ellington Leupp 1905–1909." In *The Commissioners of Indian Affairs, 1824–1977,* edited by Robert M. Kvasnicka and Herman J. Viola. Lincoln: University of Nebraska Press, 1979.

————. *Indians and the American West in the Twentieth Century.* Bloomington: Indiana University Press, 1994.

————. "A White Man's Fight: The Crow Scandal, 1906–1913." In *The American West: Essays in Honor of W. Eugene Hollon,* edited by Ronald Lora. Toledo: University of Toledo, 1980.

Pfaller, Louis L. *James McLaughlin.* New York: Vantage Press, 1978.

Prucha, Francis Paul. *The Churches and the Indian Schools, 1888–1912.* Lincoln: University of Nebraska Press, 1979.

————. *The Great Father.* 2 vols. Lincoln: University of Nebraska Press, 1984.

Regier, John F. *American Sportsmen and the Origins of Conservation.* New York: Winchester Press, 1986.

Richardson, James D., comp. *A Compilation of the Messages and Papers of the Presidents.* 10 vols. Washington: Government Printing Office, 1908.

Roosevelt, Theodore. "The Hopi Snake Dance." *Outlook* 105 (October 18, 1913): 365–73.

————. *The Letters of Theodore Roosevelt.* 8 vols. Edited by Elting E. Morison. Cambridge: Harvard University Press, 1951–54.

————. *Theodore Roosevelt: An Autobiography.* New York: Charles Scribner's Sons, 1926.

————. "A Wolf Hunt in Oklahoma." *Scribner's Magazine* 38 (November 1905): 513–32.

————. *The Works of Theodore Roosevelt, National Edition.* 20 vols. New York: Charles Scribner's Sons, 1926.

Samek, Hana. *The Blackfoot Confederacy 1880–1920.* Albuquerque: University of New Mexico Press, 1987.

Schultz, James Willard. *Blackfeet and Buffalo.* Norman: University of Oklahoma Press, 1962.

Selections from the Correspondence of Theodore Roosevelt and Henry Cabot Lodge 1884–1918. 2 vols. New York: Charles Scribner's Sons, 1925.

Sterling, Keir B. *Last of the Naturalists: The Career of C. Hart Merriam.* New York: Arno Press, 1974.

Turner, Frederick Jackson. "The Winning of the West." *The Dial* 10 (August 1889): 73.

Underhill, Lonnie E., and Daniel F. Littlefield, Jr. *Hamlin Garland's Observations on the American Indian 1895–1905.* Tucson: University of Arizona Press, 1976.

Williams, Cleveland. "Theodore Roosevelt: Civil Service Commissioner." M.A. thesis. University of Chicago, 1955.

Index